Praise for the second edition

"A 'must read' for any B2B marketer. These seminal cases not only illuminate the essentials of value based business marketing, but with detailed examples show you how to implement a value based approach in the turbulent world of today's business market. Real, Good, Practical stuff from professionals who've done it."

Ralph A. Oliva, *Director, Institute for the Study of Business Markets and Professor of Marketing, Smeal College of Business, Penn State University, USA*

"By combining an impressive list of expert analysts with real-world case studies, *Value First, Then Price* gives businesses the latest strategies and tactics needed to improve company margins and profit performance. Because the focus here is on customer quantifiable values, the book correctly shifts emphasis from a producer's features to an end-user's benefits."

Kevin Mitchell, *President, The Professional Pricing Society, Inc.*

"Todd Snelgrove's description and measurement of a new view on Total Cost of Ownership (TCO), a more holistic measurement focused around Cost, Benefit, and Value called Total Profit Added™ (TPA) is a great step in the evolution of enabling both buyers and sellers to make the right decisions based on best value not lowest price."

Thomas Choi, *Professor, Arizona State University and Executive Director, Center for Advanced Procurement Studies*

"Recent research shows that far less value (and cost reduction) is achieved through traditional negotiation than can be gained through understanding markets, needs and opportunities for creative collaboration. If you care about business and personal success, value must be your priority."

Tim Cummins, *President, World Commerce & Contracting*

"The war for value is today's biggest business challenge. *Value First, Then Price* is an invaluable, thought-provoking guide to this debate."

Nigel Barlow, *International Consultant on Innovation and Value*

"In our work with some of the world's industrial manufacturers, we've seen that companies that focus on value from both the buy and sell side enjoy a competitive edge. Top-performing industrials are eight times more likely to take a value-based approach toward pricing, and companies that measure and buy based on total cost of ownership are 35% more profitable. Buyers have never been better informed on the total cost of ownership, and companies that are still talking about features and benefits are getting left behind."

Stephen Gold, *CEO of MAPI – Manufacturers Alliance for Productivity & Innovation*

"My own research confirms McKinsey's, that only 5% of companies have value propositions. No wonder buyers have the upper hand! The world really needs this book and I congratulate Andreas Hinterhuber and Todd Snelgrove on putting together a truly fantastic piece of work."

Malcolm McDonald, *MA (Oxon), MSc, PhD, DLitt, DSc, Emeritus Professor, Cranfield University School of Management, UK*

"In business-to-business markets, managers must bridge the gap between those who say that it is only by value that firms can thrive in the long term and those who suggest that buyers will buy on price. Value can be created and captured. The bad news is that it is extremely difficult, but the good news is that a systematic approach is likely to yield dividends. In this important book Andreas Hinterhuber and Todd Snelgrove have harnessed the world's top value creation experts to provide an insightful and complete roadmap."

John Roberts, *Fellow, London Business School, UK, and Professor, University of New South Wales, Australia*

"What a comprehensive way to present value. From the discussions to the articles, a must-have guide for professionals and companies that want to buy, produce, and sell any product or services based on value."

João Ricciarelli, *Executive President America's, Leadec*

"It's not often you read a business book, learn from it and have fun doing so. *Value First, Then Price* by Hinterhuber and Snelgrove is one of those rare exceptions. I don't care whether you are on the buy or sell side of the equation, this book is for you. It is a fantastic engaging read. The material is thought provoking with great integration of theory: from value, to ROI and results. It is simply a very practical business book."

Stephen Kozicki *is on the Advisory Panel for HBR and lectures at business schools including Macquarie University, University of Technology and The Australian Catholic University, Australia*

"Much has been said and written about value in industrial markets. But how to put the idea to practice? This book focuses on what matters most: to 'challenge' customers and help them rethink their assumptions, vendors need data and value quantification. The authors provide a practical, hands-on roadmap for value pricing that both buyers and sellers can follow for achieving better business results."

Wolfgang Ulaga, *Senior Affiliate Professor of Marketing. INSEAD, France*

"*Value First, Then Price* is a much-needed work and deserves a place in most CPO and sales offices."

Keld Jensen, *Author of 'The Trust Factor – Negotiating in SMARTnership', Professor and Advisor In Negotiations*

"SAMA research emphasizes that most companies are significantly lacking in internal processes for value-based negotiation, value creation, value-based pricing and value monetization. Snelgrove and Hinterhuber provide great insights and methodologies for companies to fill these gaps."

Bernard Quancard, *Retired President and CEO Strategic Account Management Association (SAMA)*

"Quantifying and understanding the value proposition is key to business success. This book gets directly to the bottom line by taking both a buyer and seller perspective and presenting value based purchasing in a way that all purchasing professionals need to understand."

Wendy L. Tate, *PhD, Associate Professor of Supply Chain Management, University of Tennessee, USA*

"*Value First, Then Price* is a timely and rare contribution, providing not only invaluable insights, but also a practical methodology of how to perceive, quantify and capture value. From the perspective of emerging and new market economies, it offers the ultimate answer on how to escape the enduring 'lower cost – lower price' trap, and how to shift towards a sustainable, value creation driven path that leads to business and economic development."

Modestas Gelbūda, *PhD in International Business, Aalborg University, Denmark; Managing Director, Baltic Institute for Leadership Development, Lithuania, and Associate Professor, ISM University of Management and Economics, Lithuania*

"At a time when both customers and suppliers are over focused on product prices as a determinant of business transactions, this book offers a fresh way out by arguing for a new way of looking at the economics of exchange between buyers and sellers where price is just one element in determining the *true value* of what is bought and sold. More specifically, the book informs purchasing officers about the often ignored actual cost and *inherent value* (in total savings, returns on investment, etc.) of what they buy, and provides suppliers with tools to *quantify and communicate* the hidden value in what they sell. I highly recommend this book to professionals in procurement, sales and marketing, and general management."

Kamran Kashani, *IMD, Switzerland*

"The editors and their authors have tackled a problem that has faced buyers and sellers for years: how to define the concept of value that aligns with two different views of the world. Sales claims to sell based on value, and purchasing claims to buy based on value, yet both parties view this concept from fundamentally different viewpoints. This book articulates these differences, and creates a framework that can help resolve the issues, creating a mutually compatible lens for understanding this often misunderstood concept."

Robert Handfield, *Bank of America, Distinguished Professor of Supply Chain Management and Director of Supply Chain Resource Cooperative, North Carolina State University, USA*

Value First, Then Price

Value-based pricing – pricing a product or service according to its value to the customer rather than its cost – is the most effective and profitable pricing strategy. *Value First, Then Price* is an innovative collection that proposes a quantitative methodology to value pricing and road-tests this methodology through a wide variety of real-life industrial and B2B cases.

This book offers a state-of-the art and best-practice overview of how leading companies quantify and document value to customers. In doing so, it provides students and researchers with a method by which to draw invaluable data-driven conclusions and gives sales and marketing managers the theories and best practices they need to quantify the value of their products and services to industrial and B2B purchasers. The second edition of this highly regarded text has been updated in line with current research and practice, offering three new chapters covering new case studies and best-practice examples of quantified value propositions, the future of value quantification, and value quantification for intangibles.

With contributions from global industry experts this book combines cutting-edge research on value quantification and value quantification capabilities with real-life, practical examples. It is essential reading for postgraduate students in sales and marketing with an interest in pricing strategy, sales and pricing specialists, as well as business strategists, in both research and practice.

Andreas Hinterhuber is Associate Professor at the Department of Management at Università Ca' Foscari Venezia, Italy.

Todd C. Snelgrove is Senior Managing Partner at Experts in Value in Clarkston, MI, USA.

Value First, Then Price

Building Value-Based Pricing Strategies

Second edition

**Edited by Andreas Hinterhuber
and Todd C. Snelgrove**

LONDON AND NEW YORK

Second edition published 2022
by Routledge
2 Park Square, Milton Park, Abingdon, Oxon, OX14 4RN

and by Routledge
605 Third Avenue, New York, NY 10158

Routledge is an imprint of the Taylor & Francis Group, an informa business

First edition published by Routledge 2017

British Library Cataloguing-in-Publication Data
A catalogue record for this book is available from the British Library

Library of Congress Cataloging-in-Publication Data
Names: Hinterhuber, Andreas, editor. | Snelgrove, Todd, editor.
Title: Value first, then price : building value-based pricing strategies / edited by
    Andreas Hinterhuber and Todd C. Snelgrove.
Description: Second edition. | Abingdon, Oxon ; New York, NY : Routledge, 2022. |
    Includes bibliographical references and index.
Identifiers: LCCN 2021033465 (print) | LCCN 2021033466 (ebook) | ISBN
    9781032012193 (hbk) | ISBN 9781032012124 (pbk) | ISBN 9781003177937 (ebk)
Subjects: LCSH: Pricing. | Value. | Industrial marketing.
Classification: LCC HF5416.5 .V35 2022 (print) | LCC HF5416.5 (ebook) |
    DDC 658.8/16—dc23
LC record available at https://lccn.loc.gov/2021033465
LC ebook record available at https://lccn.loc.gov/2021033466

ISBN: 978-1-032-01219-3 (hbk)
ISBN: 978-1-032-01212-4 (pbk)
ISBN: 978-1-003-17793-7 (ebk)

DOI: 10.4324/9781003177937

Typeset in Bembo
by Apex CoVantage, LLC

Contents

Editors

Andreas Hinterhuber is Associate Professor at the Department of Management at Università Ca' Foscari Venezia, Italy. He has published articles in leading journals including *Journal of Business Research* and *MIT Sloan Management Review* and has edited many books on pricing, including *Innovation in Pricing* (2012/2017), *The ROI of Pricing* (2014), *Pricing and the Sales Force* (2016), *Value First then Price* (2017), *Pricing Strategy Implementation* (2020), and *Managing Digital Transformation* (2021).

Todd C. Snelgrove is the former Global Vice President of Value and Commercial Excellence at SKF, a leading global industrial engineering company. He developed and led SKF's initiatives to quantify customer value for over 16 years, to price for value, to communicate and sell value, and to procure based on best value. He now consults and helps companies in all industries, with all things value and commercial excellence. He is noted as a subject matter expert on value and has been published in various academic journals, has served as a keynote speaker at numerous global conferences, and supports executive MBA classes at schools such as Harvard, Northwestern, London Business School, and the International Institute for Management Development.

Contributors

James C. Anderson is the William L. Ford Professor Emeritus of Marketing and Whole-sale Distribution at the Kellogg School of Management, Northwestern University. For 25 years, he was the principal of James C. Anderson LLC, an international management consulting firm focused on implementing customer value management at client firms. He has consulted and provided seminars for a number of companies in North America, South America, Europe, Asia, and Australia such as American Express, bio Mérieux, Exxon Mobil, GE, Holcim, International Paper, C.P. Kelco, Orkla, PPG Industries, and Tetra Pak.

Paolo De Angeli is Head of Commercial Excellence at Borealis AG, where he is responsible for customer value management, value quantification, and pricing. He has over 10 years of experience in pricing. Previously he has worked for Syngenta and Accenture and is a graduate of Università Commerciale L. Bocconi in Milan (Italy).

Lennart Foos is a postgraduate student at Karlsruhe Institute of Technology (KIT). Currently he is enrolled in a master's degree program at KIT and at ESIEE Paris. He is interested in the application of Internet of Things technologies in the value generation process. His research includes value chain analysis, value quantification, the application of business intelligence, new product development, and innovation management.

John V. Gray is Professor of Operations at the Fisher College of Business at the Ohio State University. Prior to pursuing his PhD, he worked in operations management at Procter & Gamble, earning an MBA from Wake Forest University's evening program during that time. He teaches data analysis and an elective called global sourcing at the undergraduate, MBA, and PhD levels. Dr. Gray's research streams include studying manufacturing and supply chain drivers of quality risk and confidentiality risk, and managerial decision making in sourcing.

Susan Helper is the Frank Tracy Carlton Professor of Economics at the Weatherhead School of Management at Case Western Reserve University. She was formerly Chief Economist at the U.S. Department of Commerce and a member of the White House Staff. Her research focuses on the globalization of supply chains and on how U.S. manufacturing might be revitalized. Dr. Helper received her PhD in Economics from Harvard and her BA from Oberlin College in Economics, Government and Spanish.

Matthias Heutger is Senior Vice President, Strategy Marketing and Innovation at DHL. He leads the commercial development and innovation area of DHL's cross-divisional unit, Customer Solutions & Innovation (CSI), and drives the development of sector strategies for DHL's five focus sectors – Automotive, Energy, Engineering and Manufacturing, Life Sciences and Healthcare, and Technology. He also leads marketing and sales steering and development for DHL's top 100+ accounts, next to the customer-centric innovation activities across the DHL divisions. He reports to DHL's Chief Commercial Officer and is a member of the CSI Board.

Andreas Hinterhuber is Associate Professor at the Department of Management at Università Ca' Foscari Venezia, Italy. He has published articles in leading journals including *Journal of Business Research* and *MIT Sloan Management Review* and has edited many books on pricing, including *Innovation in Pricing* (2012/2017), *The ROI of Pricing* (2014), *Pricing and the Sales Force* (2016), *Value First then Price* (2017), *Pricing Strategy implementation* (2020), and *Managing Digital Transformation* (2021).

Pascal Kemps is Head of Marketing and Sales at TeRoCo, an IT company based in Belgium. Previously he was Head of Pricing at Securitas Europe and, before that, Sub Sector Head, Passenger Vehicles, Global Automotive Sector with DHL Customer Solutions & Innovation. He is an expert in the fields of international sales and marketing management, innovation and change management, cross-cultural management, and global integrated supply chains. Pascal holds a master's degree in economics from the University of Brussels.

Markus Kirchberger is a management accountant working for Porsche AG. He received his PhD from the Karlsruhe Institute of Technology. His research is focused around technology commercialization and value creation.

Gary Kleiner is the Value Capture Manager for Fluid Connectors and Motion Systems Groups of Parker Hannifin and has over 30 years of industrial sales and marketing experience. For the past 14 years, he has worked in pricing. He is actively involved in new product and technology growth initiatives, developing standard work processes for value capture and communication, deploying commercial value propositions, and designing customer value management programs. He has twice received the Parker Hannifin Technical Authorship Award.

Robert Maguire is an advisor to senior business leaders and works with procurement and sales teams to identify, define, and capture value. He is the author of the *Universities Guide to Best Practice in Procurement* and *Eat the Ugly Frog*, a negotiation guide. After a career of 20 years with global management consultancies and blue-chip brands, he founded his own consulting firm. He is a popular keynote speaker and regular guest on the MBA programs at London Business School and at ESADE Business and Law schools in Barcelona.

Thomas T. Nagle is Senior Advisor in Monitor Deloitte's Strategy practice. Dr. Nagle founded the Strategic Pricing Group (now part of Monitor Deloitte) in 1987 soon after publication of *The Strategy and Tactics of Pricing* – still the most widely adopted text on pricing. He has extensive experience helping B2B clients develop and implement profitable pricing and value communication strategies.

Beverly Osborn is a PhD candidate at the Fisher College of Business at the Ohio State University. She has worked in sourcing for the UN Refugee Agency at its global supply chain headquarters in Hungary and in various roles in Canada's energy industry.

Her previous degrees, both focused on supply chain management, were earned at the Zaragoza Logistics Center and the University of Calgary's Haskayne School of Business.

Evandro Pollono is Managing Director of Hinterhuber & Partners and based in Milan, Italy. He is a leading pricing expert and advises companies worldwide. Since 2014, Evandro is a visiting lecturer at the University of Alcala de Henares (Spain), where he teaches strategic pricing as part of the MBA program in international marketing.

Bernard L. Quancard was named President and CEO of the Strategic Account Management Association (SAMA) in October 2006. He retired from SAMA in 2019. He started his career in 1969 with the Boston Consulting Group. He joined Telemecanique (Schneider Electric Group) in 1975 as Vice President, Corporate Strategy, and became VP/General Manager of various divisions. In 1994, he joined the management board of AEG Schneider Automation (Schneider Electric Group) as Executive VP, Worldwide Sales and Marketing. Bernard moved to Chicago in 1997 as Senior VP/General Manager of Schneider Global Business Development (SGBD), the entity managing global strategic accounts (GSAs) for Schneider Electric worldwide. A native of France and a U.S. citizen, Bernard holds a BS degree in electrical engineering from the University of Paris and an MBA from Chicago Booth.

Risto Rajala is Associate Professor and Head of the Department of Industrial Engineering and Management at Aalto University. Rajala holds a PhD degree in information systems science from the Aalto University School of Business. His specialties include management of industrial service operations, collaborative service innovation, service-based value creation, and business model performance. His work has been published widely in refereed scientific journals and presented at academic meetings.

Robert Russell is Director of Russell Grenville Barker Limited, an accountancy services company. He is a chartered accountant and former editor of *Finance and Management Magazine*. He graduated in economics from the University of Leicester and trained with Moore Stevens Chartered Accountants.

Gerald Smith is a professor at Boston College in the Carroll School of Management, where he leads the MBA Product and Brand Management Specialization and the Brand Management Partners Program. He is the author of *The Opt-Out Effect: Marketing Strategies That Empower Consumers and Win Customer-Driven Brand Loyalty*, released 2016, and editor of *Visionary Pricing*, published in 2012. He has been an advisor in pricing and brand management to firms in a variety of industries, both B2B and B2C.

Todd C. Snelgrove is the former Global Vice President of Value and Commercial Excellence at SKF, a leading global industrial engineering company. He developed and led SKF's initiatives to quantify customer value for over 16 years, to price for value, to communicate and sell value, and to procure based on best value. He now consults and helps companies in all industries, with all things value and commercial excellence. He is noted as a subject matter expert on value and has been published in various academic journals, has served as a keynote speaker at numerous global conferences, and supports executive MBA classes at schools such as Harvard, Northwestern, London Business School, and the International Institute for Management Development.

Bo-Inge Stensson is CEO of Stensson Performance Group, a global advisory and interim firm. He is the former Senior Vice President, Group Purchasing of SKF, a leading global industrial engineering company. He has over 25 years of experience in international supply chain management and has contributed significantly to improving the supply chain performance of SKF: SKF today buys on value, as opposed to acquisition cost, and is recognized as best in class in international supplier and sustainability rankings. Previously he worked for ITT, Arla Foods, Electrolux, and Rexam.

Pekka Töytäri is Professor of Practice, Department of Industrial Engineering and Management, at Aalto University. Töytäri holds a PhD degree in industrial management. His recent research is focused on value-based exchange in industrial markets, including customer value, service-based value creation, value-based selling and sales management, as well as business model innovation. His academic work has appeared in distinguished journals such as *Journal of Product Innovation Management* and *Industrial Marketing Management*.

Tim Underhill started his career in measuring value as a visiting assistant professor at Texas A&M University, then worked for Red Man Pipe & Supply (now MRC Global) helping them sell strategic alliances based on total cost savings, and is now the president of Strategic Business Solutions. He has authored two books: *Strategic Alliances: Managing the Supply Chain* and *Team Up! Profit Up!*.

Kate Vitasek is a faculty member of the University of Tennessee's Haslam College of Business Administration. Her award-winning research has been featured in six books including *Vested Outsourcing: Five Rules That Will Transform Outsourcing* and *Vested: How P&G, McDonald's and Microsoft Are Redefining Winning in Business Relationships*. Her latest book is *Strategic Sourcing in the New Economy: Harnessing the Potential of Sourcing Business Models for Modern Procurement*.

Part I

Introduction

1 Introduction

Quantifying and documenting value in business markets

Hinterhuber, Andreas and Snelgrove, Todd C.

The essential challenge that sales and marketing managers in industrial markets face is this: converting their firm's own competitive advantages into quantified, monetary customer benefits. Doing so enables business-to-business (B2B) sales and marketing personnel to justify price differences between competing offers with a difference in monetary value. A disguised project example illustrates this fundamental principle of value quantification.

Customer value is the sum of (a) the price of the customer's best available alternative and (b) the subjective, customer-specific value of all the differentiating features that distinguish the supplier's own offering from the customer's best available alternative (Nagle and Holden, 2002). Customer value is thus the quantified sum of the customer-specific benefits accruing to purchasers as a result of purchasing the offering. This sum is the maximum price that rational buyers will be prepared to pay. The price difference between the supplier's own offering and the customer's best available alternative is then related to the difference in value between the two offerings (see Figure 1.1).

Value quantification thus enables suppliers to perform return on investment calculations: The price difference between two offerings is the investment customers make to obtain the quantified, monetary customer benefits identified.

Value quantification is arguably the most important capability in B2B selling. It is also a capability that many companies in industrial markets lack (Anderson et al., 2007); these companies, however, are at least conscious of their lack in value quantification capabilities and recognize the potential benefits of developing them (Töytäri and Rajala, 2015).

The contents of the book

This book is one of the few books – possibly the only book – exclusively dedicated to the topic of value quantification in business markets. Individuals from leading institutions, such as the Kellogg School of Management, Ca' Foscari University Venice, Boston College, Aalto University, the University of Tennessee, the Ohio State University, Case Western Reserve University, Deloitte, and Hinterhuber & Partners, and practitioners from companies including SKF, DHL, Borealis, the Strategic Account Management Association (SAMA), and Parker Hannifin, provide best practices, case studies, tools, and principles of value quantification in industrial markets. The book has two implicit premises. First, selling should be based on value first, then price. Second, procurement should also be based on value first, then price. Buyers and sellers in business markets must focus first on value, then on price, in order to increase performance.

A unique feature of this book is that it explores the topic of value quantification from the perspective of both sellers and buyers in industrial markets.

DOI: 10.4324/9781003177937-2

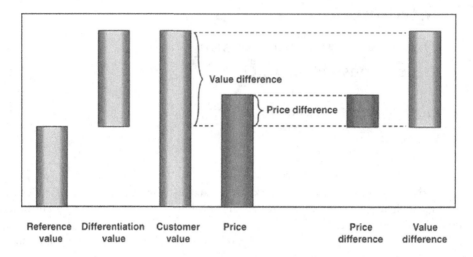

Figure 1.1 Value quantification and value-based pricing

Source: Hinterhuber & Partners

The buyer perspective: in many organizations, sourcing criteria were heavily weighted toward tangible criteria, such as price, quality, and delivery. Practitioners as well as procurement scholars have started to explore procurement models that consider an array of tangible and intangible benefits in sourcing decisions. Several chapters in this book present procurement frameworks that consider the total value of supplier contributions in the offer evaluation process. This book also presents anecdotal evidence that sourcing criteria considering the total value of benefits lead to increased firm performance and allow to create value – for example, environmental benefits – that traditional procurement models typically do not create. We need, however, more research. Specifically, we need research developing these metrics, such as total value of ownership or total value contribution (TVC) models (see Chapter 13) that reflect innovation, management capabilities, sustainability, and other elements beyond quality, price, and delivery. We also need quantitative research exploring the consequences of the use of total value of ownership models by procurement on company performance and on value creation.

On to the perspective of sales: There is now increasingly robust evidence that value quantification capabilities are beneficial for firm performance. The core focuses of this book are case studies, best practices, and recent research findings exploring the factors that enable companies to acquire and successfully deploy value quantification capabilities.

The structure of the book

Part I, "Introduction," contains this introductory chapter by *Andreas Hinterhuber* and *Todd C. Snelgrove*.

Part II, "Selling value: Value quantification capabilities," contains several chapters that address the capabilities needed to quantify and document value in business markets.

The opening chapter, "Value first, then price: The new paradigm of B2B buying and selling" by *Andreas Hinterhuber, Todd C. Snelgrove,* and *Bo-Inge Stensson*, sets the frame for the entire book. Our key argument is this: Most companies today take an inherently adversarial approach to buying and selling in industrial markets, thereby missing out on opportunities for joint value creation with customers and suppliers. Sales and procurement are too obsessed with price and not enough with value. We present a set of principles that put joint value creation at the center of the relationship with customers and suppliers. With respect to customers, the value quantification capability is the most important competency of the sales function, that is, the ability to translate a firm's competitive advantages into one quantified, monetary value reflecting both qualitative and quantitative customer benefits. Several chapters in this book (all in Part III) provide examples of quantified value propositions, for both B2B services and B2B products. With value quantification capabilities (sales) and total value of ownership models (procurement) the key element of relationship with both customers and suppliers is value first, then price.

In an interview, *Robert Russell* and *Andreas Hinterhuber* explore several key issues related to value quantification. First, since pricing is always the result of a chain of prior activities, optimizing pricing cannot involve price optimization alone. Managers should instead map the most important processes related to pricing – in B2B typically the offer development process. Once this process is mapped, once bad and best practices along every process step are described, and, finally, once managers have compared their own current practices with best practices, then opportunities to improve profits via pricing are typically identified very effectively. This interview also explores the topic of change management in the context of value-based pricing and value quantification. Hinterhuber suggests that companies benefit from holding an underlying, implicit organizational change management theory in order to effectively implement value quantification: Useful theories include the influence model by McKinsey & Company (Keller and Price, 2011), Kotter's eight-step model of organizational transformation (Kotter, 1995), the switch model by the Heath brothers (Heath and Heath, 2010), and the free-spaces theory of social movement research (Kellogg, 2008). These theories, examples, and recent research related to pricing strategy implementation are discussed in detail in another book (Hinterhuber and Liozu, 2020).

In the subsequent interview, "Muddling through on customer value in business markets?," *Todd C. Snelgrove* and *James C. Anderson* discuss two key aspects of value quantification: how to develop value quantification capabilities and how to quantify value for weakly differentiated products. The authors first suggest that companies move through three stages when building value quantification capabilities: in the first stage – the prove-the-concept stage – companies undertake several value quantification projects in order to learn the concepts, process, and tools and to obtain the benefits from these pilot projects. In the second stage – the build-the-structure-and-culture stage – companies significantly expand the scope of value quantification: They train experts, build value quantification tools and repositories of case studies, conduct more projects, measure the success consistently, and link value quantification with other projects such as the new product development process. In the third stage – the sustain-the-advantage stage – companies institutionalize value quantification by, for example, appointing champions whose primary responsibility is value quantification. A second insight of this interview is that value quantification differs between strategic and non-strategic products, that is, between products that contribute significantly to differentiating the customer's offering and those that do not: Value quantification is suitable for strategic products. For non-strategic products, by contrast, detailed value quantification is typically not possible and not even desired by customers; instead, suppliers provide customers with resonating arguments such as generic case studies – in the author's terms, with a tiebreaker – able to shift the balance in the supplier's favor. In sum, the more a supplier's product contributes to creating meaningful differentiation in the customer's products, the more value quantification has to be detailed, collaborative, and customer-specific.

In the interview "Nurturing value quantification capabilities in strategic account managers," *Andreas Hinterhuber, Todd C. Snelgrove,* and *Bernard L. Quancard* discuss the importance of value quantification capabilities for strategic account managers. Quancard is adamant: Only about 30% of account managers truly create value for customers; the remaining 70% are merely commercial coordinators. In order to truly create value, value quantification capabilities are fundamentally important. These capabilities are valuable and rare: Only 10% of companies, Quancard suggests, are able to translate into monetary terms the value they create for customers. Quancard further observes thoughtfully in what may become a noteworthy quote: "Most projects go to request for proposal (RFP), because there is not a compelling monetization of the value." In this view, a request for proposal is thus nothing else than a reflection of the supplier's inability to quantify value. Quantified value propositions, accompanied by approximate price ranges for competitive products, eliminate the need for a request for proposal and allow the isolation of collaborative customer relationships from competition. This interview also sheds light on the antecedents of value quantification capabilities: active listening skills, cross-functional collaboration, financial acumen, and an unlimited curiosity. CEO support is, like in all cases of organizational transformation, essential. A further element to consider in the process of building value quantification capabilities is the selection of customers. Not all large customers are or will be receptive to joint value creation and value quantification. Those that are not should not be strategic accounts, irrespective of their purchase volume. Account managers thus need to define criteria for determining which large customers are strategic. Only with these strategic accounts should collaborative value quantification occur.

In "Salesforce confidence and proficiency – the main cornerstone of effective customer value management" *Gary Kleiner* presents a case study on customer value quantification. This chapter stresses the importance of sales force confidence in addition to the required technical skills in order to effectively and convincingly quantify customer value.

Part III, "Selling value: Best practices in value quantification," contains six chapters highlighting best practices in value quantification. In "Value quantification – processes and best practices to document and quantify value in B2B," *Andreas Hinterhuber* presents the results of a study on value quantification capabilities in European and U.S.-based B2B companies. This chapter presents five key steps that can guide managers in industrial companies in quantifying value: generation of customer insight, value creation through meaningful differentiation and collaboration, value proposition development, value quantification, and implementation/documentation. This chapter also highlights several case studies of quantified customer value propositions, SKF and SAP among them. SKF is, of course, a special case: *Todd C. Snelgrove* has played a leading role in quantifying and documenting value for thousands of use cases at SKF.

In "Quantifying your value so customers are willing and able to pay for it," *Todd C. Snelgrove* highlights that quantified value that relies on tangible evidence and that has a high likelihood of occurrence acts as a very strong purchase motivator in industrial markets. For sales managers, value-based selling requires two conditions: ability and motivation. The ability to sell value depends on the ability to conceptualize value in a way that resonates with customers, on processes encouraging a focus on value, on the availability of value-selling tools, on initial training, and on ongoing experience in value selling. The motivation to sell value is a function of salesforce compensation, of the ability to build long-term collaborative relationships with customers where both parties are committed to creating mutually beneficial value, of a company culture led by a strong CEO committed to value-based selling and, finally, of customers who recognize the opportunity to work collaboratively with suppliers. This chapter thus takes a nuanced view of the multiple facets that companies can and should control in order to implement value-based selling and value quantification. Todd also discusses a new term, "total profit added," as a measurement for both buyer and seller to quantify total customer benefits. This approach considers not just cost reductions but also includes estimated revenue improvements.

In the chapter "An inside look at value quantification of competitive advantages" *Evandro Pollono* presents best-practice case studies on quantified value propositions. This is an important chapter. Many apparent experts advocate the importance of selling value, as opposed to selling price, without actually specifying in detail the data, the steps, and examples of quantified value propositions. *Evandro Pollono* presents four examples of quantified value propositions, that is, quantified, monetary customer benefits, calculated relative to the customer's best available alternative, from B2B products and B2B services. These case studies convincingly show that value quantification is (a) possible and (b) beneficial in industrial markets, regardless of the intensity of competition or the perceived difficulty to differentiate the product.

In "Value quantification for services" *Todd C. Snelgrove* expands on the prior chapter and presents an example of a value calculator for services. Some managers are reluctant to quantify customer value for services, possibly assuming that value quantification for intangibles is more difficult or less credible than value quantification for products. This assumption is wrong: All products are, in the end, services (Vargo and Lusch, 2004). A product has a performance promise like a service. A product customer co-creates value like a service customer. Value is future-oriented for a product as well as a service. Finally, some products are intangible (e.g., digital goods such as e-books), which means that the distinction between products and services is increasingly irrelevant. The subsequent chapter further expands on these issues.

In "Quantifying intangible benefits" *Paolo De Angeli* and *Evandro Pollono* make the point that intangibles – for example, the value of a brand, sustainability – are also an increasingly important competitive differentiator in industrial markets. Key is to make intangibles tangible by specifying how intangible competitive advantages affect key customer business metrics such as quality, revenues, or cost. This chapter provides a case study on how to quantify intangible elements with a value quantification tool.

In "Toward a shared understanding of value in B2B exchange: Discovering, selecting, quantifying, and sharing value" *Pekka Töytäri* and *Risto Rajala* highlight the importance of conceptualizing value in a way that is shared between suppliers and customers. The authors present a three-step process enabling companies to quantify value: customer insight, value proposition, and value sharing. Value quantification is an iterative process. This chapter also succinctly highlights obstacles that companies face in the process of quantifying value: different assessments of the supplier's value creation potential, inability to quantify value, and inability to defend value vis-à-vis procurement. Procurement is an obstacle for many companies aiming to implement value-based selling and value quantification. Industrial marketing and sales managers thus need to understand and influence the procurement function in order to credibly present value. The procurement function is the topic of the subsequent section.

Part IV, "Buying on value: Value quantification and B2B purchasing," contains several chapters that explore value quantification from the perspective of procurement. This is, as outlined, a unique feature of this book. Sales and account managers frequently perceive procurement as interested in price and price alone and are thus reluctant to adopt the mindset of an explorer that is fundamentally necessary in order to quantify value.

The chapters in this section convincingly debunk the idea that procurement is mainly and solely interest in price: Sales is transitioning from price to value and so is procurement. The fundamental idea is that the procurement function should not evaluate suppliers based only on quality, price, and delivery but should instead evaluate suppliers based on their overall contribution to improved customer profitability.

TVC is the name for a metric that attempts to calculate the value that suppliers create for customers, value that is substantially broader than price or total cost of ownership (TCO). The chapter "Value first, cost later: Total value contribution as a new approach to sourcing decisions" by *John V. Gray*, *Susan Helper*, and *Beverly Osborn* develops the idea in detail. The TVC name by itself promotes attention to value. TVC's structured approach begins with the question: "What do our customers, current and future, value about our products?" The TVC approach builds on insights from the literature on individual and group decision making to offset human biases and organizational incentives that emphasize cost reduction. TVC expands upon on the concept of TCO which considers life cycle costs, not just purchase price, but still is able to capture only cost-related elements. TVC, by contrast, also attempts to include benefits and supplier contributions to improve profits, innovation, or even sustainability. We are at the beginning of a process. Price and TCO are well established as supplier selection criteria but fall short of considering strategic benefits. TVC of procurement is thus a mirror concept of quantified customer benefits of sales. The concept of TVC needs to be more precisely defined – with a clear specification of categories – and it needs to be further researched – with studies documenting the link, and boundary conditions, of sourcing based on value, as opposed to sourcing based on costs, on innovation, and on profitability. To be clear: These studies exist, abundantly, for sales, but these studies do not yet exist for procurement. This is thus a very fertile ground for future quantitative, cross-sectional research.

In the interview "Selling value to purchasing," *Todd C. Snelgrove* and *Bo-Inge Stensson* discuss how to implement value quantification vis-à-vis powerful industrial procurement departments. Contrary to the commonly held assumptions mentioned before, the authors also find that procurement is frequently willing to purchase based on value if – and only if – sellers are able to present a business case highlighting how a higher initial purchase price lowers costs or otherwise yields incremental financial benefits. This interview also highlights that within SKF the procurement function has undergone a substantial change. While in the past, annual price reductions and generic indicators of supply chain performance were primary performance measures, today the procurement function is increasingly measured by indicators relating supply chain performance to the company's overall profitability and to the company's overall strategic objectives such as innovation and sustainability. This change is demanding: both for the company itself and for suppliers who must conceptualize how their performance affects the performance of their immediate customers vis-à-vis their own customers.

In "Using best value to get the best bottom line," *Kate Vitasek* contrasts three approaches that suppliers use to select vendors: price, TCO, and best value. This chapter is valuable: Understanding alternative supplier-selection methods may enable buyers and sellers in industrial markets to change them. Price-based selection criteria consider either short-term or long-term purchase price. TCO calculations consider supplier direct costs, supplier indirect costs, and a premium/discount reflecting the supplier's risk. This approach, however, has drawbacks (Piscopo et al., 2008; Snelgrove, 2012). TCO calculations do not consider the value of tangible (revenue improvements) or intangible (brand value, reputation, competencies) benefits. Total value of ownership (Snelgrove, 2012), total profit added calculations (Snelgrove, 2016), and value quantification tools (Pollono, Chapter 9 of this volume) allow the inclusion of both tangible and intangible benefits, cost, and benefits that make the customer better off. This chapter shows how to perform best value calculations. Best value is defined as the optimum benefits as defined by customers minus total supplier costs. Optimum benefits include, of course, intangible factors, too, such as reputation and quality. Selection based on best value is increasingly common in federal government procurement contracts. The chapter concludes by examining pricing models that align supplier and buyer interests; among these pricing models are performance-based agreements and vested agreements. The difference between these two approaches is fundamental: Performance-based agreements consider key performance indicators (KPIs); vested agreements consider the ultimate outcomes that truly matter to customers.

In "Value selling: The crucial importance of access to decision makers from the procurement perspective," *Rob Maguire* describes the organizational buying process in the following terms: getting the least worst answer to the wrong question from people you've met online. A key task that sellers face is, first of all, to understand what buyers want: price, a benefit, or a solution, in the authors' terms. Second, if sellers want to implement value-based selling and value quantification, they need buyers that recognize the need to purchase a solution – as opposed to purchasing an item at the lowest price. Once buyers recognize the opportunity or need to purchase solutions, sellers should practice the following steps: Investigate value creation opportunities, quantify the incremental value delivered, engage buyers in mutual value creation opportunities, sell value, and, finally, implement value-based pricing via, for example, outcome-based contracting. This chapter is thus a reminder that access to the ultimate decision maker, and not necessarily access to procurement, is a necessary prerequisite to implementing value-based selling and pricing.

In "The sourcing continuum to achieve collaboration and value," *Kate Vitasek* examines alternative configurations of buyer–seller relationships. Transactional, market-based models include basic or approved provider models. Relational models, that is, hybrids between markets and hierarchies, include preferred provider relationships, performance-based contracting, and vested business models. The author discusses the latter two models in detail in Chapter 10. Equity and investment-based models include shared service models and equity partnerships. This chapter describes these alternative configurations in detail and offers guidelines that facilitate the selection of the most appropriate model in buyer–seller relationships.

Part V, "Value quantification and organizational change management," contains two interviews with senior B2B marketing and account managers.

In this section's first interview, "Implementing value quantification in B2B," *Andreas Hinterhuber* and *Matthias Heutger* discuss value quantification for industrial services. Value quantification is, according to Heutger, always beneficial, even if organizations are strongly driven by the procurement function. In other words, even if suppliers do not require customers to quantify their value, suppliers should still do so in order to differentiate themselves from their competition. Heutger makes one point clear: Value quantification requires that suppliers understand their customers' entire supply chains, end to end. Suppliers must be able to understand the effects of their own incremental performance improvements on the performance improvements of their customers' customers. This understanding also enables gainsharing agreements – with a caveat: Gainsharing agreements require a long-term collaboration whereby both parties are committed to innovate and change. The interview also explores the antecedents of value quantification capabilities at the level of the individual sales and account manager: a strong customer focus, the ability to strategize, listening skills, and a willingness to experiment. Another important aspect of value quantification is credibility: The ability to actually deliver on the promised value may require selecting those persons within the customer's business who most appreciate the value created; it frequently entails small tests which are then rapidly scaled up. Value quantification is, in Heutger's words, a true organizational transformation that requires senior management commitment, structural changes, and changes in hiring profiles. Where to start? At the level of the individual customer. Value quantification requires a new way of interacting with customers where "trust, mutual benefits and a willingness to grow together over time" take the place of price as the main element of discussion. These words will, we hope, withstand the test of time.

In the second interview of this section, "The ring of truth – value quantification in B2B services," *Andreas Hinterhuber* and *Pascal Kemps* discuss value quantification in complex B2B services. To start off, the importance of value quantification seems to grow with the importance of customers, to a point where it is factually required by strategic accounts. Second, and more counterintuitively, Kemps suggests: The fact that some customers treat suppliers transactionally does not imply that suppliers should not treat these customers strategically. Transactional customers – customers who bid out every contract – may enable suppliers to standardize their own internal processes or to accumulate valuable competencies and insights. Treating them transactionally or, worse, writing them off would mean, according to Kemps, cutting off profitable business. Next and again controversially, collaborative customer relationships where suppliers quantify value beyond price may yield process improvements that could mean that suppliers end up selling less. This ability to solve customer problems even at the expense of the supplier's own, immediate, and certain sales forges customer relationships which are, truly, strategic. Next, Kemps warns against the folly of managing by KPIs. KPIs are typically related to business processes which have only a random fit with the few business outcomes customers ultimately want to achieve: improvements in profitability, customer satisfaction, or innovation, for example. Kemps suggests that the cultural alignment between traits of customers and traits of the account management team is the most important factor enabling value quantification and effective collaboration. So where should companies start that wish to become fully proficient in value quantification? Kemps offers two pieces of advice: Number one, patience and perseverance – once the direction is clear, perseverance is required; number two, the relentless pursuit of differentiation – the opportunities for joint value creation – is limited only by individual imagination. Finally, the ring of truth – value is a promise; results are all that matter to customers. Kemps suggests that presenting the value credibly in ways that customers can relate to and verify for themselves is fundamentally important in the context of value quantification. Companies that excel at quantifying value cut through the fog of vague data and promises. The ring of truth is thus the metaphor for the ability to summarize the fruits of much thought and labor briefly and clearly.

Part VI, "Buying and selling on value: Value quantification tools," presents three chapters discussing value quantification tools.

In "A question of value: Customer value mapping versus economic value modeling," *Thomas Nagle* and *Gerald Smith* make a strong case against customer value mapping in the context of value quantification: Only a detailed step-by-step analysis aimed at quantifying the quantitative and qualitative benefits of a differentiated product can provide insights into total customer value and maximum willingness to pay. Simply put, customer value mapping assumes (a) that customer willingness to pay is proportional to the benefits provided and (b) that customers weigh benefits and prices equally. Both assumptions are wrong. Only a detailed mapping of the subjective, customer-specific economic benefits of a product – conducted via economic value measurement (Nagle and Holden, 2002), value calculators (Hinterhuber, 2015), or value word equations (Anderson et al., 2006) – allows the quantification of customer maximum willingness to pay. The widespread diffusion of customer value mapping is no indicator of its scientific value: Bad practice, unfortunately, can persist for decades and centuries. This chapter makes a strong case for a scientifically robust (Sinha and DeSarbo, 1998) approach to quantifying value and price in B2B and B2C markets.

In "Why start-ups should consider using value propositions," *Lennart Foos* and *Markus Kirchberger* also make a case for value quantification via the customer value proposition for start-ups. In this chapter, the authors provide a step-by-step guide to developing a monetary customer value proposition. The research underpinning their work suggests that the early development of these value propositions increases the chances of selecting appropriate target markets and of successfully introducing new technologies. The development of quantified customer value propositions is thus a capability that aspiring entrepreneurs must master.

Tim Underhill, in "Creating and sustaining competitive advantage through documented total cost savings," likewise suggests that quantifying customer benefits is necessary and beneficial for suppliers. This chapter provides a case study of value quantification in industrial markets.

Part VII, "Epilogue," contains several short chapters that summarize salient aspects of value quantification and provide an outlook on the shape of value quantification capabilities in the future.

In "A call to action: Value quantification in B2B buying and selling" *Todd C. Snelgrove* invites both B2B procurement and B2B sales managers to quantify value in industrial buying and selling in order to uncover opportunities for mutual value co-creation in B2B exchange relationships.

In "Quotes and statistics to help you on your value selling journey" *Todd C. Snelgrove* presents quotes and summary statistics that attempt to highlight why value quantification is beneficial, both for sales and for procurement.

The final interview "The present and future of value quantification" by *Andreas Hinterhuber* and *Todd C. Snelgrove* sheds light on future capabilities related to value quantification. As outlined by several authors in the present book, value quantification in the future will focus on quantifying intangibles, including the quantification of non-economic benefits – likely even factors such as the value of a lower environmental impact. Value quantification capabilities are, and will be, a key differentiator between high- and low-performing companies. In the future, value quantification will be employed throughout the sales cycle with an increased focus on it in the new product development phase and an increased focus on innovative pricing models and performance-based and value-based pricing models. Finally, if value quantification is a recursive, iterative process, the availability of big data and experience will enable managers to make predictive assessments of customer-quantified benefits based on both human and artificial intelligence.

Sales and marketing are transitioning from price to value. We understand the idea of value and its multidimensional nature. In the context of quantifying value from the perspective of sellers, value is equal to the sum of quantified, monetary customer benefits, that is, the sum of quantitative customer benefits – revenue/gross margin increases, cost reductions, risk reductions, and capital expense savings – and qualitative customer benefits – such as ease of doing business, customer relationships, industry experience, brand value, emotional benefits, or other process benefits – expressed as one figure equating total customer benefits received (Hinterhuber, 2017). We know what value quantification capabilities are, and we know, via numerous, independent, converging studies, that value quantification capabilities increase firm performance. This is the perspective of sales and marketing. Here, academia is clear and ahead of practice: The research, the examples, and best practices presented in this book can help companies still selling based on price or features to transition to selling based on value. Academic research is very clear: This will improve company performance.

Procurement is also transitioning from price to value. We do have an initial understanding that traditional metrics, such as price or TCO, are unable to capture the full spectrum of benefits that suppliers bring to customers. We also have an initial idea of a metric able to quantify tangible and intangible supplier benefits – TVC, discussed in this book, is one example of such metric.

Ideally, the metric that sales managers use to sell value to procurement – quantified, monetary customer benefits (Hinterhuber, 2017) – is the same metric that procurement uses to evaluate alternative offers from sales managers. The further development of a metric able to capture all tangible and intangible benefits of alternative offers in sourcing decisions will thus, in the end, build on the value quantification and pricing literature that has already produced them.

This is extraordinary and fantastic.

This is spectacular since the development of all – well, at least a good part – of what we know in strategic pricing – the idea of customer value as sum of reference value and differentiation value (Nagle and Holden, 2002) – that is, the big bang of strategic pricing, originated from research in procurement – value engineering – in the 1950s aimed at calculating maximum purchase prices. This is the lasting contribution of Nagle, who almost single-handedly created the field of strategic pricing as we know it.

This spectacular journey started in procurement; it inspired the nascent literature on strategic pricing which now, in late adolescence, inspires the mature literature on procurement in developing strategic sourcing models. Procurement, pricing, procurement – this is the beautiful journey, based on a very simple idea. Value first, then price.

References

Anderson, J. C., Kumar, N. and Narus, J. A. (2007) *Value Merchants: Demonstrating and Documenting Superior Value in Business Markets*, Boston, MA: Harvard Business School Press.

Anderson, J. C., Narus, J. A. and van Rossum, W. (2006) "Customer value propositions in business markets," *Harvard Business Review 84*(3), 90–99.

Heath, C. and Heath, D. (2010) *Switch: How to Change Things When Change Is Hard*, New York: Random House.

Hinterhuber, A. (2015) "Value quantification – The next challenge for B2B selling," in A. Hinterhuber and S. Liozu (eds.), *Pricing and the Sales Force* (pp. 20–32), New York: Routledge.

Hinterhuber, A. (2017) "Value quantification capabilities in industrial markets," *Journal of Business Research 76*, 163–178.

Hinterhuber, A. and Liozu, S. (eds.). (2020) *Pricing Strategy Implementation: Translating Pricing Strategy into Results*, Abingdon, UK: Routledge.

Keller, S. and Price, C. (2011) *Beyond Performance: How Great Organizations Build Ultimate Competitive Advantage*, Hoboken, NJ: Wiley.

Kellogg, K. C. (2008) *Not Faking It: Making Real Change in Response to Regulation at Two Surgical Teaching Hospitals*, Working Paper, MIT Sloan School of Management, Boston, MA.

Kotter, J. P. (1995) "Leading change: Why transformation efforts fail," *Harvard Business Review* 73(2), 59–67.

Nagle, T. T. and Holden, R. K. (2002) *The Strategy and Tactics of Pricing: A Guide to Profitable Decision Making* (3rd ed.), Englewood Cliffs, NJ: Prentice Hall.

Piscopo, G., Johnston, W. and Bellenger, D. (2008) "Total cost of ownership and customer value in business markets," *Advances in Business Marketing and Purchasing 14*, 205–220.

Sinha, I. and DeSarbo, W. S. (1998) "An integrated approach toward the spatial modeling of perceived customer value," *Journal of Marketing Research 35*(5), 236–249.

Snelgrove, T. (2012) "Value pricing when you understand your customers: Total cost of ownership – Past, present and future," *Journal of Revenue & Pricing Management 11*(1), 76–80.

Snelgrove, T. (2016) *Value First the Price – Quantifying Value in Business to Business Markets from the Perspective of Both Buyers and Sellers*, Abingdon, UK: Routledge.

Töytäri, P. and Rajala, R. (2015) "Value-based selling: An organizational capability perspective," *Industrial Marketing Management 45*, 101–112.

Vargo, S. L. and Lusch, R. F. (2004) "Evolving to a new dominant logic for marketing," *Journal of Marketing 68*(1), 1–17.

Part II

Selling value

Value quantification capabilities

2 Value first, then price

The new paradigm of B2B buying and selling

Hinterhuber, Andreas, Snelgrove, Todd C., and Stensson, Bo-Inge

The problem

Most companies today take an inherently adversarial approach to buying and selling in industrial markets, thereby missing out on opportunities for joint value creation with suppliers and customers. Procurement is relegated to an administrative role, as the sales function commoditizes the value that other functions – R&D, marketing, operations – have created.

The solution

We present a set of principles that enable companies to put joint value creation at the center of their relationships with suppliers and customers.

The benefits

Focusing first on value, then on price, our research suggests, leads to higher profitability. The procurement function, typically regarded as a cost center, becomes a source of innovation and a driver of good corporate citizenship. The sales function, by emphasizing first value and then price, transforms an adversarial relationship with customers into a collaborative relationship. As a result, customers, suppliers, and society at large benefit.

Introduction

Allow us to take you on a tour, meeting your sales managers as they negotiate prices with their customers. You will see buyers who are either supremely cool or excited, but they never quite seem real – as an observer, you wonder if you are the only one to notice – and sellers who are under visible pressure. Offers fly back and forth until an agreement is reached. Buyers seem happy about the discount, and sellers seem to be busy calculating their commissions. Who won? Difficult to tell.

Follow us again to meet your buyers as they negotiate prices with their suppliers. "You can go lower!" you feel tempted to shout. "I have seen this before," you hear yourself saying, "not just now, but a hundred and a thousand times before. Did nothing change over the past decades?" And indeed, for most companies in industrial markets, the answer is no: The price is still the main element of buying and selling in industrial markets – little seems to have changed. The approach typically taken by purchasing and sales executives vis-à-vis their suppliers and customers is best summarized in one word: adversarial.

DOI: 10.4324/9781003177937-4

This need not be. Our experience at SKF, the US $9 billion manufacturer of industrial bearings and other components based in Gothenburg, Sweden, and the research we conducted with numerous other B2B companies (Hinterhuber, 2017) lead us to suggest a way to break from this vicious cycle of buying and selling in industrial markets.

Let us accompany one of the co-authors of this chapter, Todd C. Snelgrove, then SKF's vice-president of value, on a sales encounter with a global steel company purchasing industrial bearings. Industrial bearings are, to the layperson, commodities – apparently interchangeable steel used as parts of wheels and other moving objects. SKF's product has a list price of $15 (all numbers are disguised), whereas the product of its main competitor has a list price of $10. How would negotiations evolve within your own company? Most purchasing and sales executives we quiz during our workshops suggest that, depending on circumstances, both parties would compromise at around $12 in an attempt to seal a deal, with a few thousand dollars' worth of services such as training or installation thrown in for free.

This is, however, not the case in a typical sales encounter with SKF sales managers. Typically, purchasing managers – well-trained, aggressive industrial purchasing managers – pay the list price of $15. The reason is that, in a sales encounter with SKF, the discussion is first on value, then on price. The sales encounter is centered first on what the customer gets and only thereafter on what the supplier gets. This, we believe, is one simple reason why SKF is able to differentiate what many other companies would view as a commodity (see Figure 2.1).

SKF's product carries a price premium of 50% over the product of its key competitor. Yet sales managers at SKF are able to demonstrate to customers that customers end up paying less and being better off by purchasing from SKF. The company presents its price premium as an investment required to obtain clearly defined monetary benefits. In this case, an investment of $5 (i.e., the price difference between the two products) will lead to quantified customer benefits of $30 (i.e., the incremental performance advantage of SKF's

Figure 2.1 First value, then price: Value quantification drives profits at SKF (Snelgrove, 2013)

product, calculated via longer uptime, higher reliability, faster installation, lower lubrication costs, and other elements).

SKF and other high-performing companies turn sales negotiations from a discussion about price to a visualization of value and present their competitive advantages in a language that every purchasing manager understands: money, that is, quantified customer benefits (Figure 2.2).

We contend that if SKF is able to get paid for value by selling an apparently commoditized product carrying a price premium of 50% over competition, so should other companies with products that are frequently more differentiated than those of SKF. Our combined practical experience in B2B selling and buying and the research we conducted provide a roadmap for tackling this challenge.

As the example given earlier suggests, best practices within companies such as SKF differ from approaches other companies typically take: compromise on price to get the deal. The focus on value versus price is an important one among many other elements: Our premise is that, in the future, the need for collaborative value creation with customers is so pervasive that it will transform the way B2B companies buy and sell. In other words, the rules for buying and selling in the future are being rewritten, and a number of companies – SKF among them – allow us a glimpse of future best practices. We sketch out what could be called the new rules of buying and selling in B2B markets, starting with the former.

	PAST best practice	FUTURE best practice
MAIN PURCHASE CRITERIA	PRICE, QUALITY, DELIVERY	Quality, cost, delivery, innovation, management (QCDIM) Total cost and total value of ownership Performance-based contracts
CONSIDERATION OF SOFT FACTORS	GENERALLY NOT	**YES:** sustainability, risk, agility and innovation are key differentiators for suppliers
RELATIONSHIPS WITH SUPPLIERS	ADVERSARIAL BTI/BTU (bring them in, beat them up)	**COLLABORATIVE, OBJECTIVE IS JOINT VALUE CREATION WIN-WIN; SHARED KPIS**
TIME HORIZON	SHORT TERM	**LONG TERM**
INTER-COMPANY COLLABORATION	LIMITED – purchasing department operates largely autonomously	**HIGH** – cross functional collaboration with sales, marketing, R&D, manufacturing, finance and suppliers
CONTRIBUTION	TACTICAL, LOW IMPACT	**STRATEGIC, HIGH IMPACT**
MAIN EXPLICIT ASSUMPTION	PRODUCTS ARE COMMODITIES	**SUPPLIERS ARE A SOURCE OF INNOVATION**
MAIN IMPLICIT ASSUMPTION	COMPANIES COMPETE AGAINST EACH OTHER	**ECO-SYSTEMS COMPETE AGAINST EACH OTHER**
CAPABILITIES	PRODUCT AND PRICE	Understanding both supplier and customer value propositions, **END-TO-END VALUE CHAIN KNOWLEDGE**

Figure. 2.2 The new rules of purchasing in B2B

B2B buying in the future: About ecosystems and innovation

In industrial buying, best current and best future practices differ markedly. (See Figure 2.2 for an overview.)

Today, B2B procurement is concerned about price, quality, and delivery – soft factors are typically not considered. Relationships with suppliers are adversarial. In the global car industry, for example, studies measuring the quality of relationships between suppliers and manufacturers not only find that GM and Chrysler receive the lowest ratings on trust while being seen as the most demanding in terms of expected price concessions by their suppliers; these studies also find that best-in-class companies such as Porsche or Toyota do not score significantly better on these criteria (Supplier Business, 2009). Adversarial relationships with suppliers are pervasive, even among companies that today are regarded as best in class. Relationships with suppliers are thus mostly short term, and the procurement department today operates largely autonomously. This inherently limits its impact on overall company priorities to a tactical contribution at best. Implicitly, the procurement function today seems to treat every item on its shopping list as a commodity: Some companies do so quite explicitly. Shell's purchasing guidelines read, "Within Shell we do not differentiate between commoditised and non-commoditised products and services and consider all markets for which there is more than one supplier a commodity market" (Shell, 2006).

Fritz Henderson, chief operating officer of GM at that time, summarized the company's aspiration as "GM builds vehicles that people want to buy" (Henderson, 2009). The statement is trite. Most companies underestimate the monumental challenges that B2B procurement faces if it is to become a significant contributor to overall company success.

What are these challenges, then? Put simply, CEOs want more from procurement than price, quality, and delivery. CEOs demand innovation, sustainability, and ideas. The bombshell dropped, we contend, in June 2015 when six of the largest European oil and gas firms called for a globally coordinated price to reduce carbon-dioxide emissions. Take note: Heavy polluters were not the only ones to shoot for a green revolution. In September 2015, Siemens, the German industrial giant, announced the goal of becoming the first major industrial company to achieve a net-zero carbon footprint by 2030. This requires, among other monumental changes, a 50% reduction in carbon-dioxide emissions and investments of over US $100 million (Siemens, 2015).

The evidence is very compelling: The world and the strategic priorities of companies are changing, and the procurement function needs to drive this change. Profit or shareholder value maximization is not enough: Companies need to make a contribution beyond satisfying the requirements of shareholders, customers, and employees. As lofty as it may sound, the goal is to make the world a better place, and procurement, responsible essentially for everything that comes in, needs to live up to this aspiration.

Among the characteristics that characterize future best practices in B2B purchasing are a focus on innovation and management capabilities, in addition to quality, price, and delivery. This inevitably means that soft factors are the new hard factors: Sustainability, risk, agility, co-innovation, capacity management, supply chain transparency, and supplier labor standards are very important elements that cutting-edge purchasing managers consider in supplier selection. This inevitably shifts the time horizon from a short-term adversarial relationship to a long-term, collaborative relationship with suppliers aimed at joint value creation. The implicit assumption is that suppliers are precisely the opposite of manufacturers of commodities: Suppliers are a potential source of innovation that savvy purchasing managers leverage to their advantage. This is driven by the recognition that competition is manifest not only at the level of the individual company, but that it happens increasingly at the level of ecosystems (Hinterhuber and Nilles, 2021). In a nutshell, supply chains and ecosystems compete against each other, not only companies.

Apple is an obvious example, but SKF, a manufacturer of industrial components, may also serve as illustration: Through subsidiaries, alliances, and acquisitions, SKF has developed a tight network of support and knowledge partners – including research institutions – that help its industrial customers in productivity improvements. In line with the company's vision – to equip the world with SKF knowledge – the focus of this tight network is knowledge creation to drive customer profitability. SKF's ecosystem thus acts as a powerful choice driver for industrial customers.

B2B selling in the future: First value, then price

B2B selling is likewise undergoing a major change. (See Figure 2.3, which summarizes current versus future best practices in industrial selling.)

Selling today is, we learn, about communicating unique selling points (USPs) to customers. Sellers promise results to customers. The primary contact of B2B sellers is the procurement function. Sellers follow the mantra of cutting-edge marketing textbooks that present a dichotomous choice for profitable marketing strategies (Kotler and Keller, 2011): skimming (high price, low volume) or penetration (low price, high volume). Discounts are the key selling tool. Sales force compensation is linked to profit or revenue targets. The main implicit assumption is that differentiation is difficult in an environment shaped by aggressive purchasing managers who are increasingly selecting suppliers based

	PAST best practice	**FUTURE** best practice
MAIN SELLING POINTS	USP (unique selling proposition)	**DOCUMENTED AND QUANTIFIED CUSTOMER VALUE**
RESULTS	PROMISED	**GUARANTEED**
KEY CONTACTS	NARROW: mostly purchasing	**BROAD:** can include senior management
KEY GOALS	HIGH PRICE OR HIGH MARKET SHARE	**HIGH PRICE AND HIGH MARKET SHARE**
MAIN TACTICAL SELLING TOOL	DISCOUNTS	**GUARANTEED PERFORMANCE METRICS VALUE CALCULATORS**
SALES FORCE COMPENSATION	LINKED TO COMPANY REVENUES OR GROSS MARGINS	**LINKED TO CUSTOMER PROFIT IMPROVEMENTS**
MAIN EXPLICIT ASSUMPTION	BUYERS ARE PRICE SENSITIVE, PRODUCTS ARE COMMODITIES	**COMMODITIES DO NOT EXIST CO-INNOVATION WITH CUSTOMERS**
MAIN IMPLICIT ASSUMPTION	SELLING IS ABOUT RELATIONSHIPS	**SELLING IS ABOUT BUSINESS PARTNERSHIPS**

Figure 2.3 The new rules of selling in B2B

on price. In order to mitigate the impact of price-sensitive customers, today the best-performing sales organizations concentrate on forging relationships with their customers.

This is, we think, the world of selling as we know it. As the experiences of the best-practice companies in our research suggest, selling is being radically transformed. In the future, selling is not at all about selling USPs – who says, after all, that they actually improve customer profitability?

Selling is all about creating, quantifying, and documenting value to customers. Paula Gildert, then VP Global Head Strategic Sourcing at Novartis Pharma, has the following advice for any sales manager knocking on the company's doors: "Suppliers often don't come to us with a business case. But it's what we want. Sell your value in our numbers to get our attention. But if you can't quantify your value, don't be surprised at the failure of procurement to do so" (Snelgrove, 2018: 252).

Witness SKF's Documented Solutions Program, which guarantees performance outcomes to customers and allows SKF to achieve premium prices vis-à-vis customers. This means results are not promised – results are guaranteed (Hinterhuber and Snelgrove, 2020).

As the introductory example illustrates, in this case both SKF and its customers win. Metso, a technology supplier to the mining industry that evolved into Metso Outotec, is another pertinent example. "Expect results" was the company's tagline as a stand-alone company. Perttu Louhiluoto, president of the Mineral Services business area, notes that "suppliers need to be able to demonstrate and quantify the economic value of their offering beyond cash cost" (Louhiluoto, 2017: 10). Consequently, the company's CEO stresses the importance of "value quantification to the customer" noting that a solid understanding of customers' business enables the company "to quantify the business impact for the customer" (Kähkönen, 2012: 21). The increased importance of value quantification as a new capability of sales managers is also reflected in changes in the company's service offering: Traditionally, Metso – but many other companies as well – offered "break-fix support"; now the company is offering consulting contracts that optimize total cost of ownership and performance-based contracts that optimize customer operations (Silvennoinen, 2014: 20). Simplifying a bit, in these cases the service offering evolves from "done to" to "done with" to, finally, "done for" the customer. In the latter two cases, value quantification capabilities are, of course, of central importance. This approach to selling also allows a company to overcome the false dichotomy between high price and high market share: SKF, like Apple, is a market share leader and premium price producer at the same time. A focus on value enables high market share and premium prices to coexist.

Sales force compensation is linked not only to profit or revenue goals – these are, after all, internal indicators – but it is increasingly linked to outcomes that matter to customers, such as customer profit improvements or customer satisfaction. Implicitly, these companies feel very strongly that commodities do not exist. There is no product that cannot be differentiated. Shell, for example, illustrates that even a tradable commodity like gasoline can be differentiated, as in the highly successful introduction of V-Power (Hinterhuber, 2016). The end result is that selling is about forging business partnerships with customers.

International logistics company DHL is a superb example. Pascal Kemps, sector head for passenger vehicles, frequently observes that the shipping operations of large customers – for example, global car manufacturers – are not optimized: When customers ask DHL and its competitors to submit a quotation, competitors will submit a proposal for, for example, 80 containers, as specified in the bidding documents. DHL, by contrast, typically will suggest freight optimization first, which means DHL ends up selling less (Hinterhuber and Kemps, 2017). DHL quotes a price for 70 containers, for example, and highlights the steps to implement route optimization. This reduces revenues short term: "You need to make an investment to service a customer in order to achieve a longer-term sustainable success" (Hinterhuber and Kemps, 2017: 173). This sacrifice, Kemps suggests, builds invaluable trust with customers.

Forging partnerships requires, as the experience of DHL suggests, a cultural change. In Japan there is a beautiful expression: "You have to be prepared to sit on a rock for three years," observes Kemps,

> which means that sometimes you have to be in a difficult, painful situation before you get results. I know that's difficult for many of my colleagues, but fortunately I'm in an organization where it's understood that things may take time and it's accepted that sometimes you need to make an investment to service a customer in order to achieve a longer-term sustainable success. I'm well aware that that's not the case in all organizations.
>
> (Hinterhuber and Kemps, 2017: 173)

Accordingly, DHL links sales force compensation to customer-related outcomes, such as profit improvements or customer satisfaction, and not only to company-related outcomes, such as sales or margin budgets.

The dual focus on value in both purchasing and selling allows SKF and other companies to thrive in a very competitive environment. In a stagnating environment, SKF, for example, has grown substantially vis-à-vis competitors. The procurement and supply chain functions have taken a proactive stance, moving from knowledge and compliance toward commitment and contribution as good corporate citizens. The performance has been honored as best in class by the Dow Jones Sustainability Index.

More broadly, several independent, quantitative studies with hundreds of respondents in B2B conclude that companies that sell on value are substantially more profitable than companies that sell on costs (Hinterhuber, 2017; Hogan, 2008; Liozu and Hinterhuber, 2013; Nagle and Müller, 2018) and that companies buying on total cost of ownership are again substantially more profitable than companies buying on price (Manufacturers Alliance for Productivity and Innovation, 2012).

Buying and selling in B2B is not a zero-sum game: Customers, suppliers, and the society at large benefit from a joint focus on value and innovation occurring at the extreme ends of the organization – in buying and selling. Putting value ahead of price transforms a traditionally adversarial relationship into a collaborative partnership that unleashes profits and innovation.

Note: Part of this research was undertaken previously while Andreas Hinterhuber, Todd C. Snelgrove, and Bo-Inge Stensson were working in different roles: Andreas Hinterhuber, Partner, Hinterhuber & Partners; Todd C. Snelgrove, Vice President Value, SKF; Bo-Inge Stensson, SVP Group Procurement, SKF.

Acknowledgment

Reprinted, with permission, from Hinterhuber, A., Snelgrove, T. C., & Stensson, B.-I. (2021). Value first, then price: the new paradigm of B2B buying and selling. Journal of

Revenue and Pricing Management, 20(4), 403-409. https://doi.org/10.1057/s41272-021-00304-3;

References

Henderson, F. (2009) "Re-inventing GM: GM investor presentation," www.autonews.com/assets/PDF/CA59644122.PDF. Accessed 30 August 2014

Hinterhuber, A. (2016) "The six pricing myths that kill profits," *Business Horizons 59*(1), 71–83.

Hinterhuber, A. (2017) "Value quantification capabilities in industrial markets," *Journal of Business Research 76*, 163–178.

Hinterhuber, A. and Kemps, P. (2017) "Interview: The ring of truth – value quantification in B2B services," in A. Hinterhuber and T. Snelgrove (eds.), *Value First, then Price: Quantifying Value in Business Markets from the Perspective of Both Buyers and Sellers* (pp. 161–177), Abingdon: Routledge.

Hinterhuber, A. and Nilles, M. (2021) "Digital transformation, the holy grail and the disruption of business models," *Business Horizons.* https://doi.org/10.1016/j.bushor.2021.02.042.

Hinterhuber, A. and Snelgrove, T. (2020) "The present and future of value quantification," *Journal of Creating Value 6*(2), 295–303.

Hogan, J. (2008) *Building a World Class Pricing Capability: Where Does Your Company Stack Up?* Cambridge: Monitor Group Perspectives.

Kähkönen, M. (2012) "Creating long-term value," Metso Capital Markets Day Presentation, 11 December, Vantaa, Finland.

Kotler, P. and Keller, K. L. (2011) *Marketing Management* (14th ed.), Upper Saddle River: Prentice Hall.

Liozu, S. and Hinterhuber, A. (2013) "Pricing orientation, pricing capabilities, and firm performance," *Management Decision 51*(3), 594–614.

Louhiluoto, P. (2017) "Three horizons of profitable growth," Metso Capital Markets Day Investor Presentation, 1 June, Vantaa, Finland.

Manufacturers Alliance for Productivity and Innovation. (2012) *Approaches Towards Purchasing on Total Cost of Ownership*, Arlington: A MAPI Council Survey.

Nagle, T. and Müller, G. (2018) *The Strategy and Tactics of Pricing: A Guide to Growing More Profitably* (6th ed.), New York, NY: Routledge.

Shell. (2006) *Shell Procurement Guide to Online Bidding.* quoted in: Effective strategies for dealing with procurement, Huthwaite Inter- national, 2008.

Siemens, A. G. (2015) Siemens to be climate neutral by 2030: Siemens press release, Munich 22 September.

Silvennoinen, J. (2014) "The leader in value-adding services," Metso Capital Markets Day Investor presentation, 26 November, Amsterdam, The Netherlands.

Snelgrove, T. (2013) "Creating value that customers are willing and able to pay for," Presentation at the Product Management Forum of the Manufacturers Alliance for Productivity and Innovation (MAPI), Rosemont, IL.

Snelgrove, T. (2018) "Creating, calculating and communicating customer value: How companies can set premium prices that customers are willing and able to pay," in A. Hinterhuber and S. Liozu (eds.), *Innovation in Pricing: Contemporary Theories and Best Practices* (2nd ed., pp. 244–256), New York, NY: Routledge.

Supplier Business. (2009) "2009 OEM-Supplier relations study, planning perspectives international," www.autonews.com/assets/PPT/CA66291725.PPT. Accessed 15 July 2015

Funding Open access funding provided by Università Ca' Foscari Venezia within the CRUI-CARE Agreement.

3 Interview

Processes and capabilities for value quantification

Hinterhuber, Andreas and Russell, Robert

ROBERT RUSSELL: Andreas, you've been working with companies for many years on pricing. What's the first thing you do when you have a new client?

ANDREAS HINTERHUBER: I have a lot of respect for the medical profession: Excellent consultants are like doctors – they improve the lives of their clients. The most important part in this process is diagnosis. If we get the diagnosis wrong, even the best, scientifically most advanced treatment will lead nowhere.

ROBERT RUSSELL: How do you apply this insight to the world of pricing?

ANDREAS HINTERHUBER: Over the past years, we at Hinterhuber & Partners have invested a very substantial amount of time and intellectual effort to develop state-of-the-art diagnostic instruments in pricing. We use rigorous pricing tools and checklists to analyze what we term the "3Cs": customers, competitors, and the company itself. To understand customers we use the customer needs profiler to gain relevant insights; to understand and map competitors we use the competitive advantage profiler. To understand the client company we use the competitive advantage profiler and our value quantification tool. We further assess company pricing capabilities via a scale, PRICECAP, that we've developed, and we map all processes that involve pricing decisions, typically the sales process in B2C and the offer development process in B2B. We complement this with structured interviews with key executives in marketing, sales, and pricing; with interviews with customers and distributors; and with an analysis of company documents on profitability by product, sales rep, region, customer, and segment. This provides us with, first, very important insights about the current situation of the client . . .

ROBERT RUSSELL: . . . but does not yield any specific insights related to pricing?

ANDREAS HINTERHUBER: Correct, in principle. To understand why, we have to remember that pricing decisions are usually the result of a chain of prior decisions, typically either horizontal chains, i.e., different departments within an organization, or vertical chains, i.e., different hierarchical levels. We cannot improve pricing by changing prices. We have to work on the chain of effects to understand which prior decisions, which structural configurations, or which other elements influence the effectiveness of pricing.

ROBERT RUSSELL: Maybe you could provide an example to illustrate this point.

ANDREAS HINTERHUBER: We recently completed a pricing project with a German B2B company with sales in excess of €5 billion. As part of the diagnosis, we mapped the key processes where pricing decisions were made. The key process in B2B is, as mentioned, the offer development process – most industrial companies have a similar process in place that covers the following seven elements: generation of customer

DOI: 10.4324/9781003177937-5

insights, identification of market opportunities, evaluation of market opportunities, offer development, quotation, negotiation, and, finally, offer delivery. Figure 3.1 provides an overview. The client illustrated in Figure 3.1 had an offer development process in place, but the analysis revealed that profitability suffered as a result of a poor design on nearly all elements in this process. Customer insights, for example, were not shared between sales managers and regions, so the salesforce was perceived as out of sync by some customer segments. Likewise, executives did not systemically collect, let alone share, information on price levels or offer configurations of competitors. Sales managers responded passively to requests for proposals rather than actively developing new markets and cross-selling new products to existing customers. Sales managers used revenues and not gross margins to evaluate market opportunities, meaning that the company's best available technical talent was regularly assigned to large but unprofitable deals. Also, the offer development reflected what salespeople thought customers wanted instead of taking customer insight to develop the value proposition; solutions were thus frequently over-engineered or quoted at rock-bottom prices unnecessarily.

Quotations were strictly done on a cost-plus basis: The company had a pricing tool, which upon close inspection was nothing but a revamped costing tool. Sales managers thus did not have the capabilities or tools to incorporate considerations on customer value – how much customers were willing to pay – into the price quotation. Furthermore, there was no follow-up on quotations the company did not win: Sales managers could not indicate, even if they wanted to, why any given tender was lost. To state it clearly, best-practice companies understand why deals are lost and analyze the relative frequency of, for example, reasons related to product, price, availability, relationship, quote speed, project cancellation, service, or quality. This win/loss analysis is a fundamental part of improving pricing in competitive bidding situations, but it was completely absent in this case. Negotiations were sometimes ineffective, simply because sales managers did not know how to sell and price out supplementary services to customers. Furthermore, discounting guidelines did not exist: Sales

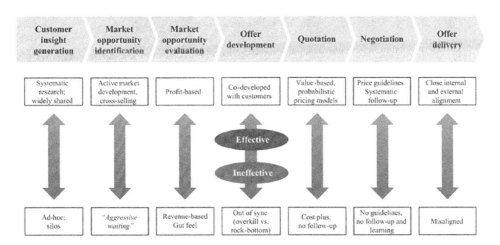

Figure 3.1 The offer development process in B2B: Effective and ineffective practices

Source: Hinterhuber & Partners

managers were simply encouraged to "do their best" to sell at list prices, but there was no follow-up, no learning, and no improvement in net price realization. In this process alone, our analysis identified several million euros in profit improvements. Delivery was the only element in this process that worked really well – that was the only part in the process we recommended not to touch at this stage. In summary, in order to drive profits via pricing, we frequently need to examine the entire chain of effects, and in this case the offer development process was probably the single best starting point. While this situation is unique, I would contend that the quality of the diagnostic part is a fundamental aspect of all pricing projects.

ROBERT RUSSELL: What specific improvements in the area of pricing do you then implement?

ANDREAS HINTERHUBER: In 2012, we published an article in the *MIT Sloan Management Review*, "Is It Time to Rethink Your Pricing Strategy?" This article distinguishes between "price setting" and "price getting": Combining these two elements gives us our pricing capability grid (see Figure 3.2; Hinterhuber and Liozu, 2012).

Price setting refers to the different approaches companies use to determine selling prices: cost-based pricing, competition-based pricing, and customer-value-based pricing. Price getting refers to different abilities to actually get the price set out in the first place: Some companies are very good at realizing their list prices, via, for example, value communication, customer value quantification, or price controlling. Other companies are less effective, and prices erode as a result of poor negotiation, poor value communication, or weak price-realization capabilities. Salesforce incentives may play a role as well. We use this framework to map where our clients stand today – that is, where they stand today in terms of price setting and price getting – and we use this framework to jointly define a 1- to 2-year target: Together with

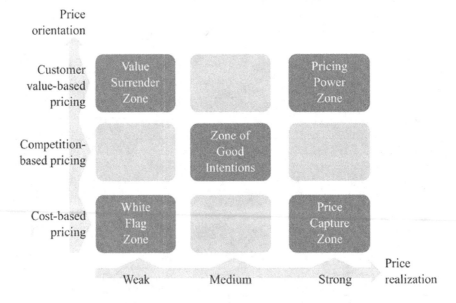

Figure 3.2 The pricing capability grid. Reprinted from A. Hinterhuber and S. Liozu, 2012, "Is It Time to Rethink Your Pricing Strategy?" *MIT Sloan Management Review* 53(4), 69–77. © 2012 from MIT Sloan Management Review/Massachusetts Institute of Technology

senior executives we define where the company as a whole should be in terms of price setting and price getting. This typically leads to very specific actions and projects in these two areas.

ROBERT RUSSELL: Does pricing need to be customer-specific?

ANDREAS HINTERHUBER: Yes. Many companies have pricing processes that are, counterintuitively, both too rigid and too flexible. Too rigid, because many companies basically have a one-size-fits-all pricing strategy. Too flexible, because there are too many price exceptions. On the former: Take the case of how airline companies set ticket prices until about 30 years ago. They sold tickets like bus companies sell tickets today: one price for one destination. And this, of course, fails to capture the value that different customer segments may place on a ticket. For some, value means evening return flights; for others it may mean flexibility, or service quality, or status miles. Today the airline companies use an understanding of customer willingness to pay in order to set prices differently based on differences in value provided to their customers. Revenue management is, of course, practised nearly universally by the airline industry, and it is a key contributor to profitability also in a number of other industries, like the hotel industry, the rental car industry, and even in some B2B contexts. So, yes, pricing needs to be customer-specific and thus flexible. But pricing needs an element of rigidity as well: We need rules, guidelines, and policies. Tom Nagle – a pioneer in pricing – defines pricing criteria as the requirements that customers or orders must meet in order to qualify for lower prices (see Nagle and Holden, 2002). The key insight is this: Sales managers implement pricing policies, but they cannot have primary responsibility for defining these policies in the first place. In this respect and in this respect only, pricing needs to become more rigid, especially in B2B companies where prices are generally negotiated.

ROBERT RUSSELL: You were asked at a recent event at the Institute of Chartered Accountants of England and Wales (ICAEW) about service pricing. Services account for 60% to 80% of GDP in advanced economies. Services do have specific traits which may pose challenges for pricing. The value may be intangible. Determining relevant costs is frequently arbitrary. So in many service industries the hourly rate is frequently the dominant pricing approach, be it in law firms, advertising agencies, or even top-tier management consultancies like McKinsey, BCG or Hinterhuber & Partners. But you suggested, then, that this was an outmoded method. How easy would it be to go into a company and suggest that they radically reform their pricing? This may mean, of course, massive cuts to their costs.

ANDREAS HINTERHUBER: This question is excellent because it implies that changing pricing practices involves far more than changing list prices. I agree: Changing pricing practices is, in many cases, a case for a true organizational transformation. It's a bit like changing the company DNA. Pricing is part of the company culture, and changing pricing practices requires a change in capabilities, in culture, in structure, in incentive systems, and in how the company interacts with customers. This applies also to the change from hourly rates to value-based or outcome-based pricing. Any company aiming to change from cost-based to value-based pricing is well advised to treat this change as a true organizational change management program. Here, the eight-step change model of Kotter (1995) can provide a useful framework for kick-starting this organizational transformation related to pricing (see Figure 3.3). Companies need to establish a sense of urgency, they need to form powerful guiding coalitions, and they need to establish a compelling vision. They also need to communicate this vision,

	Main Steps	*Key Activities*
1	Establishing a sense of urgency	Examining competitive realities Identifying crises or major opportunities
2	Forming a powerful guiding coalition	Assembling a group with enough power Encouraging the group to work together
3	Creating a vision	Creating a vision to direct the change Developing implementation strategies
4	Communicating the vision	Using every vehicle to communicate Teaching new behaviors by example
5	Empowering others to act on the vision	Eliminating obstacles; changing structure Encouraging risk taking
6	Planning for and creating short-term wins	Planning and creating key improvements Rewarding employees involved
7	Consolidating improvements and producing still more change	Using increased credibility to changing structures that don't fit; adding projects
8	Institutionalizing new approaches	Articulating the connections between the new behaviors and corporate success

Figure 3.3 The eight-step change model

Source: Kotter, 1995

remove the inevitable obstacles to change, and they need quick wins able to demonstrate that pricing works. Companies need to build on these quick wins and they need to, finally, institutionalize the new approach to pricing in their culture.

A change in pricing practices is an organizational change management program. As such, it needs CEO support. In a recent research project (Liozu and Hinterhuber, 2013), we polled 358 CEOs of mostly medium-sized companies and documented that CEO championing of pricing leads to both increased pricing capabilities and improved firm performance in industrial firms. CEOs thus can play a very important role by acting as champions of pricing and the pricing function. This is something that few companies have fully understood.

ROBERT RUSSELL: If I were, say, a lawyer delivering a service at a rate per hour and if I had an existing customer who was used to paying so many thousand pounds a year who then said, "Okay, we want you to tender now," and I said, "Okay, I'll give you value added," how would I know the value?

ANDREAS HINTERHUBER: There is one golden rule. If you are a lawyer you should not ask what you do for your client. What you should ask is what the client is able to do as a result of working with you – as opposed to working with your closest competitor. You have to ask what your competitive advantage is incrementally worth to customers in monetary terms. In your example, this lawyer could thus tie the professional fees to quantifiable outcomes, jointly defined with clients: Relevant outcomes could be the level of compliance achieved, lawsuits won, or other indicators which matter to clients. I need to make one point clear. Value-based pricing requires differentiation. One of my favorite quotes – our clients say that we actually coined this quote – is "If you are not perceived as being different, you will be benchmarked on price." So the idea that you can define outcomes, implement value-based pricing for standardized, fully commoditized products or services, is wrong. Although I strongly believe that commodities do not exist, I do recognize that, in any industry, there may be products or services where differentiation is not economically feasible, at least not in the short term. Take a supply contract for a ton of standard-grade office paper. In these or similar cases, after a conscious decision on whether or not to participate in a bid, I suggest reverting to competitive pricing, adjusted to reflect differences in offer quality, if relevant.

ROBERT RUSSELL: Microsoft has decided that Internet Explorer is basically dead. So they're going to kill it off metaphorically and replace it with a new interface for the Internet to compete more effectively with Chrome. So the point is: some companies may have to decide that their product line does not have value.

ANDREAS HINTERHUBER: Fair observation.

ROBERT RUSSELL: I don't suppose they would call you in and you would say there's no point to have a price for this because it has nothing left.

ANDREAS HINTERHUBER: I think I would make two observations. End-of-life-cycle pricing frequently allows price increases. Take the pharmaceutical industry as one, representative, example: Once a product goes off patent and before literally dozens of generic competitors rush to the market, the patent holders increase the price. A back-of-the-envelope calculation with the three variables *contribution margin, break-even sales analysis*, and *post-patent price elasticity* shows that pharmaceutical companies lose more margin by dropping prices than they do by increasing prices. This pattern holds, I suspect, also in other situations where products reach the end of their life cycle and where a small but loyal segment of customers exists. The other, equally important observation is that killing products is a necessary component of good management practice. Most companies do this too late. Many companies make the mistake of carrying a large product portfolio, which of course also carries the risk that salespeople focus then on the wrong products. And so it takes courage to ask, "Where am I truly competitive? In which areas am I able to deliver outstanding value?" It takes courage to then say, "Okay, I withdraw from products or segments A, B, and C because this is not where I want to be in the future and instead I do something else."

ROBERT RUSSELL: There is an example in Britain of a brewing company. They used to make beer, and now they run coffee shops and hotels. So they killed off their entire product. I find that extraordinary. That they reinvented themselves, presumably by looking at the profitability of beer and the profitability of coffee and deciding that this is a better way to go. But that kind of radical reform isn't something that many companies do.

ANDREAS HINTERHUBER: Yes.

ROBERT RUSSELL: This type of radical change is probably rare: in addition, when companies implement such radical change, they probably do not call in top management consultants like you for advice. But, then again, I may be wrong on this one.

ANDREAS HINTERHUBER: Interestingly, we are called in also at an early stage where companies truly want to understand their strategic direction, including the strategic direction of pricing for the future. And in this case, articulate, analytical, and independent thinkers can be quite helpful. Since we are not attached to a company's history and we don't fully understand the politics, our only concern is the future, and maybe that is an advantage.

ROBERT RUSSELL: Many companies, both in B2B and B2C, struggle when having to set prices for innovations, especially when these innovations are radical.

ANDREAS HINTERHUBER: The pricing of innovations is a particularly interesting and challenging area – simply because for true breakthrough innovations there is no reference value, there is no benchmark against which to compare a new product.

ROBERT RUSSELL: How do you set prices for breakthrough innovations?

ANDREAS HINTERHUBER: We unbundle first, and we aim to increase the perceived value with a strategic approach to pricing in a subsequent step. First, we decompose the innovation into the three or four benefits delivered and determine customer willingness to pay for each of these component benefits. This approach, summing customer willingness to pay for the components and adjusting the sum for any interactions if relevant, allows us to quantify customer willingness to pay for breakthrough innovations very, very accurately. An example will illustrate the principles. A few years ago a major, global tobacco company approached Hinterhuber & Partners ahead of a planned new product launch: a smokeless cigarette. This product is tobacco-based, thus satisfying smokers' cravings, but it does not emit smoke, thus consumable wherever smoking restrictions apply. We used ethnographic research to understand how this new product could fit into the lifestyles of current customers. This research indicated that the most likely, closest substitutes for this new product were energy drinks and coffee, which potential customers consumed when smoking was not an option and when they felt in need of a boost. This insight and a bit more research, some modeling, and a few other steps allowed us to attach a very precise price point to a product which can be considered a major, potentially breakthrough, innovation: This process allowed us to substantiate that willingness to pay for this innovation was closer to the price levels of energy drinks or coffee than to the price of a single cigarette. The second step in pricing breakthrough innovations is a conscious effort to increase customer willingness to pay. In a recent article (Hinterhuber, 2015) I highlight how companies can favorably influence customer perceptions of value and price without actually lowering the price. Understanding the psychological elements of pricing, understanding how customers perceive prices, allows companies to create and raise customer willingness to pay. Examples of companies that have a superb understanding of the psychological effects of pricing in order to increase customer willingness to pay are Apple in B2C or Xerox and Monsanto in B2B. Figure 3.4 provides the full overview of how companies can use an understanding of consumer psychology to increase customer willingness to pay.

ROBERT RUSSELL: That is brilliant, and I would like to ask another question. Let us discuss retail pricing. Take food or apparel retailers in the United Kingdom. Many of them are struggling because they are trying to justify the price differences they inevitably have over competing retailers. I think all these companies are now seeing massive changes to the way that customers behave. And I know that I wouldn't like to say this, but everyone will face it at some point: If people don't look at their pricing during times of calm, they may be forced to make radical changes during times of radical change.

ANDREAS HINTERHUBER: This, Robert, is a quotable quote indeed. Executives would be well advised to remember this. I agree: Once you enter rough waters, you lose degrees of freedom. So the best time to change your pricing strategy is when you don't have to.

ROBERT RUSSELL: What are some of these changes in retail pricing?

ANDREAS HINTERHUBER: One is a thing called the Internet, clearly. For retailers this requires a rethink away from standard, fixed mark-ups to mark-ups that reflect the

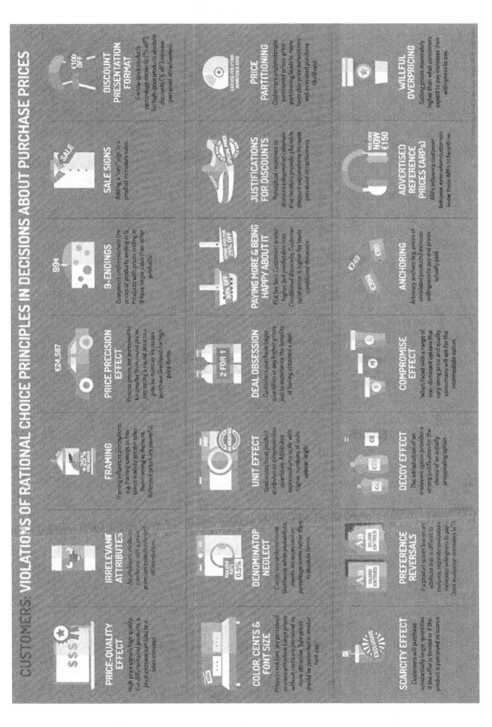

Figure 3.4 An overview of the psychological effects that shape customer perceptions of value and price. Reprinted with permission from A. Hinterhuber, 2015, "Violations of Rational Choice Principles in Pricing Decisions," *Industrial Marketing Management* 47, 65–74. Copyright Elsevier 2015, all rights reserved

incremental value that store-based retailers provide. When this value is there – because of services, warranties, immediate product availability, assortment – there are margins. When value is absent, margins go as well. The other change is the adjustment of prices based on the role that any given product plays for the customer. Products bought on impulse or as complements allow pricing freedom. Products that customers use to evaluate the overall price attractiveness of a retailer or products where price awareness is high require a different – frequently an aggressive – approach to retail pricing. Best-in-class retailers understand very well the role that any given product plays for customers and adjust prices accordingly.

Next is the disappearing middle ground. In many industries we see that the middle ground – companies that are neither the low-cost nor the most-differentiated suppliers – come under pressure, from both the low end and the high end. These companies are not well positioned, and this has a direct reflection on their pricing strategy. Take the car industry: Opel lost market share both to low-end Korean manufacturers and to high-end, premium car manufacturers. Similarly, in retailing, growth is happening largely at the extreme ends of the markets, in the low-price bracket and the premium price segment.

ROBERT RUSSELL: What are the implications for pricing?

ANDREAS HINTERHUBER: The implications are relatively straightforward: Many apparent pricing problems are in reality positioning problems. Companies need thus to understand their strengths and weaknesses, as perceived by customers. They need to understand how much value they create for their customers, as perceived by their customers, and not, I emphasize, how much value senior managers think these companies create for their customers. Once they have clarity on their competitive advantages and the monetary value of these competitive advantages to customers, then we can explore pricing. And it also links back to what we said before about pricing as the last decision in a chain of prior decisions. For a company such as Marks & Spencer, for example, to change their pricing strategy would probably be ridiculous. They may need to change their pricing, but first they need to change a whole range of other elements in their customer value proposition: probably assortment, maybe store layout, selection, services, loyalty cards, etc. And only after the senior leadership team has established a compelling value proposition – including an understanding of customer willingness to pay – will the time be right to explore adjusting the pricing strategy.

ROBERT RUSSELL: What are some of the emerging issues you see in pricing?

ANDREAS HINTERHUBER: Over the past five years, Hinterhuber & Partners has completed a major research project investigating how companies quantify their value proposition. For many companies the capability to quantify value is the single area where improvements are needed most. Our research also suggests quite clearly that those companies with the most developed capabilities to quantify the value proposition to customers in monetary terms are also the companies that outperform their competitors in profits and sales growth. On top of the agenda of any B2B senior sales or marketing manager worth her salt is the question of tools, processes, and capabilities to document and quantify value to customers. And this, I think, really is the litmus test of pricing.

ROBERT RUSSELL: You suggest that the ability to quantify value is the true indicator of whether or not companies are truly good at pricing?

ANDREAS HINTERHUBER: Yes. We have to remember that the most important feature of selling in industrial markets is the need of sellers to quantify value: Selling in industrial markets requires the ability to document in monetary terms ($/€/£/¥) how much incremental profit a proposed product or service delivers over the customer's next best alternative. Buying and selling in industrial markets is thus increasingly akin to performing ROI calculations. Buyers evaluate the monetary benefits against costs and prices of competing offers. Sellers justify any price premium by documenting that the quantified value to customers is substantially larger than any price premium over the customer's best available alternative. Surprisingly, very few suppliers have developed the capabilities to quantify and document value. Most suppliers in industrial markets sell features, specifications, or benefits: They struggle to convert their competitive advantage into quantified customer benefits.

ROBERT RUSSELL: Your research suggests that the industrial purchasing function is increasingly forcing companies in B2B to quantify value?

ANDREAS HINTERHUBER: Yes. This is the simple answer with far-reaching consequences. Take SKF, a Swedish company with about €8.5 billion in sales and a leading supplier of industrial bearings and other equipment to the automotive and machinery industry. SKF is operating in a heavily competitive industry, and the company's product range frequently carries a price premium of 20% to 50% over the customer's best available alternative. Yet SKF is thriving in this industry, with profitability and growth levels substantially higher than its direct competitors. How does SKF do this? SKF has established a function, led by Todd C. Snelgrove, Global VP of Value, in charge of documenting and quantifying value to customers. Take the following example (see Figure 3.5). SKF uses a value calculator to document to customers that the product of SKF, sold at a premium of 50% over the customer's next best alternative, is delivering

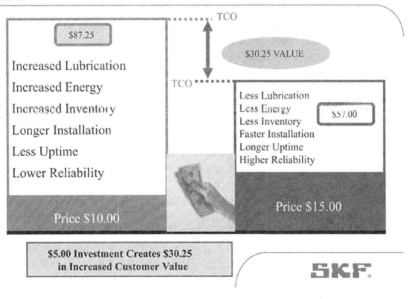

Figure 3.5 SKF case study: A best-practice example of quantifying and documenting customer value

Source: SKF

monetary benefits that substantially exceed this price premium (Hinterhuber and Snelgrove, 2012). Industrial bearings are, for the layperson, commodities: apparently interchangeable steel products. SKF is able to document to customers that, despite a substantial price premium over the next best available product, customers end up paying less and being better off by purchasing from SKF.

ROBERT RUSSELL: This is fascinating.

ANDREAS HINTERHUBER: Marketing, pricing, and sales managers in B2B should take notice: If SKF is able to quantify the value of industrial bearings, so should other companies with products that are frequently even more differentiated than those of SKF.

ROBERT RUSSELL: So you suggest pricing in B2B is all about value documentation and quantification?

ANDREAS HINTERHUBER: At the risk of over-simplification, yes. This is the area where I see a huge investment of many companies in B2B. This investment is directed at equipping their salesforce with the capabilities, the tools, the processes, and the value calculators which enable them to quantify and document value to their customers. And in the past, this was clearly not the case. In the past, the traditional approach was, if we play out the example above: My asking price is 15, the competitor is 10, so we meet somewhere in the middle around 12, and we both walk home happy.

Best-in-class companies, such as SKF, DHL, HP, Maersk, SAP, Tieto, Metso, Grainger, Monsanto, pharmaceutical companies, and others, do not sell like this anymore. Those days are gone. All these companies have developed tools and processes to convert their competitive advantages into quantified customer value. This increases both profits and customer satisfaction. What SKF today does is this: The price premium is five over the customer's best available alternative, but the company documents, quantifies, and guarantees to customers that the incremental value to customers is 30. The sales message is this: It would be an error of omission not to buy the more expensive product since the most expensive product actually costs less. So SKF phrases this as an investment: "You, hard-nosed purchasing manager, would be doing your company a disservice by purchasing the lower-price product because it would cost you more." Today and, I would contend, in the future, leading-edge B2B companies will equip their salespeople not only with the confidence but also with the tools – for example, value calculators and value quantification tools – that empower them to convert competitive advantages into quantified monetary customer value. The tools and the confidence will help the salesforce resist customer pressure for lower prices.

ROBERT RUSSELL: Many companies struggle to defend their price premiums vis-à-vis Chinese suppliers, for example . . .

ANDREAS HINTERHUBER: . . . and the only remedy is investments to develop capabilities and tools to quantify value. As a result of this research, for example, we have built up a database of well over 100 customer value calculators that B2B companies actually use to document and quantify value to their customers. The insights gathered during this research have enabled us to develop our own value quantification tool (VQT) which, in the eyes of a senior vice president of purchasing at a €10 billion B2B company, is today the globally most advanced tool for quantifying value to customers. So I would contend that, at least for some B2B segments, competition comes down not only to the quality of products and services but also to the quality of thinking that enables the sales manager to justify price premiums to customers.

ROBERT RUSSELL: Andreas, thank you. I think we've covered a number of key issues in pricing. That's brilliant. I enjoyed our conversation.

ANDREAS HINTERHUBER: Very well; thank you likewise, Robert.

References and further reading

Hinterhuber, A. (2015) "Violations of rational choice principles in pricing decisions," *Industrial Marketing Management 47*, 65–74.

Hinterhuber, A. and Liozu, S. (2012) "Is it time to rethink your pricing strategy?" *MIT Sloan Management Review 53*(4), 69–77.

Hinterhuber, A. and Snelgrove, T. (2012) "Quantifying and documenting value in B2B, professional pricing society online course," www.pricingsociety.com/home/pricing-training/online-pricing-courses/quantifying-and-documenting-value-in-business-markets

Kotter, J. P. (1995) "Leading change: Why transformation efforts fail," *Harvard Business Review 73*(2), 59–67.

Liozu, S. and Hinterhuber, A. (2013) "CEO championing of pricing, pricing capabilities and firm performance in industrial firms," *Industrial Marketing Management 42*, 633–643.

Nagle, T. and Holden, R. (2002) *The Strategy and Tactics of Pricing: A Guide to Profitable Decision Making* (3rd ed.), Englewood Cliffs, NJ: Prentice Hall.

4 Muddling through on customer value in business markets?

Snelgrove, Todd C. and Anderson, James C.

Jim and Todd have had many conversations about customer value management (CVM) over the years. Todd's company, SKF, has graciously contributed best-practice examples to Jim's management practice work (e.g., Anderson et al., 2007, 2010).

Implementing customer value management in a business

TODD C. SNELGROVE: What do companies seeking to implement customer value management (CVM) need to do to make this strategy work?

JIM ANDERSON: We find that businesses seeking to implement CVM, in order to make it really work, progress through three stages: Prove the CVM concept, build the CVM structure and culture, and sustain the CVM advantage. In the *prove the CVM concept* phase, a business undertakes several CVM projects to better understand the monetary value of changes in its market offerings to target customers. While the business obtains specific results for the offerings that it studies, along with learning the concepts, process, and tools of CVM, the overarching goal is to demonstrate that CVM can work in the business. The experience with CVM at this stage provides proof that CVM will improve profitability and that it's practical for the business to do. Teams working on the projects create "success stories" which create momentum and enthusiasm within the business for CVM change. It is often viewed as a cliché that senior management commitment and support is needed to bring about any enduring change in a business, but it's nonetheless true. Even more critical, though, is gaining the commitment and support of first-level managers and those who work for them, such as field sales reps and tech reps. We find that there are three sorts of folks in businesses: progressive thinkers, open-minded individuals who need to see change demonstrated in their own setting, and laggards. The progressive thinkers are a small minority who can look beyond their own business and envision how developments in other industries or geographies can be adopted or adapted for use in their own business. They "get" what CVM could do for their business from others' experiences. The majority of individuals in a business are open to change, but they want to see evidence that the proposed change works in their business, often in the form of pilot programs, before they are willing to implement it. These are the individuals who are critical to win over during this first stage. Finally, there are a minority of laggards in any business who are not open to change. They've seen it all and want to continue doing what they've been doing. "We tried that twenty years ago and it didn't work!" is a typical laggard reaction to whatever new is proposed. Never mind that the business likely is significantly different from what it was twenty years ago or that whatever

DOI: 10.4324/9781003177937-6

was tried then is not the same as what is being advocated now. Fortunately, persuading the open-minded individuals that it is worthwhile doing more CVM enables a business to move to the next CVM stage. In the *build CVM structure and culture* stage, the business expands its CVM capability by designating and training customer value experts or specialists who can assist others with CVM projects. The business undertakes more projects, builds more customer value models, and begins a repository of value word equations for others to use, which makes their task of conducting customer value research easier. The business provisions value-based sales tools that its salespeople are *able* to use and *want* to use. The business establishes linkages between CVM and existing processes in marketing, sales, and new product development. There may be interest, for example, in applying CVM earlier in the new-product development process. Finally, the business defines success metrics and designs training for the CVM rollout. In the *sustain the CVM advantage* stage, the business scales new CVM capabilities across the organization. CVM champions work throughout the functions and geographies of the business. Most of them will have this CVM work simply as part of their responsibilities in their positions, but it's essential that several individuals in the business have CVM as their sole or primary responsibility. Some individuals need to have ownership or stewardship of CVM in the business, where their mission is to keep CVM vital, renewing and updating the CVM capabilities and culture. What critical incidents can you share, Todd, about progressing through these stages at SKF, and what are you doing to keep CVM vital at SKF?

TODD C. SNELGROVE: It's an ongoing program, but when I look back I can clearly see the three stages you refer to. In the *prove the CVM concept* stage, I remember two different situations that were powerful. I had become increasingly excited in the late 1990s about the rise of procurement and the need to convert our technical value into monetary terms for procurement. A new product was created called System 24 that had some unique features that created customer cost savings. However, with a price premium of 35% or so, I needed to demonstrate that the annual actual cost would be less. I was at a call with a large customer, who was using thousands of our competitor's version of the product. Given a 35% price premium, I needed to demonstrate the benefits in dollars of switching to our version. On the back of a piece of paper, I showed how, because of the increased number of flow-rate options our system offered (the technical feature), the customer in some instances would increase the accuracy of the product delivery and, in other cases, reduce the number of units required. The net result was that the customer got a better product and spent 18% less on the system in dollars per year. We got an order. That night I sat with my laptop and created a calculation in Excel. Management got very excited about this, so we created a calculator for one product, with the goal of adding other new solutions as they were getting ready to launch. Over the next two years I was a fanatic! I acquired the name Bulldog, as I kept pushing this concept to become more of a company focus for all that we do. It was 2001 and the global recession was in full swing. A large industrial customer had a new VP of procurement who was demanding a price reduction to keep the contract for the next 5 years (let alone no price increase). Since large, spherical bearings (costing six figures or more) have very long lead times, our business was in jeopardy. Our North American president gave our key account manager the authority to offer a 5% price discount to keep the business. A few days later he said, "Snelgrove, why don't you go down and see if you can find a way to guarantee the value instead of the price discount?" Long story short, we agreed that we would guarantee a 5% annual cost savings (not price savings) and that if we failed to do so, we would write them a check. For a customer that buys $4,000,000 a year over 5 years, the saving to us – if we could deliver and prove our value – was enormous. The $1,000,000 price difference would fall to our bottom line. All we needed to do was make it happen. The *build CVM structure and culture* stage happened right after the large value deal was signed. Within a week I was told by the North American president, "Guess what? That is all I want you to focus on." At the time no structured tools existed, and we knew we needed to have a better system for calculating and logging our value than just an Excel template. Our company uses Lotus Notes, a back-end system that runs our corporate email, but also a place where a database could be created. It allowed us to have one system for the whole company, constant live updates, new solutions pushed out when created, and a way to log the cases that were created, and eventually accepted. As the programmers were working on the system, I was busy with product divisions, challenging them to help me convert technical features and benefits into monetary savings. We needed the formulas and some realistic numbers to put in the opening templates. Our industry and application engineers were a great support. Eventually the story and news of the tool spread in the company across geographies, and I was placed in a global role to develop, champion, roll out, and support our value initiative for our end-user accounts and industrial distributors. The *sustain the CVM advantage* stage is a never-ending focus and journey. First off, our CEO bought into the concept that if we create value we must be able to prove that value and even get paid based on the value being created. He also realized that value is different for our different divisions (what is of value to an original equipment manufacturer is different from what is of value to an end user, or to an automotive or aerospace customer, but they all want to receive value). Therefore, my role was moved from being a global role for one division to a role supporting the whole company. To keep the focus and everything at front of mind, I've focused on a few things. First is to make sure the tool is easy to use and includes the right information. In 2015 we launched an iPad version, which is simple and quick to access. I've made the value quantification logic part of our new product launch creation, rollout process, and pricing. We started a Key Accounts group a few years back, and those people have helped push the need to keep the system full of cases for their customers. We have or we want to have agreements around value, so we need the examples and proof. Finally, I spend a lot of time in the marketplace trying to get customers to rethink how they segment suppliers. I need customers to see us as a strategic buy and to choose suppliers based on best value, not on lowest price that meets a minimum criterion or specification. In sustaining the focus, it doesn't hurt that our CEO talks about the concept constantly, that we announce the number of cost-saving cases and value created in our annual report, and that each division president has it as part of their scorecard. We don't want to just focus on creating cases; we want to find ways to really save customers hard money and for us to get paid based on that value.

Customer value management for value selling versus tiebreaker selling

TODD C. SNELGROVE: In a recent piece, "Tiebreaker Selling" (Anderson et al., 2014), you discuss the difference between value selling and tiebreaker selling. Can you explain how the practice of CVM varies between these two approaches?

JIM ANDERSON: The management practice research for "Tiebreaker Selling" was a revela-
tion for us. We have been emphasizing for many years that suppliers practicing CVM
should demonstrate and document the value of their offerings to customers relative to the next best alternative for those customers. *Demonstrate* means persuasively
showing the customer before purchasing the offering what cost savings or added
value the customer could expect from the offering. *Document* means working with
the customer after a suitable period of time using the offering to find out what cost
savings or added value the customer actually has received from using it. Demonstrating and documenting superior value each require that customers actively participate
and share their data on comparative use. What we found in the management practice
research is that customers in business markets have become more strategic in their
purchases. They make a fundamental decision about each purchase: Is it strategic or
not? Simply put, strategic purchases are ones that the customer has decided contribute significantly to differentiating its offerings to its customers. Not surprisingly, most
purchases turn out to be non-strategic. Most of us in marketing and sales have heard
of the "20–80 rule": 20% of our customers should account for 80% of our sales and
profits. What we have heard from purchasing and supply managers is that they now
are following an "80–20 rule": 80% of their time should be spent on the 20% of the
purchases they consider to be strategic, and 20% of their time spent on the 80% of the
purchases they consider to be non-strategic! As one can imagine, there are considerable time constraints in making non-strategic purchases. Purchasing managers and
other customer managers simply do not want to spend the time it takes to demonstrate and document the value of non-strategic purchases. Instead, they initially seek
suppliers that can meet their basic specifications at a competitive price, and then they
ask the finalists for "something else" (other than price concessions) to justify choosing one offering over the others. That is why we coined the term *justifier* for this: It
enables the purchasing manager to justify to others in the business why one supplier's
offering was selected, and, through getting a noteworthy extra that the customer
finds valuable without analysis, it justifies the purchasing manager's contribution to
the business. Although customer managers are not willing to take the time to find out
what the specific value of a non-strategic offering is for their business, they nonetheless appreciate the supplier giving them a rough estimate of what it might be. This
realization suggests an approach to CVM that will be essentially the same early on,
whether the supplier's offering is strategic or non-strategic. Later on, though, what
the supplier does will diverge dramatically. We contrast value selling with tiebreaker
selling in Table 4.1. As the table makes clear, these two kinds of selling are dramatically different from each other. Nonetheless, conducting customer value research
during a pilot program before the commercial launch of the offering (or updated
versions of it) will be worthwhile. Learning the value of the offering relative to the
next best alternative by working with a handful of customers in a pilot program will
teach the supplier about the points of difference between offerings and what they are
worth to the pilot-program customers. What these points of difference are, though,
will vary depending on whether the core offering is highly differentiated and strategic or undifferentiated and non-strategic. For the highly differentiated, strategic
core offering, the estimates of the monetary value of the points of difference will be
used to provision a *value calculator* (Anderson et al., 2007). For the undifferentiated,
non-strategic core offering, the estimates of the monetary value of the points of difference will be used to provision what we call *justifier value cases*, which are named or

Table 4.1 Value selling versus tiebreaker selling

	Value selling	*Tiebreaker selling*
Supplier's core offering	Highly differentiated: The product or service has unique features that customers appreciate	Undifferentiated: The customers want only their basic specs met at a competitive price
Customer's view of purchase	Strategic: The purchase significantly contributes to differentiating the customer's offerings	Not strategic: The purchase is not critical to differentiating the customer's offerings
Customer willingness to extensively evaluate offering's value	High	Low
Deal winner	The offering provides quantifiably higher value than that of competing offerings, which more than compensates for its higher price	The supplier offers a justifier – a noteworthy extra that the customer finds valuable without analysis and shows the purchasing manager's contribution to the business
Supplier's goal	Gain business at a significant price premium (>5%)	Gain or retain business at a slight price premium (3–5%)

Source: Adapted from "Tiebreaker Selling: How Nonstrategic Suppliers Can Help Customers Solve Important Problems," by J. C. Anderson, J. A. Narus and M. Wouters, 2014, *Harvard Business Review 92*(3), 90–96.

unnamed case studies from pilot-program customers that broadly suggest the monetary value of the studied justifiers. Each of these becomes a sales tool that salespeople use in their selling efforts. Each of these kinds of selling tools enables the salesperson to provide the kind of proof of superior value that the customer managers want. The result is that these tools enable the salesperson to achieve a better price, whether it is a significant or a slight price premium. Do you find that the justifier concept and tiebreaker selling are applicable at SKF? What challenges does SKF face in putting them into practice?

TODD C. SNELGROVE: Great question. I've thought about this research for a while. I think the first thing SKF needed to think about is "what are we actually selling?" If it's a specific engineered product, then you're right; either it's demonstrably better and we can quantify the value to allow the purchaser the customized business case to justify the investment, or we have general business cases with industry numbers that we can present if the customer doesn't want or need a customized business case. However, sometimes, in certain product ranges either the differences are minor or, more important, the performance differences are less about the product itself and more about the implementation of a program. In these cases we say to customers, if they are of sufficient size and so forth to justify the resources, let's not focus on the specific product being better or different, but through – as you say, Jim – applying our Systems, Support and Implementation Programs, we can guarantee a hard annual saving. We then explain the program – the SKF Document Solutions Program – that is tied to our system and where we document our value. The savings might be not in a specific bearing, for example, but in which bearing was chosen, how they were installed, if the right lubrication has been selected, if the correct seal has been applied that keeps the dirt out, or in the maintenance practices around the machines to help them last longer and run at a lower total cost of ownership. Also, I think that many times procurement makes assumptions about how they should source a certain category. They base it on dollars spent or on risk (see Chapter 7, which discusses this in detail). The takeaway is that if procurement assumes you are easily substitutable with another competitor because you have an International Standards Organization product and other suppliers are almost as good, and your spend is low compared to other things they buy, then they might look for the differentiator. I spend a lot of my time challenging this assumption. It might not be the client's biggest dollar spend, but the impact that a supplier can have on your profitability is huge. To do this, though, I need to inform and engage procurement way before they make this decision, not in the middle of a negotiation or in response to a request for quote, as they have already decided what they will measure, and it's tough for them to open up and say, "Wait, I should re-think this."

Muddling through on customer value

TODD C. SNELGROVE: Do you notice a trend in the practice of CVM and value selling?

JIM ANDERSON: Recently I did a search for large-scale, management practice studies that have been done on CVM and value selling. I expected to find at least several studies but I could find only one, done by the Aberdeen Group (2011). They surveyed 214 businesses about their value-selling practices. Aberdeen aggregated the businesses' responses on three performance measures to segment them: customer retention rate, average year-over-year growth in overall company gross profit, and average year-over-year increase in average closed deal size or annual contract value. Based on their aggregate responses to these three measures, Aberdeen grouped them into three performance classes: the top 20%, which they term "best-in-class"; the middle 50%, which they term "industry average"; and the bottom 30%, which they term "laggard." Juxtaposing the findings that they report in two sections of the report produces some surprising comparisons. I share this juxtaposition of findings in Figure 4.1. On the left we see the results for the statement "We clearly translate features/benefits of our solution into economic value we can articulate to customers," and on the right we see the results for the statement "Sales process includes distinct steps, activities, tools to reinforce value delivered to customers." Notice the considerable percentage decrease for each performance class on these two measures. For example, 74% of the best-in-class performers agree with the statement that their business is translating features or benefits to economic value it can articulate to customers, while only 51% agree that their sales process has some distinct means to reinforce the value delivered to customers – a decrease of 23%! What accounts for these differences, we can only speculate on. Perhaps the technical or marketing folks are doing the translation on the left but are not providing value-selling tools that salespeople find persuasive and want to use. If one regards the results on the right as reflecting where "the rubber meets the road" in conducting business on value, we would conclude that most businesses are muddling through on value. Barely half of the best-in-class businesses agree that they have the means to reinforce the value that their offerings deliver to customers. Looking on the bright side, most businesses that believe they are doing poorly in CVM and value selling can take comfort in knowing that they are not alone and that there's considerable room for improvement!

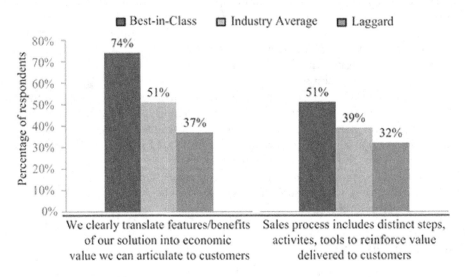

Figure 4.1 Value realization: Muddling through on value

Source: Adapted from "Value-Based Selling: Building a Best-in-Class Capability for Sales Effectiveness" [Research Brief] by Aberdeen Group, October 2011, retrieved 26 October 2015 from www.zsassociates.com/publications/whitepapers/aberdeen-study-value-based-selling.aspx

JIM ANDERSON: Todd, do you know of any other studies done on CVM and value selling?

TODD C. SNELGROVE: One of my favorite pieces of research was conducted by Deloitte and published in April 2013 in *Harvard Business Review* as "Three Rules for Making a Company Truly Great." They looked at data for over 25,000 publicly traded U.S.-based companies over 44 years to see what characteristics made them the most successful. They found a way to strip out other factors. They came up with three rules for companies that continually were more profitable than others in their industry. They found the number-one quantitative reason was a focus on being Better Before Cheaper – on creating a product or service that is of value versus being "a me-too, almost as good copycat." The second rule was Revenue Before Cost – working on getting paid for value before focusing on stripping away internal costs. We all know that internal waste should be avoided, but the research shows that having ways to get paid for value is significantly more important than cutting internal costs. Finally, rule number three was There Are No Other Rules; nothing else – such as R&D spend, number of patents filled, or brand recognition – was statistically significant. In focusing on creating something of value, we use value quantification or engineering for value, as others call it, to see what attributes we should focus on new products having that create the most customer value. The ability to quantify our value and sometimes enter into agreements to get paid based on the customer realizing that value helps improves our top line and allows customers to buy our solutions.

JIM ANDERSON: Do you have an explanation you would like to offer for the difference in results in Figure 4.1?

TODD C. SNELGROVE: I think your conclusion is correct. Someone at the head office sent a Power Point presentation that shows some global success for some customers. It might even show the breakdown of how the value was created; however, there's no systematic tool that allows the salespeople to run the calculation for their customer in their country using the customer's own numbers. Either that, or the calculations were so complicated that no one understood how they worked. Sometimes I find that engineers feel that more information is better. If people don't understand or believe the value quantification, then it doesn't matter that you have a spreadsheet that has numbers on it. Why are CVM and doing business based on value not more widespread?

JIM ANDERSON: CVM and doing business based on value isn't easy. It takes time and money, knowledge and skill, visible senior management support, persistence, and creativity. These last two – persistence and creativity – are especially critical to overcoming the obstacles that inevitably arise in doing CVM, particularly in customer value research. Many suppliers in business markets believe their offerings are so complicated that it's impossible to express their value in monetary terms. But think about this for a moment. If we do believe our offerings are so complicated that it's not possible to express their value in monetary terms, then how can we expect the customers to adequately understand their value in monetary terms? And, if that's the case, how can we expect to get an equitable return on the value that our offerings provide to customers? Believing that their offerings are so complicated that they cannot adequately express their value stops many suppliers before they even start with CVM. That's why we counsel suppliers to start small, with a pilot program of several projects, to prove the CVM concept for their business. Selecting the projects for this pilot is critical. We believe it's best for a supplier to start with projects for new or significantly improved offerings, which the supplier believes are differentiated and that have demonstrably superior value for target customers, but the supplier does not know what that's worth in monetary terms. Suppliers need to resist the temptation to put "problem child" offerings in this initial pilot program. Similarly, trying to use a CVM research project to obtain a higher price for the superior value that the supplier has already given away at a low price is a non-starter. Simply put, there must be something new or different about the offering that the supplier believes would be valuable to persuade customers to participate in the research. To even start with CVM requires a champion at the business who advocates giving CVM a chance. You played this role at SKF, Todd. What compels this individual to become a CVM champion? It may be a critical incident that occurs in the business, someone coming to the business who has had success with CVM elsewhere, or a progressive thinker who simply becomes tired of muddling through on value. Why do you believe doing CVM and business based on value is not more widespread? Based on your vast experience, what advice can you offer for how suppliers in business markets might do better?

TODD C. SNELGROVE: Yes, it does take someone to drive the program. If it had just been an idea that I'd had, and it sat in one of numerous projects I am involved with along with my daily job, it never would have worked. Any culture change project – which selling on value is – requires a long-term shift in people's thinking, motivation, and skills. To make this happen, a person or team needs to drive it. Too often I see sales saying they want this and then throwing it over the fence to marketing to say "Build it." A tool might get developed, but it won't be used and become robust if that's the case. We have had four different versions of our tool, and numerous updates and ongoing improvements. As the retired CEO said, "Todd, you will always have a job, as this is a never-ending journey to show customers that best value is more important than lowest price." Also, I think sometimes sales wants something perfect. You have to start and say, "We think this should last twice as long based on these engineering studies" – this then becomes a proposal; over time something actually happens and you were either right or wrong. Or during product development you run test cases so you do have benchmark data. If I could guarantee every customer that my option would last twice as long as a competitor's, then I wouldn't need salespeople. Start with reasonably defendable assumptions, then track what actually happens. In 2001 we had one case in our system that was approved by a customer; now we have over 64,500 versus 58,000 signed off on by customers. So now I have enough data to do probabilities, share best- and worst-case scenarios, show numerous examples, but that all started somewhere. What's that saying – "Every journey starts with one step"?

JIM ANDERSON: From your experience at SKF and talking with other companies, what advice comes to mind on how to spread the practice of CVM and doing business on value?

TODD C. SNELGROVE: Well, as we've discussed, it starts with having a corporate directive that says that we're going to be the value player in our industry. If your company is not a value player, then creating a tool to prove value will not solve this, and eventually customers will realize that your "value program" is really just a sales and marketing strategy with no meat on its bones. Next, have someone drive it as a full-time job; no one can become an expert on something doing it part-time. I live, eat, breathe this stuff. I believe in it, and my having the freedom to focus on one strategy has allowed us to realize the benefits of value selling based on our ability to quantify value. Start in a region with one product so that when you're ready to roll it out, you have some stories, and some examples, to show other salespeople that it does work. Don't just focus on the tool; think of all the other things that are needed to support and move your company in this direction. What do they say? "A fool with a tool is still a fool"? I remember our CEO in the early days when I sent reports of wins saying a few interesting things. He asked, rhetorically, "How many ways do our salespeople have to offer a discount or do something for free? Too many! How many tools do they have to prove our value? Guess that's our answer: We need to create the tools and processes." During another meeting when I was demonstrating the measurable effect I was having for our company, he said to me, "Every minute you spend documenting the sales you have created, the agreements to guarantee value versus discounting, you're not out doing what I want you to do [i.e., quantifying and documenting value]. I trust you, and I know the value in what you're doing." Finally, he asked if I would speak at a conference that had nothing to do with our business, as another CEO was chairing the event and had asked him for the favor. He said, "Do not always look directly for 'What's in it for me (or SKF)?' to do something. Get the message out anywhere, to anyone, about buying on value, and the benefits will come somewhere." I can truly say that he was right.

References

Aberdeen Group. (2011, October) "Value-based selling: Building a best-in-class capability for sales effectiveness, research brief," www.zsassociates.com/publications/whitepapers/aberdeen-study-value-based-selling.aspx. Accessed 26 October 2015

Anderson, J. C., Kumar, N. and Narus, J. A. (2007) *Value Merchants: Demonstrating and Documenting Superior Value in Business Markets*, Boston, MA: Harvard Business School Press.

Anderson, J. C., Narus, J. A. and Wouters, M. (2014) "Tiebreaker selling: How nonstrategic suppliers can help customers solve important problems," *Harvard Business Review 92*(3), 90–96.

Anderson, J. C., Wouters, M. and van Rossum, W. (2010) "Why the highest price isn't the best price," *MIT Sloan Management Review 51*(2), 69–76.

5   Interview

Nurturing value quantification capabilities in strategic account managers

Hinterhuber, Andreas, Snelgrove, Todd C., and Quancard, Bernard L.

ANDREAS HINTERHUBER: Why and how does value quantification matter for the strategic account manager?

BERNARD L. QUANCARD: As we speak today, if I look at all the companies that have a strategic account management program or initiative, I would say that unfortunately between 50% and as much as 70% of the strategic account managers (SAM) are actually doing commercial coordination. There is some value in doing commercial coordination, but it's not what we mean when we talk about strategic account management. The core of the strategic account management initiative is the first phase of creating value for the customer. So, as we speak, a dominant proportion of SAMs are commercial coordinators, and only a minority, likely around 30% of account managers, are the actual conductors – the orchestrators – of the value creation process. So, in the future, the core of strategic account management will be the value creation process. The key capabilities of SAMs will be to drive the value creation process effectively. This requires, first and foremost, that the account manager be an active listener and at the same time a strategic thinker. Although they are pushing products, SAMs must also be listening to customer problems; they need to understand the customer's business model and truly understand customer value. This requires understanding how the output of company activities impacts the customer's bottom line. SAMs thus need to be able to manage the overall strategic customer relationship as well as continuously find new opportunities for value creation. When we talk about value creation, we obviously have to talk about value quantification. This is where the SAM needs to have experts in the company, whether they come from marketing or whether they come from expert centers within the company and act as Chief Value Officers. But the fundamental insight is that SAMs need to have a lot of expertise in value quantification in order to be able to monetize the value created through the SAM process.

ANDREAS HINTERHUBER: Value quantification is a key capability. I, of course, agree. But there is a potentially unexplored sideline to this capability: Value quantification requires collaborating with customers. Now, some customers may be very reluctant to share with the SAM what their product/solution does for their profitability because they fear this knowledge could be turned against them. Put differently, once the SAM knows – thanks to their customers! – that their products produce benefits that are sometimes greater than those the SAM had imagined, the SAM factually has an incentive to increase the price. What is your take on that? How do you quantify value with customers who appreciate your offer but do not want to share information?

DOI: 10.4324/9781003177937-7

BERNARD L. QUANCARD: This is an extremely important topic, and my answer is very, very simple but difficult to implement. The key to a strategic account management initiative is managing critical customer relationships and also having an Executive Sponsor at the customer and an Executive Sponsor in your company. The key is not to have a price discussion. The key is not to have a value discussion. The key is to have a high-level business discussion. How do you impact your customer's financial model or business results? To take a concrete example: When I am a SAM at Schneider Electric, I am not talking about electrical cabinets with circuit breakers to protect the electrical systems in a plant. I am talking about energy management and the electricity bill. I am having a business discussion with the Executive VP of Operations. I am the SAM; I am with my Executive Sponsor. When I meet the customer, I visit the Executive VP of Operations, and I have a business discussion. Price to value is only a consequence of the business discussion, and the creation of value has to come from solving business issues and business problems. So that's what makes the SAM approach so critical and so different. It's that from a business discussion you create value, and the price is only a consequence of the value created. The collaboration is first about a strategy of relationships and business discussions, and then you collaborate, implementing the consequences of that business discussion with multifunctional teams in your own company.

TODD C. SNELGROVE: Value quantification requires information from customers. My take is that in many instances customers do not share information, not because they do not want to, but simply because they do not have the information themselves. Many times, I have been at procurement conferences, and procurement people have said to me, "SAMs seem to think that we have the answers to all these questions." "We do not," is the near-unanimous answer from procurement. So we don't provide information because we don't know how long that motor will last or what the average mean time between failures is. It's not that we are not giving the information because we know it and don't want it to be used against us. The answer is simple: We are not giving the information because we do not have it. And I think this is plausible. There are many things I don't know about the specific operations of our manufacturing process. Based on current research, I think you would agree on a pricing model ahead of time. So it's a model that we agree on. If this does X, then a percentage of Ys occurs; then we're less concerned about the exact number, because the more value is created, then yes, the price may go up, but because we agree with the structure of that – a percentage or whatever it is – customers will want it to be even bigger because then they get a much bigger benefit. But if the pricing model is discussed afterward, yes, they can see their unwillingness: If I tell you how good it was, I can end up paying more. But if we agree ahead of time on the model not the numbers, people would seem to be more open. And, of course, if it is about co-creation, one of the benefits of being part of the co-creation is that we are looking to get a test customer to validate the value proposition, and, of course, in most situations they would get an even greater benefit . . .

BERNARD L. QUANCARD: . . . and the model would often be more efficient and explainable to the customer if it started with a business discussion. I always take the example of energy management at Schneider Electric, where it's about doing an energy audit of the plant; it's about a plan to remove the energy-leaking equipment, changing old equipment; it's about putting new methods in place. So we are talking about a complex solution, solving an important business issue, and the issue of value comes before the price. The price is just the consequence of value – and yes, probably the price would have a premium. But as you said, the model, the pricing model, is so compelling in terms of gains to the customer that the price level, then, is far less important.

TODD C. SNELGROVE: From my own perspective at SKF, I would fully agree. We are talking about a bearing that, by itself, seems to be irrelevant. Our take is: How can we make your operation run more efficiently at the lowest total cost? Where are those opportunities, whether it is energy or inventory, or whatever it is? So, starting with the business discussion and saying (a) here's what best-in-class looks like and asking (b) what it would be worth to move you to best-in-class? And at this point we would then like to start a business discussion. This leads then to the next point that Andreas raised earlier: How do you start this discussion? The customer might not know the information or they might not be willing to share proprietary information, so I suggest starting with the business case: I find people are much more open to saying "that number is high" or "that number is low." But if you ask a lot of open-ended questions – which people are taught in field training – it actually confuses the customer. So start with some specific numbers, let's say a best-in-class performance on a given item, and move from there. This seems to make people more comfortable, as opposed to asking 20 open-ended questions which they may be unable to answer.

ANDREAS HINTERHUBER: Bottom line: do your homework and start with some specific data points that you have collected from competitors, suppliers, and customers . . .

TODD C. SNELGROVE: . . . or industry benchmarks. I had a conversation once with a person about energy savings, and she didn't know there's a government calculation. And I just pulled it up on the Web, and she said, "that's good enough." So it's not a closed-end question, but it will help to move the conversation along by having some reference data points that are industry- or application-specific. So do your research ahead of time to have some sample data points to help move the conversation along.

TODD C. SNELGROVE: Bernard, what other companies do you see that have really embraced the need to (1) have a SAM and to (2) quantify value as part of an effective account management program?

BERNARD L. QUANCARD: Well, today when you start with a business conversation and a value creation conversation, you won't go anywhere if you don't monetize the value you create compared with your competitors, and that monetization has to be approved by the customer. Now, how many companies do that? I would say less than 10% of those companies that are involved in strategic account management. It remains a scarcity, and this is why most projects go to request for proposal (RFP), because there is not a compelling monetization of the value. If there were a compelling monetization where you show that you bring much more money to your customer compared with your competitor's solutions, there wouldn't be any need for an RFP. Really! You would have to show that we are within a price range that makes your value proposition compelling. You could have graphs of price ranges from you and your competitors, but that would be sufficient. The goal of strategic account management is to eliminate the bidding process, from my point of view. So monetization is essential to doing that – monetization of the value – but very, very few companies do that. Why don't they do it? Only because the staff does not have the right conversations at the right level with customers, but certainly because there is no real expertise internally on how to monetize the value proposition.

TODD C. SNELGROVE: I fully agree: most companies lack the skills, techniques, and processes needed to quantify value. And I can speak just from my background: at least industrial companies have such a technical background, and they believe that technology automatically will make the business case. So that's probably one of the reasons why they cannot seem to get their hands around how to monetize value: their background is technical, not commercial.

BERNARD L. QUANCARD: This is very true. From an organizational standpoint, in many companies there is still a fundamental misalignment between customer-facing people and marketing. Marketing thinks they're the best ones to do the value proposition, and they do it non-collaboratively with the customer because they do it from their desk. And in most cases, customer-facing people will find those value propositions by marketing to be irrelevant, not adapted, or not customized and therefore poorly aligned with real customer needs. So that misalignment might be very painful. Marketing says, "You know, we should do the strategy; we are the ones who understand." Sales says, "Marketing is trying to impose standard solutions on us that don't fit real customer needs."

TODD C. SNELGROVE: How do you align marketing and sales?

BERNARD L. QUANCARD: Marketing and SAM should work together, very early, very upstream in the process of value discovery, upstream in the process of the customer's core discovery, when we uncover the customer's problems and the value needs for the supplier. Misalignment occurs because marketing comes way too late in the process.

TODD C. SNELGROVE: What's the role of the CEO in this process? Do you believe the CEO's buy-in, excitement, and involvement are necessary to implement this cultural step change in their organization?

BERNARD L. QUANCARD: No question. Collaborative value creation with your most important customers is a transformation that companies do not know how to make because they lack the capabilities or because there is internal misalignment. Only top-driven initiatives will transform the organization and align the resources and get results. I strongly believe in top-driven transformations or initiatives for value creation and value quantification.

TODD C. SNELGROVE: I remember the many SAM conferences where you have a CEO come in from one of the best-practice SAM organizations. And as you see them speak with passion and belief that they must provide value, deliver that value, and quantify that value for customers, it really reinforces the point that a CEO standing behind these initiatives seems to make a big difference.

BERNARD L. QUANCARD: Absolutely. Organizations are full of people who have their own routine; organizations are silos. Value creation around the customer and value quantification can only be top-driven, because only the top can erase the negative issues of silos, the negative issues of insufficient capabilities, and only the top can change the mind-set and the routines of the key people in the organization.

TODD C. SNELGROVE: Let's return to the "how" of value quantification: Certain things are very quantifiable – energy consumption, for example – but often you get into these subjective, less-quantifiable things like brand values, perceived safety, or other intangible elements. Do you have any opinions on or experiences with how companies either quantify those or address those with their customers?

BERNARD L. QUANCARD: Excellent question. My answer might surprise you. If you don't have a sense of urgency, you're not going to go anywhere. Let me give you an example. Maersk Line, the big logistics company, sells totally commoditized products. It is impossible to find a more commoditized business, and yet Maersk Line has been relentlessly investing in improving the customer's bottom line. Maersk says,

> We, Mr. Customer, we are 97% on time and our competitors are at 93%. That is four points of more reliable delivery on-time for Maersk. This is worth millions of dollars to you, Mr. Customer, and we are computing it.

Or:

We have a much lower carbon footprint than our competitors, and that carbon footprint fits directly within your philosophy, Mr. Customer, of being a green company. We are going to help you on your journey toward becoming the greenest competitor in your industry. Let us quantify it for you: This is the much lower carbon footprint of our ships vis-à-vis our competitors.

There's no limit if you have a sense of urgency about value creation and value quantification. It's just that we have to get out of the routine, and we have to be creative, collaboratively with the customer, to discover areas of value and of creating that value. Take Morton Salt, a company that sells the salt used to melt snow after a snowstorm. Well, the logistics – how you package the salt – will make a huge difference. Customer A may need a little bag, customer B next door may need different packaging, and they have different logistical needs. So, personally, I am a big fighter against the concept of commodity. There's no such thing as a true commodity. It's the new economy, the Internet, and the sharing economy that are leading to so many service opportunities and so much value creation that no commodity is ever condemned to remain a commodity. It is a mind-set, it is a question of capability, and it is a question of top-driven transformation. It is not a question of "help me, my product is a commodity!"

TODD C. SNELGROVE: It could be that, or that the value you add around the product, the services you add around the product, the implementation, are where the value is created.

BERNARD L. QUANCARD: Exactly. There's no limit to what you can do. You have to look at the value stream leading from the raw materials all the way to shipping to the end customer.

TODD C. SNELGROVE: Agreed. There are no such things as commodities.

ANDREAS HINTERHUBER: Let's get down to the individual SAM. What are, in your view, characteristics – that is, personality traits – of SAMs that excel in quantifying value? What are, by contrast, personality traits or behavioral characteristics that make the individual SAM less effective at value quantification? Can you think of some personality traits that differentiate these people?

BERNARD L. QUANCARD: Oh, absolutely. One is the ability to listen instead of the ability to push a product. Some lone wolves, some big salespeople, will be terrible SAMs because they do not listen. We at the Strategic Account Management Association (SAMA) say that active listening is active only when you listen to things at very low noise levels: listening to some of the things the customer tells you that do not seem important but are very important. So when the plant manager out there was telling me, "Well, you know, I have a couple of 15-year-old transformers; they leak energy, but that is not a problem. They are not active." It is a problem. It's a lot of the customer's energy bill going down the drain, just like that. Listening to the low-noise things, capturing those things, is what we call active listening. Active listeners are a rare commodity, especially among salespeople. Salespeople are hunters; they jump at you;

they don't listen. They want to sell; they want to push the product. So active listening is number one. Number two is the ability to collaborate with multi-stakeholders at the customer inside your own company. But again, pure salespeople are very often lone people. They're lone wolves, as we say. They don't collaborate. They're unable to motivate multifunctional teams. There's no value creation if you're by yourself – a lone wolf. Value creation is impossible. Value creation is common at the intersections. Value creation requires the ability to interpret weak signals. Value creation will come at the intersections of things, intersections of technology, intersections of the customer's issues, whatever they are. So the ability to work with multi-stakeholders is the second key characteristic of a good value creator and a good value quantifier. Third is having financial acumen, not being afraid of the numbers and the dollars. Again, a lot of salespeople know how to cut prices, but they are frightened by dollars in terms of value quantification. They have no financial acumen. They don't know a darned thing. So those would be my three key characteristics: active listening, ability to work collaboratively with multi-stakeholders, and financial acumen.

TODD C. SNELGROVE: I couldn't agree with you more on all three.

BERNARD L. QUANCARD: And it is a culture – it is a culture. It's almost a cultural trait, and it cannot be taught. Some people will never have it in them. I'll talk about myself: I was in sales for many years. I had to really police myself to listen. I slapped my face, and I said, "Come on, listen; you're not listening. Listen! Listen! You're not listening. You're just talking." The worst enemy of SAM is the inability to listen.

TODD C. SNELGROVE: Very good points. What's your take on customer selection in the context of Strategic Account Management Programs and value quantification? Obviously, value quantification will matter less for some types of customers or purchasing organizations.

BERNARD L. QUANCARD: You raised a critical point which we call in our SAM organization "the selection of the right accounts." It's a difficult problem and issue. Personally, large accounts can be critical, but they could be 100% transactional. If after a journey of three to five years you don't have a share of these large, critical customers who are open to talking value, you should keep that customer on the list of large customers, but not on the list of strategic accounts. A strategic account has to have some openness to value. That being said, some strategic accounts will buy a lot of stuff transactionally, but key are the dynamics and the journey: Do I have a share at my strategic accounts that's based on value creation and quantification? Is that share growing out of the total sales to that customer? These are the key metrics you have to look at to encourage you to continue along the value journey. But if after three to five years you are 100% transactional, you have to cut your costs and abandon value creation and quantification. That is where some organizations could be hopeless. Even if you go above them or with them at the business management level, the relationship will return to being commoditized and price-only in the end. If this happens numerous times in a three- to five-year journey, get out; those are not strategic accounts. I think it's courageous to recognize that.

TODD C. SNELGROVE: This is very interesting. You have to set a time frame. I see a lot of SAMs not walking away. But what do they do? They try to give their customers even more value, assuming that eventually they'll be willing to pay for that value. So I think that, as you said, after a preset time, if you can't convince them, you should walk away and stop delivering the value. Don't try to deliver more value where it is not recognized or not being paid for.

BERNARD L. QUANCARD: This means that when you increase your cost to serve in order to try to deliver more value, most customers start to represent losses. And there's no good strategy built on losses. It doesn't exist and should be banned. A good strategy gives you a return on investment after three to five years.

TODD C. SNELGROVE: There are organizations where procurement is focused on price and price only. Are there things you can do to get them to start thinking that maybe they should do things differently?

BERNARD L. QUANCARD: I think the key is to find an area in the organization – the customer's organization. Sometimes it might be R&D; sometimes it might be new product development. The key is to find an area that will be hungry for value creation and quantification. And once you have an ambitious business case, even a small one, at the organization, you've got to start a journey to expand into other areas. It has to be what I call a "positive cancer." You start in an area . . . again, very often my own experience shows that starting in the new product development area offers a big payback, because that area is where you create everything, everything is upstream, you can make the difference very upstream in the value. I call it positive cancer because you start with a business case of value and then you expand and expand and expand. This positive journey allows you to show that you've grown the bottom line more based on value than on price, and it's the truth.

TODD C. SNELGROVE: Can you think of any industries where value quantification wouldn't work?

BERNARD L. QUANCARD: It might be when a product is very commoditized. It might be that competitors copy you very quickly. Whatever value you bring, in logistics or whatever – take the examples we discussed before of Morton Salt or Maersk Line – it depends on how quickly your competitors catch up. If your competitors catch up very quickly, then it's really, really difficult. I would look at it more from a competitive standpoint than from an industry perspective alone. I do not believe there is a specific industrial sector. Again, I push back on a commodity. I think commodity is a concept that can be "refused," but if your competitors catch up very quickly, that makes it very difficult.

TODD C. SNELGROVE: If you can have a sustained differentiation in the product, in the processes and services . . .

BERNARD L. QUANCARD: . . . exactly, if that creates the differentiation that will force your competitors to be slow in catching up, that's the way to go.

TODD C. SNELGROVE: Some value quantification now clearly takes place in B2C, too: Take white goods, and cars and houses and things where people take the time and energy to do some research. Do you see a skill set moving from B2B to B2C?

BERNARD L. QUANCARD: We have a lot to learn from B2C in B2B, frankly. The reason is that the Internet has a much greater impact on the consumer than on the business buyer, although it's catching up with the business buyer. So we have a lot to learn because B2C is more competitive. Competitors are catching up faster, I think, in B2C. In B2B, it's much more complex. The value chain is much more complex. The number of stakeholders and the decision processes are much more complex. So we have the benefit of having a much more complex world in B2B, but if we were to apply some of the lessons we learned from B2C that could have a huge impact. Take crowdsourcing: How do I crowdsource an issue, a value proposition, to make it complete and valuable? How do I use social media and technology in B2B? We could learn a lot from B2C and apply it to B2B.

TODD C. SNELGROVE: This is very well pointed out. Many times, B2B companies do not even think or want to learn, but there's a lot to be learned from B2C. What other pieces of advice do you have for companies that do create value in their industry but are having a hard time getting paid for it?

BERNARD L. QUANCARD: I really believe that the question raised earlier – how quickly competitors catch up – is the key element that will lead to what customers value. In the end, demonstrate value; and if you have and bring more quantified value than your competitors, and if you threaten procurement that you will walk out, the business case will keep you in. So I think the lack of value quantification is about the competitive environment more than anything else. And that is where I believe the SAMs have to be very good and very well trained on what I call strategic negotiations, how to negotiate for value, away from price. If you look at companies, they typically will tell you that out of 100 SAMs, they have at least half or more who let the price go; they don't find the value because they're convinced that competitors will catch up, but they haven't even checked it. So I would really say that in the end, the art and science of negotiations of value versus price will have the biggest impact on whether the customer recognizes the value you bring.

TODD C. SNELGROVE: The ability to quantify that value gives you the tools to help negotiate based on it?

BERNARD L. QUANCARD: And understanding your competitors' value and how much more you bring versus your competitors – that's going to be the key to negotiating for value and getting paid for it.

TODD C. SNELGROVE: Very well said. I very much appreciate your time. I would just like to say: I appreciate what SAMA does for the profession, driving the research, driving the opportunities to share best practices, and I thank you for your time today in showing the importance of value quantification.

ANDREAS HINTERHUBER: Thank you both for sharing your time and expertise.

6 Salesforce confidence and proficiency – the main cornerstone of effective customer value management

Kleiner, Gary

Introduction

Account managers make a dangerous assertion when they express statements such as "I have a great relationship with my customers; they know what I do for them." Customers may indeed be aware of a few select things the salesperson recently did for them, but those memories fade quickly. What is even more foolhardy than assuming that the customer is fully aware of the items the seller has provided is the supposition that the customer knows what everything was worth in quantifiable financial terms.

The absence of real value creates parity among suppliers

When customers perceive equality between two suppliers, it is easy for them to default to the one that offers lower pricing. If the only quantifiable data point containing a currency symbol that a seller has to engage a customer with is their unit pricing, they will be at a severe disadvantage during any type of negotiation. This lack of solid data will work against them especially if they're either the highest- or the lowest-price provider. Note the keyword in the first sentence – "perceive." It's unfortunate, but far too many people today base decisions on their perceptions rather than on facts.

The old phrase "What you don't know will hurt you" will plague sellers during pricing and business negotiations with customers if they're unaware of the tangible value delivered. Qualitative, abstract, and general statements of activities and perceived benefits cannot effectively combat the thinking that "I can get the same thing cheaper from many other suppliers." Likewise, similar types of intangible statements of supposed benefits cannot consistently and effectively offset price objections for superior products, services, or technologies. Even if the seller and their organization are truly responsible for effectively implementing technology or process improvements that have increased efficiencies and/ or reduced external expenditures, the customer will perceive that no formal value has been created. Unless there is documentation of the value-added activity and a subsequent review with the customer, no value will have been officially received or implemented. This is why it is imperative for a seller to routinely document their value-producing activities and to review these events with their customers regularly.

A case study on value quantification

A recent example better illustrates how a lack of real documented value creates parity among suppliers. A longtime supplier of components and assemblies to support

DOI: 10.4324/9781003177937-8

production requirements has been providing products and services to a customer for several years. Exceptional responsiveness, attention to detail, and routinely high degrees of service and support enabled the supplier to develop incomparable personal relationships with key decision makers. The customer was less than an hour away from the supplier's facilities, and the supplier had a technical salesperson on site at least 2 days a week. The supplier had participated in two or three engineering review sessions each year to reduce design and manufacturing complexity, weekly on-time deliveries of products were standard practice, no-charge evaluation samples were provided, and the list went on. At one point in the previous year the customer's material planning system had failed to ensure that enough materials were on hand to complete a major order. The supplier worked well into the evening to get the needed products to the customer so that they could ship to their customer. On another instance, they had spent 2 days on site to inspect competitive products because the customer's quality department had neither the skill sets nor the tooling needed to identify and rework suspect parts from another supplier. This, too, allowed the customer to complete shipping products to their customers on time.

Yet through all their exemplary service efforts, the supplier failed to properly document the resulting value of their ongoing actions because they "assumed" their customer knew of the services they provided. The supplier received a telephone call one day from a key contact stating that the family had decided to sell their business to a larger manufacturer of complementary products. Shortly after the acquisition was completed, the supplier received a subsequent phone call from supply chain stating that a price comparison was performed with another supplier and that it revealed nearly a $100,000 difference. Because of this disparity, the new owners intended to shift their annual spend to an out-of-state provider strictly because of price. The incumbent supplier successfully lobbied for the opportunity to formally present why they believed they should maintain the business. Their presentation detailed a lengthy list of their services along with service examples, and the summary slide of their initial draft presentation was similar to the one shown in Figure 6.1.

When this presentation was previewed with their key contacts, the supplier learned that the new management wanted to see actual examples of quantifiable contributions to the bottom line and not a capabilities overview. Fortunately, this advice permitted the supplier to regroup and refocus their presentation so that it emphasized less what they had provided and more what the customer had received. The supplier subsequently invested many additional hours revising the presentation to include several specific examples of their services and resulting value.

- Local representation on site 2 days per week
- Orders fulfilled from local inventory
- Weekly product deliveries
- Value-added solutions provider
- Annual VAVE support to improve designs
- After-hours emergency support
- Rush-order capabilities
- Onsite inspection and troubleshooting capabilities

Figure 6.1 Add-on services at Parker Hannifin

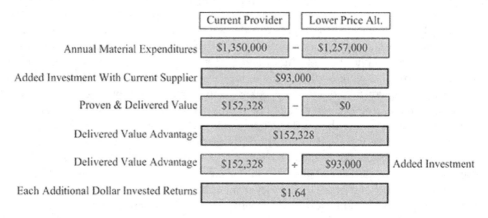

Figure 6.2 Value quantification for add-on services

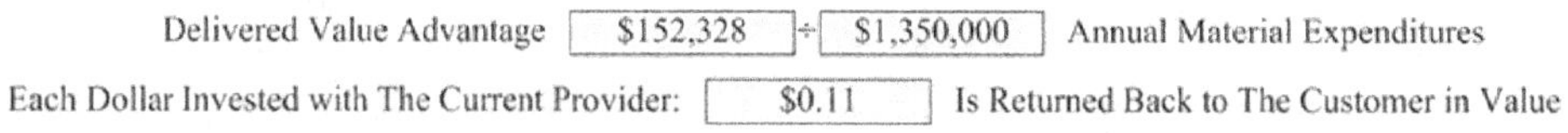

Delivered Value Advantage $152,328 ÷ $1,350,000 Annual Material Expenditures

Each Dollar Invested with The Current Provider: $0.11   Is Returned Back to The Customer in Value

Figure 6.3 ROI calculations for add-on services

While revising their proposal, the current supplier estimated that the competitive price difference was closer to $93,000. This pricing differential represented approximately a 6.9% reduction in customer expenditures from current pricing levels. With this information the incumbent supplier wanted to confirm that they still had a competitive value advantage, so they performed a side-by-side cost-to-value comparison. The results showed that their delivered-value advantage was still high enough to offset the likely difference in competitive price. In performing the analysis they divided their delivered value advantage of $152,328 by the added pricing investment of $93,000 that the customer was making with them. This showed that for each additional dollar invested (or spent) with them, the customer received a return of approximately $1.64. Investing $1.00 and getting $1.64 in return from operational efficiencies produced a convincing and quantitative reason to remain with them.

In deciding the best way to present this information to the customer, one of the sales managers felt that they should refrain from providing any "assumptions" of competitive pricing and only deal with the facts that were known and available to them. With that consideration they revised their side-by-side value comparison to show the value return based on the customer's current purchase price investment. This amended analysis took their delivered value advantage of $152,328 and divided it by the annual spend of $1,350,000. The results showed that for every dollar in customer purchases, approximately $0.11 was being returned to them in delivered value. This was basically an 11% cost reduction and was still greater than the estimated 6.9% price reduction being proposed by the competitive supplier.

Their presentation structure and summary page layout were revised from a qualitative and abstract format to a quantifiable summary of economic benefits received similar to what is shown in Figure 6.4.

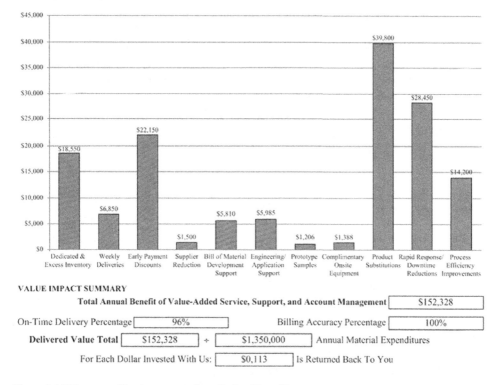

Figure 6.4 Value quantification case study at Parker Hannifin

When the opportunity finally came to formally present to the new owners, the quantifiable and compelling results enabled the supplier to retain the business. An additional benefit of their presentation is that the customer and the supplier both committed to future quarterly reviews of value-added contributions using a similar reporting format. When everything was concluded and the supplier had had a chance to review the results with their key customer contacts, both agreed that this detailed value-reporting format permitted them to keep the business. Without it, they would have lost the business entirely or would have had to make significant price concessions to retain it.

Concerns of management

A concern that sales managers may voice is that the documentation process for value-added events will consume a valuable portion of their sellers' time and equally reduce the already limited amount of customer-facing time. It is a valid concern of management that activities outside of securing orders, building customer relationships, and developing new business can be considered non-value-added for generating immediate revenue; however, the value-added documentation approach and customer value management actions actually complement these activities.

Although extra time outside of routine sales-call activity is required to demonstrate and document value-added efforts, it's a worthwhile investment. In some cases (as we detail later), we are taking just a few minutes to set aside and make a few notes in a planner or on a tablet about the support provided to the customer and what economic benefits resulted. In cases where more complex solutions are being supplied, the time investment will be noticeably greater. In the first sentence of this paragraph the word "investment" was used to describe the time required for documentation, and that word was carefully selected. Value-added documentation and customer value management programs are investments in the future. One good definition of "investment" is

> an asset or item that is purchased with the hope that it will generate income or appreciate in the future.
>
> ("Investment," n.d.)

We can easily reword this description to make it more closely relate to the value-added documentation approach:

> A document or visual example that is created with the intent to generate income or to appreciate in the future.

Value-added documentation is not intended to satisfy immediate needs of the day but to fulfil future needs. A key to good investing is to start early and to make regular deposits with the intent of generating future returns. If you constantly delay depositing funds into an investment or retirement account, you run the risk of that account being deficient when you need to make a withdrawal. In the anecdotal case given earlier, the account manager and company were deficient in making the necessary investment of time to build a good value-added investment portfolio. Fortunately, as the scenario developed, they secured good feedback from their key client contacts prior to presenting; in most cases, however, sellers do not have this luxury. Unfortunately, the lack of a good proactive investment approach caused the supplier to expend a significant amount of time researching and building their presentation because there were no data available. Additionally, their ability to reactively quantify the value impact was further challenged because some key customer contacts were no longer available to gather the necessary data. A proactive documentation approach does indeed take time to implement and manage, but it takes far less time than reactively responding to customer or competitive pressures. Additionally, the quality of the documentation is higher when the event can immediately be documented rather than built from reactive estimations of value received.

A second concern of managers is that presenting the economic value from all of the "good" the supplier was responsible for delivering may bring back painful memories of the added costs the customer incurred when the supplier fell short and "bad" things happened. This is a valid potential concern of management of any level when considering implementing a value-added program. When a supplier fails to live up to their end of the business relationship, they certainly must be held accountable, and a supplier will always receive "grief" when their actions directly, or indirectly, cause their customers to incur added costs. However, when they are responsible for implementing cost-reduction initiatives and/or reducing external expenditures through value-added services, those same suppliers should also receive "gratitude" for their contributions when it is due. If you are eligible for getting the "grief" when things go wrong, you should also be entitled to getting the "gratitude" when things go right.

When will this approach not work?

Providing real, meaningful, and monetized value is an exceptional way to build and maintain a competitive advantage, but it is not the "magic wand" that offsets organizational deficiencies. B2B and B2C companies must possess several attributes just to be in business, among them knowledgeable salespeople, appropriate levels of inventory, timely responses, competent inside support staff, good relationships with key customer decision makers, and application fluency. A keen understanding of value is not a substitute for a lack in one or more of these areas. As noted, using value to compensate for operational shortcomings may actually exacerbate an already tense customer relationship.

Likewise, if you do enjoy operational proficiencies with service, supply, and support, there are still customer dynamics to consider. Some customer policies will create situations where value-added contributions will not create an effective differentiation between price and cost. The most prominent condition is dealing with companies who only care about one thing: obtaining the lowest purchase price. In many situations, businesses with this management philosophy do not permit sales representatives to interface with anyone but supply chain representatives, and it is very challenging, if not impossible, for suppliers to receive recognition for any value-added contributions. On a similar note, some organizations carefully restrict access to engineering, and meetings are permitted only with a representative from the supply chain present, also making it very difficult to effectively build a position of value.

Starting off in a straightforward and simple manner

We spent several paragraphs covering the business cases for better customer value management, and we can now delve into what sellers and seller organizations should begin to do in order to optimize their customer value relationship. As previously stated, routinely documenting the measurable value-added contributions in quantifiable terms will ensure that your delivered value is known by the customer.

People naturally gravitate toward things they feel comfortable with and will go to great lengths to avoid awkward situations. The most important principle of getting sellers and customers on board with formal recognition of the value-added benefits received is to apply a variation of the K.I.S.S. principle. This new variation of the age-old acronym is "Keep It Straightforward & Simple." The initial messages of value must be simple enough for both parties to process and understand.

Complicated messages of value to an audience unfamiliar with receiving and processing value-added communication will be quickly dismissed. If someone doesn't know how to swim, you cannot teach them by pushing them into the deep end of the pool and expect them to begin swimming on their own. It will be a traumatic experience for them, and if they make it back to the pool deck, they will undoubtedly not go into or near the pool again. A more logical approach would be to first introduce them to the shallow end of the pool and get them comfortable with the water. When they get comfortable with the environment of the shallow end, you can then help them progress to the rope that separates the shallow end from the deep end of the pool. Once they are comfortable in that area, you can then again help them progress to deeper water. Developing and delivering complex messages of value in products, services, and/or systems is the equivalent of swimming in the deep end.

This swimming lesson analogy also applies to the pricing department that has attained process effectiveness in developing sound and credible value-based pricing strategies. Achieving operational excellence in the value-based pricing area is a noteworthy accomplishment; this distinction is quickly lost, however, if the sales team cannot communicate it and/or if the customers cannot understand it. Likewise, if your sales team becomes highly proficient in developing more complex, quantifiable value-based messages but your audience is not used to seeing them, you will again be at the opposite ends of the pool.

Instilling confidence, comfort, and credibility in the organization

The most basic foundation of an effective customer value management strategy can be distilled to the three Cs: confidence of the seller in their abilities, their level of comfort in developing and deploying value-added documentation, and the credibility of the message they're creating. Here are some additional guidelines to follow to ensure that the value messaging is clear and compelling for the seller to develop and for the receiver to accept.

1. Keep your calculations simple, show all of them, and create a corresponding word problem that explains them. Producing a figure alone with no supporting detail or means of calculation will always lead to speculation. Showing a formula with no descriptions of the input values will also lead to conjecture.
2. Use customer-supplied data or conservative and reasonable estimations if customer data are not readily available. If you cannot get solid customer data on labor rates and related costs, you can use your internal company data or information from local peer companies as a starting point. The U.S. Labor Department is also a wealth of information, providing labor rate ranges by occupation and geography.
3. Err on the conservative side with low estimates. It is better to have the customer look at the number and think it understated than to have them perceive your estimates to be too high. You'll be in a better position by having the customer talk the number up, since this means they are taking an interest in your message and attempting to make it more accurate.
4. Don't try to quantify everything. You can add support to your quantifiable value with bullet points of additional benefits the customer is receiving. These added benefits can be non-measurable or extremely complex to measure and will add validity to the amount of value you produced through your calculations.
5. Speak of value in terms of ranges rather than single numbers. Here is an example of this:

   > Our process improvement of providing pre-inspected finished good assemblies removed between 400 and 485 annual labor hours required for assembly and final inspection. We estimate this annually displaced between $34,000 and $41,225 from the total direct assembly and inspection labor content of your cost of goods sold.

6. Present your value in person as soon as possible once the event or solution has been provided. Presentation of the value should occur promptly after the event or after the solution was found to be acceptable by the customer. The value you create is worth the most shortly after it has been delivered, and it erodes over time. As stated earlier, memories of good events fade quickly for both the customer and the seller.
7. Deliver the value-added documentation to the person whose budget line you positively impacted. Although they play for the same team, the materials manager is not

going to get overly excited to hear that your process improvement reduced final inspection and test times by 5%. People are motivated most by how they are measured, and if your message positively impacts them, they will be more receptive to it. You will even find that your customers will advocate for you on future opportunities when you can link your value-added contributions to their budget and/or productivity metrics.

8. Sellers need to maintain a positive mind-set when approaching customers with examples of value-added documentation. Many professional sellers and managers have played organized sports in the past or have coached sporting teams for their children or communities. A coach would bench or release a player from the team if they routinely showed a losing or defeatist attitude. Athletes and coaches approach every game with the mind-set that they will win. A value-added seller should approach delivering and communicating value to every customer with the same winning mind-set. Henry Ford once said, "Whether you think you can, or you think you can't – you're right" (Anderson, 2013).

9. Real and meaningful value is less about what you do and more about what the customer receives. Many sellers feel that value is what they do or provide to the customer; however, that's only a small part of the overall equation. There is both a science and an art to value-added documentation. The science component includes those things provided that have commercial billable value – such as an emergency after-hours delivery from local inventory. At the minimum, the seller should document billable services, support, and items provided to the customer at no or a reduced charge. This is the easy part and the equivalent of swimming in the shallow end of the pool. The pitfall of only documenting items of this nature is that the customer can easily rebut them by saying "this is your job," "this is what we expect," or "your competitor can do the same thing." The art of value-added documentation and communication is identifying what the customer received as a result of your efforts. Typically what the customer receives is worth many times more than what you provided. Let's use the example of an emergency after-hours delivery from location inventory. If you waived the call-out charge and subsequently developed a value-added document for what you did (the science), the document would show $250 in cost avoidance. However, as a result of your responsiveness, that after-hours delivery of critical components may have reduced 2 hours of unscheduled downtime at $5,000 per hour. The "science" side of your documentation is worth $250, but the "art" provided them $10,000 in value. When you understand and communicate the "art" of your value, you are now in an area where many customers cannot compare you with the competition. They can refute those items of your job that you quantify, but they are hard-pressed to dismiss the benefits they received from you performing your job with a high degree of efficiency and precision.

10. One of the worst words in a salesperson's vocabulary is "free." First, customers are smart and realize that somewhere along the line they are actually paying for those "free" items. Second, there is zero value associated with items that are "free." The word "free" should be stricken from the vocabulary of the value-added seller and replaced with a better description such as "provided at no charge." Appropriate documentation should then be used to show the economic value provided for those billable items that were provided at "no charge."

11. The number you deliver to the customer is not the end of the conversation but rather the starting point. Value is not affirmed and real unless the customer agrees to it. Even

- Communication should be direct & straightforward
- Show & explain your math
- Use customer data
- Don't try to count everything
- Be conservative
- Use ranges rather than specifics
- Present as soon as possible
- Deliver it to the right person
- Have a positive winning attitude
- It's less about what you do & more about what's received
- "Free" items create no value
- Prepare to negotiate the value
- Be selective – don't overshare

Figure 6.5 Guidelines for effective value quantification

if you are presenting reasonable and compelling value, prepare to negotiate over what it is finally worth in the eyes of the customer. In many cases the customer may contradict the numbers that are part of the "science" of what you delivered by categorizing them as part of "your job." This is why the "art" of value-added documentation is important, because the customer was more profitable as a result of you doing your job with a high degree of proficiency.

12. Use judgment about what you share and what you don't share. Social media has grown exponentially in popularity and usage over the past few years. Some people share very few details of their life; thus, you take notice and find it interesting when they do post updates to their social media profile. Conversely, there are others who grossly overshare every aspect of their day. With these people, you eventually grow weary of their posts and become desensitized to them. Keep that in mind when you are developing your value communications.

Figure 6.5 summarizes these considerations.

Closing comments and considerations

The Chinese philosopher Lao Tzu wrote in the *Tao Te Ching*, "The journey of a thousand miles begins with one step," and the basic details provided in this chapter are an ideal first step in the value management journey for many. Implementing sound value-management programs takes time, and you can expect a few bumps in the road while on that journey. A natural learning curve follows the implementation of any new process or strategy, and you can expect to encounter a few slip ups along the way in implementing a customer value management program. Making mistakes is a natural part of life and is generally seen as acceptable. Don't let your journey end once you have read the last page and closed the cover of the book.

References

Anderson, E. (2013, May 31) "21 Quotes from Henry Ford on business, leadership and life," *Forbes*. www.forbes. com/sites/erikaandersen/2013/05/31/21-quotes-from-henry-ford-on-business-leadership-and-life/ #2715e4857a0b3fe6625b370

"Investment". (n.d.) "Investopedia," www.investopedia.com/terms/i/investment.asp

Part III

Selling value – best practices in value quantification

7 Value quantification – processes and best practices to document and quantify value in B2B[1]

Hinterhuber, Andreas

Introduction

The requirements for a high-performing sales function are changing. In the past, communicating product benefits and features was a key element of sales activities. This is no longer enough. Today, the sales function is increasingly asked to document and quantify value to customers. Consider the results of a survey of 100 IT buyers at Fortune 1000 firms (Ernst and Young, 2002): 81% expect vendors to quantify the financial value proposition of their solutions (see Figure 7.1).

Similarly, a subsequent survey asks 600 IT buyers about major shortcomings in their suppliers' sales and marketing organizations (McMurchy, 2008): IT buyers see an inability to quantify the value proposition and an inability to clarify its business impact as important supplier weaknesses (see Figure 7.2).

These survey results suggest that the ability to quantify and document the financial impact of the value proposition is critical for sales executives. How well equipped are today's sales managers in this respect? Extant research suggests that B2B purchasers rate the ability of sales managers to quantify the value proposition as unsatisfactory (Ernst and Young, 2002). The conclusion: B2B sales managers must improve their capabilities to quantify and document value.

About the research

Over the last five years, my colleagues and I analyzed the value propositions of 125 B2B companies: These companies vary in size and include Fortune 500 companies as well as many small- and medium-sized companies. We complement this research with discussions at dozens of large- and medium-sized companies across a wide range of industries, including automotive, IT services, chemicals, B2B services, pharmaceuticals, forestry, and machinery. In these companies our interlocutors are sales directors, pricing managers, senior executives, and first-level sales managers. Our aim is, first, to collect global best practices in quantified value propositions and, second, to gain insight into the processes that guide the effective development and implementation of quantified value propositions. As a result of this research, I present in the following section a framework for the effective development of quantified value propositions. I also present selected case studies that – based on this research – are current global best practices.

The process

Value quantification requires a process. Based on the research, within high-performing sales organizations this process includes the following steps (see Figure 7.3).

DOI: 10.4324/9781003177937-10

B2B VENDORS ARE EXPECTED TO QUANTIFY THEIR VALUE

E & Y survey of 100+
Fortune 1000 IT buyers

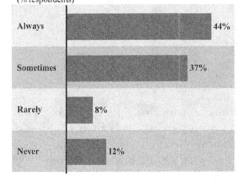

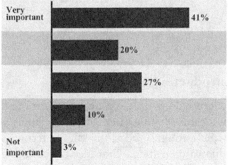

Before funding a project, how often do you expect IT vendors to quantify the financial value proposition of their solution? (% respondents)

- Always — 44%
- Sometimes — 37%
- Rarely — 8%
- Never — 12%

How important is a vendor's ability to quantify their financial value propositions in your vendor selection process? (% respondents)

- Very important — 41%
- 20%
- 27%
- 10%
- Not important — 3%

Source: Ernst & Young survey of 100+ Fortune 1000 IT buyers; Fortune 1000 IT buyer Survey, Ernst & Young, 2002

> **81% of IT buyers expect vendors to quantify their value proposition in financial terms.**

Figure 7.1 Value quantification: A critical requirement in B2B sales

WHAT IT PROVIDERS DO NOT DO

Gartner survey of 600
Fortune 2000 IT buyers

What are the shortcomings of IT provider sales & marketing? (% respondents)

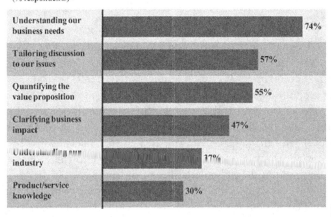

- Understanding our business needs — 74%
- Tailoring discussion to our issues — 57%
- Quantifying the value proposition — 55%
- Clarifying business impact — 47%
- Understanding our industry — 37%
- Product/service knowledge — 30%

Source: Gartner survey of 600 IT decision makers of Fortune 2000 companies; Neil McMurchy, Tough Times in IT, Gartner 2009 presentation

> **IT buyers see the inability to quantify the value proposition as a major shortcoming in IT sales and marketing.**

Figure 7.2 Value quantification: A major shortcoming of B2B sellers

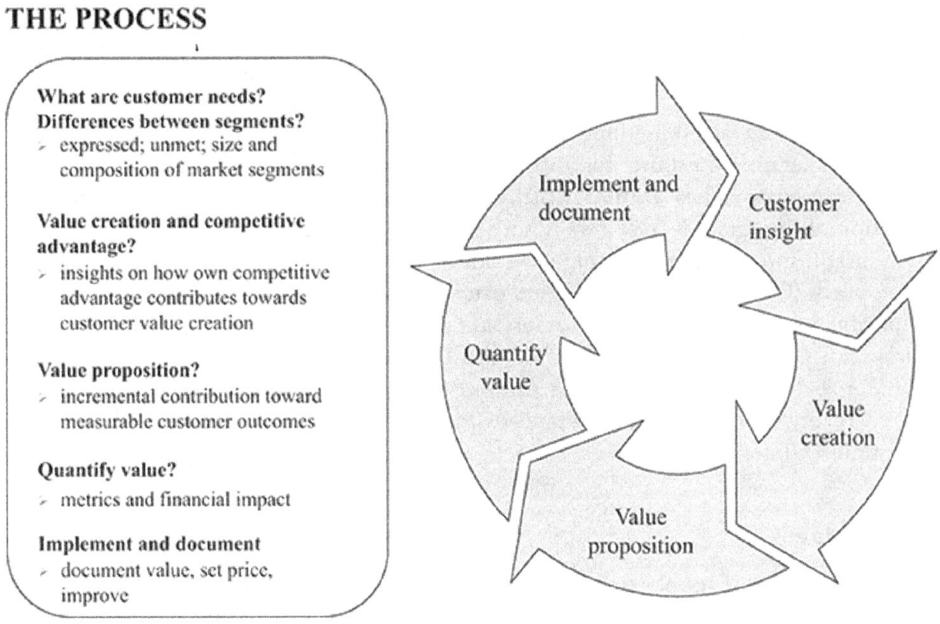

THE PROCESS

What are customer needs?
Differences between segments?
- expressed; unmet; size and
  composition of market segments

Value creation and competitive
advantage?
- insights on how own competitive
  advantage contributes towards
  customer value creation

Value proposition?
- incremental contribution toward
  measurable customer outcomes

Quantify value?
- metrics and financial impact

Implement and document
- document value, set price,
  improve

Implement and document

Customer insight

Value creation

Value proposition

Quantify value

Figure 7.3 The process of value quantification
Source: Hinterhuber & Partners

To be clear, in some organizations, the process leading to a quantified value proposition is more complex than the steps outlined later. In other companies, the actual process is much simpler than outlined: well-developed salesforce capabilities ensure that the quantification of the value proposition is a routine component in all major sales pitches, done without explicitly performing all steps outlined in every sales call. Nevertheless, we find that all high-performing sales organizations perform the five steps outlined in one way or another.

Customer insight

The first step in this framework is customer insight. Few companies have developed systematic capabilities in this respect. According to our research, companies that master the development of quantified value propositions strive, first and foremost, to achieve leadership in customer insight. A fundamental component of achieving leadership in customer insight is developing the ability to listen to customers. Jeff Immelt, CEO of General Electric, says, "Listening is the single most undervalued and under-developed business skill" (Clegg, 2014). Carol Meyrowitz, CEO of TJX, states, "In all our training we emphasize the importance of listening" (Meyrowitz, 2014: 47) – even for apparently inward-oriented functions such as corporate purchasing.

Listening is a key requirement that leads to performance improvements at the level of individual sales managers (Drollinger and Comer, 2013), but current research and executives of innovative companies concur that listening to customers does not and cannot imply following customers. The CEOs of Ford, Sony, Apple, and other companies all warn explicitly against taking customer input at face value. Steve Jobs, during his tenure as CEO of NeXT, said,

It sounds logical to ask customers what they want and then give it to them . . . You can't just ask customers what they want and then try to give that to them. By the time you get it built, they'll want something new. (Gendron and Burlingham, 1989)

Key to generating customer insight is an ability to interpret customers' unmet needs. Two research approaches are noteworthy: ethnographic research and outcome-driven innovation. Ethnographic research is today the gold standard enabling researchers to obtain insight into customers' thought worlds in order to uncover existing, but currently unmet, needs (Cayla et al., 2014). This research method enables researchers to experience the specific, naturally occurring behaviors and conversations of customers in their natural environments. As a result, insight into unsatisfied needs may emerge.

Outcome-driven innovation relies on a combination of qualitative and quantitative research to uncover latent customer needs in order to develop ideas for breakthrough innovations (Hinterhuber, 2013).

Create value

The rule is simple: If suppliers are not perceived as being different, then customers will benchmark them on price. The second step in the process of value quantification is thus differentiation along categories that matter to customers. To be clear, differentiation from competitors does not per se add value. It might lead to a sustained investment in product features that add no value for customers. Product differentiation strategies thus have to be preceded by an understanding of the real sources of value for customers (Hinterhuber, 2004). Customer insight − step one in our process − has to guide differentiation.

The objective of differentiation is to increase customer willingness to pay or total customer value. What is customer value? The definition of customer value in B2B must be based on the following five fundamental principles.

Value is, first of all, always defined by customers and their success metrics. Value is thus subjective, customer-specific, relative, and contextual. Customer insight is the first premise that guides the definition of value. Second, value is always created collaboratively with customers and must be recognized by customers if suppliers expect customers to pay for value. Collaboration is thus the second principle that guides the definition of value. Third, value is the sum of quantitative, financial, and qualitative, intangible benefits delivered to customers. Value is both hard and soft. Value quantification thus requires that suppliers develop capabilities to quantify the impact of both quantitative and qualitative benefits on key customer success metrics. Quantification of the business impact is thus the third principle that guides the definition of value. Fourth, all value is based on differentiation. Value is always based on the differentiation relative to the customer's perceived best available alternative. Differentiation is thus the fourth principle that guides the definition of value. Finally, value must be substantiated. For suppliers, value is a promise. For customers, value is an expectation. Suppliers must convert their promises into credible, verifiable, and simple deliverables in order to provide customers a realistic assessment of their abilities to deliver the expected results. Figure 7.4 summarizes these fundamental principles that guide the definition of value in B2B.

WHAT IS VALUE?

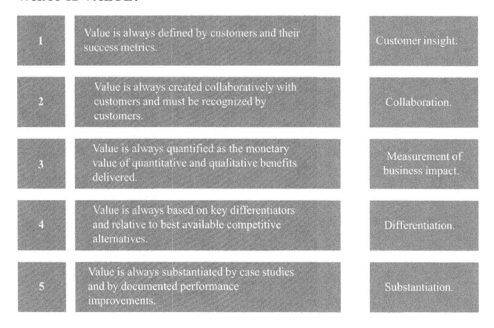

1	Value is always defined by customers and their success metrics.	Customer insight.
2	Value is always created collaboratively with customers and must be recognized by customers.	Collaboration.
3	Value is always quantified as the monetary value of quantitative and qualitative benefits delivered.	Measurement of business impact.
4	Value is always based on key differentiators and relative to best available competitive alternatives.	Differentiation.
5	Value is always substantiated by case studies and by documented performance improvements.	Substantiation.

Figure 7.4 Customer value – basic premises

Customer value is a multifaceted concept; differentiation can thus occur along a number of dimensions. Most important, differentiation is also possible for apparent commodities. Consider the following project, recently completed (Hinterhuber and Pollono, 2014).

Executives at a global basic chemical company assume that they are operating in a commodity industry and believe that – in order to achieve meaningful sales – prices for the chemical product in question need to be lowered to the price levels of a low-cost product from China that recently entered the market (indexed at 100 in Figure 7.5). Workshops with executives and focus groups with core customers and distributors allow us to uncover a number of differentiating factors between the low-cost competitor and the company's own offering. Although in no single area do the two products differ dramatically, we find a number of areas where there are small, albeit meaningful, differences between them. Through internal expert estimates and field value-in-use assessments, we quantify customer value for these differentiating features as follows.

We find that small differences in logistical know-how, in product quality, in ordering costs and complexity, in vendor competence, and in customer knowledge add up to a positive differentiation value of 8%, thus allowing the company to set prices up to 8% above the customer's best alternative. The highest possible price is, of course, not the best price: it leaves no incentive for the customer to purchase. After applying a series of price optimizations, competitive simulations, and estimates of customer reactions, we recommend a final selling price of 105. This represents a price premium of 5% over the customer's best available alternative, but this price is, nevertheless, attractive for customers, since their quantified benefits are higher than the price they are expected to pay.

VALUE-BASED PRICING IN B2B COMMODITIES

Hinterhuber &
Partners project

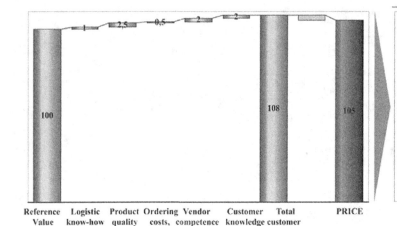

Key learnings
- even "commodities" can/need to be differentiated
- sum of many small differences makes a big difference
- price premium of 5% leads to dramatic differences in profitability
- need to sustain price and value premium

Figure 7.5 Value-based pricing and value creation for B2B commodities

As main learnings of this short case study, we highlight the following points: (a) even apparent commodities can and need to be differentiated, (b) the sum of many small differences in product characteristics can add up to a significant difference in customer value, (c) small price premiums over competitive products (e.g., 5%) translate to significant profitability differences between companies, and (d) the price and value premium between two competitive offerings need to be sustained over time via continuous improvement.

Develop the value proposition

The value proposition (Lanning and Michaels, 1988) or, alternatively, the value word equation (Anderson et al., 2006), is an instrument designed to translate customer value into quantified, monetary benefits. Anderson et al. (2006: 96) note that "a value word equation expresses . . . how to assess the differences in functionality or performance between a supplier's offering and the next best alternative and how to convert those differences into dollars." Numerous studies suggest that very few sellers can quantify the value proposition for their customers (Anderson et al., 2007; Hinterhuber, 2008). The capability to quantify value is, however, essential. Todd C. Snelgrove, chief value officer of SKF, states: "Best in class companies have taken the time, effort, and focus to quantify the value of their products and services. If you can't, purchasing will have no choice but to ask for a lower price" (Snelgrove, 2013).

On the basis of our research, I have developed a checklist of elements essential to best-practice value propositions (see Figure 7.6).

BEST PRACTICE VALUE PROPOSITIONS

Check	Item	Key issue	Rate
	Is the target customer group clearly identified?	segment	
	Is the key business issue we resolve a real pain-point for this segment?	relevance	
	Is it clear that the value proposition is superior for this customer group?	better	
	Does the value proposition reflect our competitive advantages?	advantage	
	Is the value proposition relative to the customer's best available alternative?	competition	
	Are customer benefits quantified? Is the quantification the result of quantifying both financial as well as qualitative benefits?	quantify	
	Is the value proposition based on sound customer and market research?	research	
	Does it reflect changing customer priorities? Is it relevant ... tomorrow?	update	
	Can you substantiate the value proposition with case studies or evidence of quantified performance improvements delivered?	substantiate	
	Can you articulate the value proposition in 1-2 minutes?	short	

Figure 7.6 Checklist for developing a best-practice value proposition

Source: Hinterhuber & Partners

Quantify value

Quantifying value means translating competitive advantages into financial customer benefits. Competitive advantages typically deliver either quantitative or qualitative benefits or both. Quantitative benefits are related exclusively to financial benefits, whereas qualitative benefits are related to process benefits – they allow customers to achieve the same goals in a better way. Quantitative benefits come in four categories: revenue/margin improvements, cost reductions, risk reductions, and capital expense savings. Qualitative benefits include ease of doing business, relationship benefits, knowledge and core competencies, the value of the brand, and other process benefits.

Customer value is the sum of quantitative and qualitative benefits. Value quantification tools visualize the total customer value, that is, the sum of quantitative and qualitative benefits, the price of the company's own product/solution, and the costs of the best available competitive product. These value quantification tools thus allow ROI calculations: the ROI is the result of relating the price premium to the quantified difference in customer value.

Leading B2B companies routinely perform value quantifications. An example from SKF is illustrated in Figure 7.7 (Hinterhuber and Snelgrove, 2012).

Industrial bearings are, for the layperson, commodities: apparently interchangeable steel products used in industrial manufacturer's rotating equipment. SKF is able to document

Price vs. Total Cost – It's about measuring all the factors…

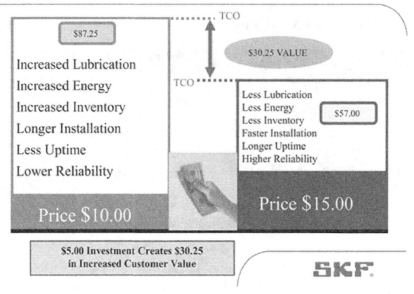

Figure 7.7 Value quantification at SKF

Source: SKF

to customers that, despite a price premium of 50% over the next best available product, customers end up paying less and being better off by purchasing from SKF.

Marketing, pricing, and sales managers in B2B should take notice: if SKF is able to quantify the value of industrial bearings, so should other companies with products and services, which are frequently even more differentiated than those of industrial parts.

Implement and document

The final component in the process of value quantification is implementation and documentation of results. The promises outlined in value quantification tools – such as the one in Figure 7.7 – account for nothing unless the value is actually realized in customer operations. In high-performing sales organizations, the following guiding principles underpin this process (see Figure 7.8).

Customer orientation

Customer orientation may appear to be a trite attribute of companies that successfully quantify the value proposition, but it is not. Our research suggests that low-performing sales organizations push their value propositions to customers regardless of whether these value propositions apply in the current context: customer needs may have changed, the next best available competitive alternative may have changed due to new competitors, the customer's objectives may have changed, or customer capabilities may have shifted.

IMPLEMENT, DOCUMENT, AND IMPROVE

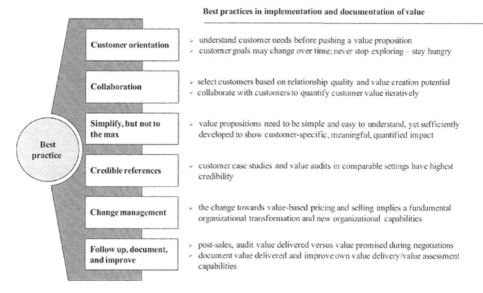

Figure 7.8 Implementing and documenting the quantified value proposition

Nothing, our research suggests, destroys the credibility of sales managers quicker than presenting a value proposition to customers without first having gained an in-depth understanding of current and future customer needs. The adage "Seek first to understand, then to be understood" is also valid in this specific context.

Collaboration

Quantified value propositions are the result of a tight-knit collaboration between vendors and suppliers: credible quantified value propositions cannot be developed in isolation and require that customers give suppliers access to the profit implications of the supplier's offerings for customer operations. This is tricky. In some instances the request for access to customer data highlighting the profit implications of supplier offerings on customer operations can trigger a countervailing request by the customer for access to supplier cost data (Rosenback, 2013). This request is reasonable. As a result, negotiated prices for differentiated offerings will settle not between the price of the customer's best available alternative and total customer value, as the literature on value-based pricing suggests (Nagle and Holden, 2002), but between (the likely lower) supplier costs and total customer value.

In this context, customer selection is important: Rather than selecting customers based on size or reputation, high-performing sales organizations select customers based on the quality of the relationship and the potential for joint value creation. Furthermore, high-performing sales organizations take time and invest resources to fine-tune the value proposition through multiple iterations, whereas low-performing sales organizations tend to take a hit-or-miss approach. Typically, the latter leads to value propositions that are more generic and less relevant to any particular customer.

Simplify, but not to the maximum

The essence of a quantified value proposition consists of translating the company's competitive advantages into quantified, expected performance improvements. This requires an understanding of competitors and their price and performance level; an understanding of the firm's own competitive advantages; and, finally, an understanding of customers, their needs, and their business models (Hinterhuber, 2004). Modeling these relationships is complex: effective value propositions, like all models, are thus always a simplification of reality – but not to the point where simplification leads to meaningless generalization.

Credible references

References enhance the credibility of quantified value propositions. These references can take many forms: summaries of pilot projects, customer case studies, value audits, or documented performance improvements countersigned by customers.

Change management

Institutionalizing value quantification as organizational capability requires organizational change management (Liozu et al., 2012). New approaches to selling, marketing, and pricing frequently require new capabilities, a new organizational structure, different goal and incentive systems, new processes and tools, and new organizational priorities. From an organizational perspective, the implementation of value quantification across the organization must be treated like an ongoing change management process as opposed to a project with a finite life (Hinterhuber and Liozu, 2014).

Follow up, document, and improve

As a final element in value quantification, high-performing sales organizations rigorously follow up on actual versus expected quantified value delivered in 6- to 12-month intervals. This enables both customers and suppliers to learn, to analyze causes of performance deviations, and to implement measures to close performance gaps. This documentation also enables suppliers to build up a library of documented and quantified performance improvements, by, for example, client function, industry, size, and geographic area. SKF, for example, has built up a library containing more than 63,000 case studies of documented and quantified value delivered by SKF, countersigned by customers. This library, SKF's Documented Solutions Program, is a very powerful selling tool for sales managers when participating in competitive bids with new customers: extant data can be used to estimate likely quantified performance improvements based on a long history of performance improvements in similar situations that customers have actually realized. This documentation is thus an important enabler of organizational learning within suppliers: suppliers learn about typical roadblocks to the realization of expected quantified performance improvements; suppliers also learn about all those areas of their own offering where the realized value is higher than the value they themselves expected to realize.

These positive and negative deviations from initial performance expectations are important foundations for gaining an even better, more fine-tuned and granular understanding of the effect of a firm's own competitive advantages on customer operations. As a result, these deviations will, over time, likely diminish.

Examples of effective quantified value propositions

In the course of our research, we encountered a dozen or so companies that have highly effective quantified value propositions. These well-crafted value propositions support sales and marketing executives during the bidding phase. The ultimate outcomes of effective quantified value propositions are higher prices and higher win rates. As a further benefit, respondents report that the conversation with B2B buying centers shifts: price is less a central concern and the focus shifts toward the quantified performance improvement. Realization of this performance improvement requires that customers and suppliers work together closely. Effective quantified value propositions thus fundamentally change the nature of the customer – supplier relationship, requiring a tight-knit collaborative attitude whereby barriers between the organizations of customers and suppliers start to fall. This ultimately benefits customer satisfaction and customer loyalty.

Recently, Hinterhuber & Partners has worked with a global IT service company to define profitable pricing strategies. This company had clear-cut competitive advantages, yet managers struggled to translate these competitive advantages into quantified customer value. As a result, aggressive competitors regularly undercut the company on price. The dilemma was thus: Should the company reduce price in the uncertain hope of gaining volume, or should the company maintain price and risk losing even more revenues?

Hinterhuber & Partners helped this company to escape from these self-imposed limitations. After interviewing managers, customers, distributors; after collecting data on competitive price levels; and after, finally, employing a robust process to identify and quantify key value drivers, we developed a customized value quantification tool that helped the company to understand, precisely, the amount of value a specific product generated for a specific customer segment. Deployment of this tool (see Figure 7.9) led to immediate, substantial profit improvements. A disguised example illustrates the principles: Instead of submitting an offer at a cost-plus-driven price of approximately 400,000€ that sales managers would usually heavily discount, the company is now in a position to confidently offer its solution at 465,000€; this price is low compared with the total quantified customer value of over 800,000€. This process thus enables the company to sell its products with a robust ROI calculation attached: There is a price premium over low-price competitors, and this is graciously acknowledged. The main point, however, is that an investment of approximately 100,000€ (i.e., the price premium versus the low-price competitor) leads to incremental customer benefits of over 400,000€ (i.e., the difference in customer value between the two offers), thus leading to an ROI of 300%.

This is, in sum, a key benefit of value-based pricing and value quantification: turning the conversation from a discussion on price differences to an exploration and documentation of quantified customer benefits.

Value quantification is especially effective and in many cases mandatory when the supplier has a price premium over a relevant competitor. For many suppliers the key question is, is it possible to convince customers that customers end up paying less by purchasing the most expensive offer? The quantified value proposition of SAP (Raihan, 2010) provides

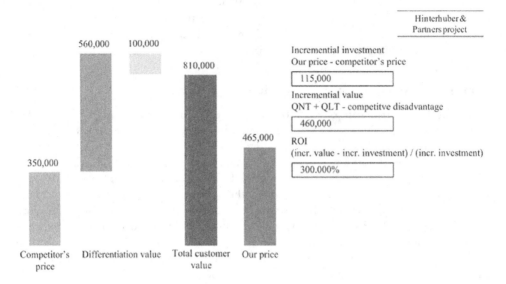

Figure 7.9 Quantifying the value proposition – a case study in B2B services

Source: Hinterhuber & Partners

an alternative way of presenting a premium-price offer: not as one that will lead to lower costs of ownership, but one that reduces customer risks (see Figure 7.10).

SAP sells enterprise software: In this specific project case the company's price is 20% above the price of a comparable competitor. SAP argues that the true cost of the competitive solution is higher than its own price, mainly because risks have not been accounted for. SAP identifies several categories of risk: solution risk (lower business functionality, regulatory risk), supplier risk (only local presence, long-term viability), technology risk (lower scalability), operational risk (lower flexibility), and, finally, implementation risk (lower experience). These risks can be quantified and should be, at least according to SAP, added to the price of the lower-cost solution. The risk-adjusted price of the apparently low-cost offer exceeds the price of SAP's solution by a substantial amount. According to SAP's experience, this helps the company win deals even though the list price of its solution is substantially higher than the price of the customer's next best alternative. Lower risks thus can justify price premiums.

Further considerations

Value quantification capabilities may be the most important capabilities of high-performing sales companies today. Building these capabilities requires a deep personal and organizational change. An interviewee at a global B2B IT service company observes: "What we started to realize was: It is not what your products or services do for your customers. It is what your customers are able to do as a result of using your products and services."

The preliminary results of this research indicate that companies with well-developed value quantification capabilities are able to realize higher prices and higher win rates. Relationships with customers benefit as well: collaboration increases. As companies

The Risk-Justified Project Cost Is Higher Than the Actual Proposed Project Cost of the SAP Solution

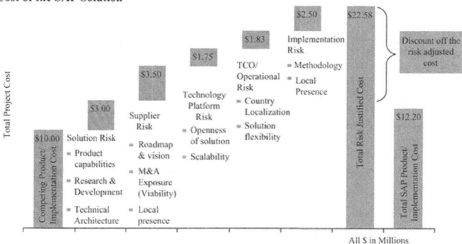

Figure 7.10 Quantifying the value proposition – the example of SAP

Source: SAP

implement the process outlined here – (a) customer insight, (b) value creation, (c) value proposition, (d) value quantification, and (e) implementation and documentation – customer satisfaction and loyalty typically increase. Thus, developing these capabilities may lead companies to achieve a sustainable competitive advantage.

We lack, however, quantitative empirical studies documenting the link between a company's value quantification capability and performance. This would make for a fascinating study.

Note

1 This is a fully updated and expanded version of the article: Hinterhuber, A. "Value quantification – The next challenge for B2B selling" in Hinterhuber, A., Liozu, S. (Eds.), *Pricing and the Sales Force*, Routledge, 2016. Copyright (c) 2016 Routledge. All rights reserved. Reprinted by permission.

References

Anderson, J. C., Kumar, N. and Narus, J. (2007) *Value Merchants: Demonstrating and Documenting Superior Value in Business Markets*, Boston, MA: Harvard Business School Press.

Anderson, J. C., Narus, J. A. and Van Rossum, W. (2006) "Customer value propositions in business markets," *Harvard Business Review 84*(3), 90–99.

Cayla, J., Beers, R. and Arnould, E. (2014) "Stories that deliver business insights," *MIT Sloan Management Review 55*(2), 55–62.

Clegg, A. (2014, October 21) "The quiet art of being a good listener," *Financial Times*, p. 12.

Drollinger, T. and Comer, L. B. (2013) "Salesperson's listening ability as an antecedent to relationship selling," *Journal of Business & Industrial Marketing 28*(1), 50–59.

Ernst & Young. (2002) "Fortune 1000 IT buyer survey: What could shorten sales cycles and further increase win rates for technology vendors?" *Economics & Business Analytics White Paper* 1–15.

Gendron, G. and Burlingham, B. (1989) "The entrepreneur of the decade: An interview with Steven Jobs," *Inc. 10*(4), 114–128.

Hinterhuber, A. (2004) "Towards value-based pricing – An integrative framework for decision making," *Industrial Marketing Management 33*(8), 765–778.

Hinterhuber, A. (2008) "Customer value-based pricing strategies: Why companies resist," *Journal of Business Strategy 29*(4), 41–50.

Hinterhuber, A. (2013) "Can competitive advantage be predicted? Towards a predictive definition of competitive advantage in the resource-based view of the firm," *Management Decision 51*(4), 795–812.

Hinterhuber, A. and Liozu, S. M. (2014) "Is innovation in pricing your next source of competitive advantage?" *Business Horizons 57*(3), 413–423.

Hinterhuber, A. and Pollono, E. (2014, May) "Value-based pricing: The driver to increased short-term profits," *Finance & Management 221*, 21–24.

Hinterhuber, A. and Snelgrove, T. (2012) "Quantifying and documenting value in B2B: Professional pricing society online course," www.pricingsociety.com/home/pricing-training/online-pricing-courses/quantifying-and-documenting-value-in-business-markets

Lanning, M. J. and Michaels, E. G. (1988) "A business is a value delivery system," McKinsey & Company Staff Paper No. 41.

Liozu, S., Hinterhuber, A., Perelli, S. and Boland, R. (2012) "Mindful pricing: Transforming organizations through value-based pricing," *Journal of Strategic Marketing 20*(3), 1–13.

McMurchy, N. (2008) "Tough times in IT: How do you exploit the opportunities?" Gartner presentation, Stamford, CT.

Meyrowitz, C. (2014) "The CEO of TJX on how to train first-class buyers," *Harvard Business Review 92*(5), 45–48.

Nagle, T. T. and Holden, R. K. (2002) *The Strategy and Tactics of Pricing: A Guide to Profitable Decision Making* (3rd ed.), Englewood Cliffs, NJ: Prentice Hall.

Raihan, R. (2010) "Leveraging IT to drive business value," Presentation at the Information Resource Management Association of Canada (IRMAC), Toronto, Canada.

Rosenback, M. (2013) "Antecedents and obstacles to total cost of ownership analysis in industrial marketing – A case study," Paper presented at the 29th IMP Conference, Atlanta, Georgia.

Snelgrove, T. (2013) "Creating value that customers are willing and able to pay for," Presentation at the Product Management Forum of the Manufacturers Alliance for Productivity and Innovation (MAPI), Rosemont, IL.

8 Quantifying your value so customers are willing and able to pay for it

Snelgrove, Todd C.

How does one get paid for value created? The question has been asked by every premium player in every market of the world. Given that the financial benefits of value creation and pricing are well known, why do so many companies fail to achieve the desired results after they've done the work to create something of value? For those that do invest and create customer value, it's time to do the work to get paid for it!

PV ≥ Cost = Action

I have begun to look at this as a formula. If the perceived value (PV) of a good or service is greater than or equal to the cost of buying it, then an action such as a purchase should occur. In more detail, it is the PV from the customer's perspective; however, if that value can be expressed monetarily, it will be a harder value than a PV that is not. Cost includes the asking price, plus all other associated costs (shipping and handling, research time, cost of capital, etc.). If I perceive that I will obtain more value than the cost of doing so, it probably will result in a purchase. The greater the difference between PV and cost, the higher the percentage of people who will buy. For example, if the quantified customer-specific value is $100, and the cost of acquiring it is $42, then a value surplus or incentive to buy of $58 exists and for most that surplus is large enough to motivate most people toward the desired action of purchasing. However, let's assume that PV is a feeling (no number is assigned to it); in this case, fewer people would buy. Finally, if the PV were only $43 and the cost were $42, far fewer people would invest in buying to receive the one dollar of benefit.

Looking at the example in Figure 8.1 of an offering for a tool called a laser alignment system, we see a list of PVs; let's assume for each item there's a value that, based on industry averages or customer-specific numbers, totals $10,000 and that the total costs of acquiring the tool are $4,200, leaving a value surplus or "incentivization" benefit of $5,800. If the numbers are a hard value, believable to me as a buyer, then I will find a way to get the $4,200. In general, the harder and more monetary the value numbers are, the less value surplus is needed to get an order.

Companies that employ a good value-based pricing strategy are 20% more profitable than those that have weak execution on value pricing, and 36% more profitable than those that are good at executing a cost- or market-share-driven strategy (Hogan, 2008). Thus, I would argue that value pricing works only if additional areas are also addressed. A company must create value, communicate that value through sales and marketing, and quantify that value in monetary terms; only then can it get paid for the value created.

DOI: 10.4324/9781003177937-11

	Perceived value ≥ Costs = Action	
Less energy consumption		
Faster installation	Price of tool	
Longer machine life	Cost of adding or using existing vendor	Order or no order
Easier installation	Time to wait for delivery of tool	
Less machine vibration		
$10,000	$4,200	$5,800 value surplus

Figure 8.1 Example of perceived value calculation for a laser alignment tool

Think about it for a second: if a company is great at three of these but not the fourth, it won't get paid for value.

As I travel the world, I hear too often from CEOs the refrain "I want our salesforce to sell based on value but they do not . . . why?" The answer is "simple." No one size fits all, and no silver bullet exists. Selling on value takes focus, management support, tools, and training, and product or service differentiated attributes to see the results. In talking with other thought leaders in the value space, I have come to realize that numerous other things need to happen to make value-selling work for a company.

For a salesforce it comes down to two main focuses: Do they have the ability to sell value? And do they want to sell value? I find that most companies focus on the ability area and assume that the salesforce wants to sell value and that they just need to go and do it. So what's needed?

Why spend the time and effort to quantify your company's value?

The first step in the journey is to realize that quantifying value is something your customers want and need you to do, something that will allow them to justify buying your option, unless you're consistently the lowest-priced offering. In the world of buying and pricing, two competing forces exist. From a customer's perspective, these are the *willingness to pay* (WTP) for value and the *ability to pay* (ATP) for that value. In the days when the user of a product or service was the decision maker, and purchasing was more of a clerical function, the process was easier – easier in the sense that the user of the solution you were offering could justify in their own mind what better, longer, easier, faster meant because they were the ones who would receive the benefit. However, in the last two decades, the activity of "purchasing" has evolved into the strategic focus of "procurement." The difference is important: now procurement decides what is of value, what they are willing to pay for – and because they are not the ones who will see and receive the benefits, they are less likely to pay for them. Second, in today's budget-constrained world, the question is whether the customer has the money or budget to buy the better offering. The case studies, research, and anecdotal stories that follow show that if value can be quantified in the universal language of dollars and cents, then obtaining new budgets or reallocating money from another budget can easily happen, and procurement will be willing to invest.

For example, I might say to a potential customer (user of a product or service), "This solution will allow you to do the job 22% faster, and the quality of the job will be 10% better" (assuming data exist to reinforce this). How willing and able would that customer be to pay for that value? It would depend on what those impacts would mean to them and on comparing this buy with other competing purchases. They might sense that mine is the better solution, and then they would have to take this argument to their boss, procurement, and finance and explain that time is money, for example. However, what if a customized business case showing that the company's solution would save their company $225,000 a year in overtime, parts, reduced scrap, and less rework? Which scenario has a better chance of getting the order? Now they would know what the solution was worth and where it would rank with competing requests for the two very scarce resources of time and money. In today's world, where your offering is competing for funding and priority over other options, the one that has the best business case, with the hardest values, and the highest probabilities of realization, will be the offering that is purchased. If you cannot quantify the value of your offering, it will be placed in the dreaded no decision, or low-priority, bucket. Or the purchase will be seen as a commodity and you will be compared with your competitors based on price and delivery. Instances of decision-by-committee have increased, and "let's not make the wrong decision" seems to be a dominant driving force. It's easy to point to "we got all the minimum requirements at a lower unit price" to support a bad supplier selection if ultimately things don't work out. However, with a vetted business case, all functions involved in the decision can point to the payback, ROI, and cash flow of the business case provided to justify why that project or solution was approved over the other options. Even when there is no budget, if the payback is believable or guaranteed, money can easily be reallocated or found when a quantified business case exists.

So once you see the need for and benefit of quantifying your value, what else needs to happen to enable your company to sell and get paid for that value? Let's look at the internal and external resources, requirements, and focuses needed (see Figure 8.2). These are not ranked by order of importance; however, you need to address all of them to be truly successful. Over the last decade I have had the chance to sit with the Guru of Value, Professor James C. Anderson, and discuss what's working, what's not, and why, in our company and others' "Value Merchant" strategy. After one discussion, Jim created the diagram shown in Figure 8.2. I was amazed at how clearly he was able to represent the main

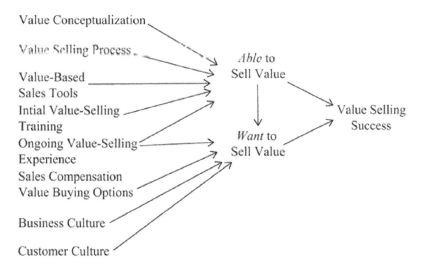

Figure 8.2 What causes value-selling success?

points and show how they support the two areas of ability and willingness to sell value. Checking to make sure we address all areas listed in this diagram ensures that we cover all the basics for a vital, ongoing, robust program based on value that allows a company to differentiate its offering from that of the competition.

The ability to sell value component

Value conceptualization

What is your company's value to your customers? What does it help them do better than the other options? Value selling begins with the basic step of making sure your company creates something of value. Whether it's a product or a service, it needs to have an attribute that is not only different but also of value to someone within your target audience. Most academics use the term "unique selling proposition" or USP; however, just because something is unique doesn't mean it is of value. At our company's 100-year celebration, our CEO took the stage and memorably said, "Value is not in the minds of our engineers and what we think value is; value is what customers value."

Years ago, while interviewing for my job at SKF (a Swedish-headquartered global leader in industrial engineered products), I asked our Canadian president why customers would choose to buy an SKF bearing over a competitor's offering, when we had a price premium. I will never forget the stone-faced glare of our Swedish president, who said – almost in disbelief that I didn't already know why – "We are Swedish." I began to chuckle and then realized that he wasn't joking. So our head office is in one country, whereas our competitors' are in others. This is unique, but it's not something of value (to me, at least). What I heard him say was that our head office is in Sweden. What he meant was that we make the highest-quality products in the world and that we've generated more innovations and patents than all our competitors (Swedish culture is highly innovative and focused on quality). So the first phase of value selling is to make sure that you create something that is of value to your customers – whatever that may be.

Since publicly traded companies have a shareholder responsibility to create sustained profit, let's make sure we help them do this in the right way by adding real value and taking out real cost. To get buy-in, this value must be quantified.

Value-selling process

Second, value has to be part of your selling process. Are you merely reacting to customers' requests, or are you proactively engaging customers, solving problems, and articulating that value during your sales process? The Corporate Executive Board (CEB, 2015), a U.S. think tank, recently found that of more than 1,400 B2B customers' sales interactions, those customers completed, on average, nearly 60% of a typical purchasing decision in researching solutions, ranking options, setting requirements, benchmarking pricing, and so forth before they even talked with a supplier. So if the customer has decided that three suppliers meet their minimum criteria, then price is the only measurable thing of difference. In this case, it's hard to come in and say, "Hey, you need to rethink your requirements: what you really need to do is measure value or total cost of ownership." However, based on experience, we've been able (although it's harder when it's later in the sales cycle) to say,

> Should we be discussing the $5,000,000 in annual parts that you buy and a price savings of 5% on that if you give me an additional $2,000,000 in business ($350,000 theoretical price savings), or the $4,000,000 in CAPEX and OPEX savings (hard EPS improvements) our company can help drive to your bottom line by getting your facilities to a world best-in-class average? An opportunity for profit that is 11.5 times bigger.

All the customer can now ask are questions like "Has this happened before? What's the probability that it will happen? How will we measure it? What happens if you hit or miss your target? What payment relationship should we have?" These all move into the discussion of implementation to realize value.

Can your salesforce have an intelligent discussion with procurement, finance, engineering, and even the customer's CEO to explain how lowest price is not the same as lowest cost? Can your company affect, measure, and reduce costs and increase value in using your product or service during the phases of acquisition, installation, operation, maintenance, and disposal? Can your company also increase the benefits your customer receives, such as increased production, reduced risk, increased safety, increased sell-through? By looking at the total cost of ownership (reduction of costs) along with the total benefit of ownership (increase in benefits of value), you can now understand and demonstrate in numbers how you can affect and measure the impact of your offering on their total value of ownership – which is the difference in reduced costs plus increased benefits minus any price difference – thereby making them measurably more profitable. Actually a better term to use is "total profit added" (TPA). This would be the most holistic measure of all the costs saved (total cost of ownership [TCO]) and all the increased benefits created, thereby allowing for a clear demonstration if the price being charged will lead to the highest profit for the customer, versus other options, over the total life of the product or service. TPA is the next evolution measuring and choosing based on best value (see Figure 8.3).

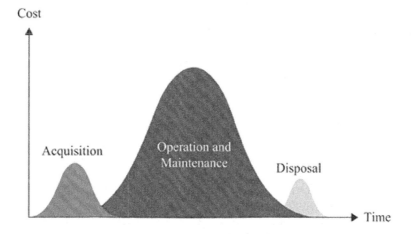

Figure 8.3 Total cost of ownership

Value-based sales tools

Most companies mistakenly think that having a value-based sales tool is the holy grail and the end of the value journey. As companies have said to me in the past,

> If we just had a methodology to sit down with customers and document for them where and how much more money they can make or save using our offering versus the next best alternative, all our problems would be solved.

This is one of the foundational building blocks; however, it is only part of the journey.

At SKF, in the early 2000s, we realized that all the superior technical benefits in the world of our products wouldn't matter to a VP of finance or procurement unless we could convert what those features and benefits meant into cold, hard cash. With that in mind, we created a tool called Documented Solutions Program™ (see Figure 8.4). It is our methodology for sitting down with the user of the solution and running an expected and eventually an actual business case ROI. This financial justification for the customer can now be used to show their bosses the benefits in hard cash of choosing to work with SKF or to buy a specific solution. We are not the lowest-price provider in our industry, but we can help customers realize the lowest costs by using our services and products. These tool and methodology have become a mainstay of our business, and each year we report the numbers generated. At the end of 2015, we had over 66,301 accepted or verified cases with customers, with savings of over U.S. $5 billion, covering all five of our technology platforms. You can imagine the power of sitting down with a customer and demonstrating how this same offering has helped their own company at a different location in the world, or someone within the same industry, save so many dollars by implementing this solution. The conversation goes from "how much does it cost?" to "when can we get this started so I can start saving money and solving a problem?"

For a value quantification tool to really work, it must be easy for the technical and financial person to understand. Remember, a good TCO tool is not a sales tool in and of itself. It's a process and methodology for benchmarking, finding, prioritizing, customizing, and quantifying expected values in financial terms so that customers can see if it makes sense for them to invest in your solution. Too often I see company-made templates that are really just a sales tool called something else.

Characteristics of a good TCO quantification tool:

1. Benchmarks data ranges and reference points.
2. Allows customers to change input data.
3. Is clear and concise. Sometimes engineers overcomplicate things and think the more detailed, the better.
4. Shows the results as your customer would like to see them, for example in terms of ROI, net present value, cash flow break even, dollars saved.
5. Is functional – allows users to save cases and work through a process to go from proposal, to accepted, to verified.
6. Builds in an archive so that cases can be saved, searched, and sorted by industry, application, country, distributor, customer, and so forth.
7. Provides live updates when connected to corporate server; links to reference material.
8. Is easy to use – available in a light version such as for an iPad (SKF launched in 2015), multiple languages and currencies, and so on.

Figure 8.4 SKF documented solutions

Initial value-selling training

Now that you know your offering has value, your sales process incorporates value, and you have tools for demonstrating and quantifying value, you'd better make sure your sales-force is comfortable with selling based on value versus price or technology. During initial training, spend time discussing why this is a good strategy for them and your company and why customers want and need proof of value. Programs that come as edicts from the head office usually encounter resistance in the field that is not needed. Bring the team along on the journey; don't ram it down their throats. Of course, they need to understand and practice with the tool's functionality. Also, if your salesforce is technical, then you will need to spend even more time getting their buy-in. For SKF this has been an issue, because we hire engineers, for whom the technology itself explains the value. They tend to be happier talking about product features and benefits such as the hardness of the steel or the precision of the manufacturing process – and if the solution proves the value, why would one need to convert that value into dollars and cents? When talking to other engineers, they're right; they understand what these things mean – but finance does not. Over the years, we've launched and used a great outside global sales consulting group to ensure that our teams feel comfortable with and know how to sell based on value and that they're comfortable with terms like "return on investment," "return on equity," and "net present value," and how we affect a customer's earnings per share. If your salesforce doesn't understand these terms or know how your company's offering can affect your customer's profit, then some training is required.

In the ability-to-sell-value stages we focused on the basic underpinnings needed. Next we discuss what else needs to happen to keep the culture change program alive and thriving with your team and with your customers.

The want to sell value component

Ongoing value-selling experience

However, training is not a one-and-done thing; it must be ongoing. Just as athletes train daily, so should salespeople. At SKF, we have just begun to do roleplaying in which a senior manager acts as the customer and challenges our salesperson's presentation and offering and asks, "What's the value for me, the customer?" You will only be good at and comfortable with value selling when you know and have answered similar questions hundreds of times. What will procurement's response to this offer be? Let's practice and think through what their possible objections might be so that we're prepared on game day. I also like regions and countries of the world that include the discussion of value during every meeting, where someone presents a case, what numbers were used, how the process worked, and key learnings.

Sales compensation and value buying options

If you can prove value, companies can pay for it. Sales compensation will have an impact on how your people behave. Do you incentivize volume targets? If so, then you shouldn't have to ask yourself why your salespeople are so eager to cut prices. In some organizations I have seen sales targets set as a threshold, with no consideration of whether a deal was struck by providing discounts. Some companies might think of themselves as advanced because they reduce the sales amount to the net discounted price. However, for a company with a 10% net profit margin, a 5% price cut is the equivalent of realizing only half the profit dollars. Also, remember that free services, free samples, free training, extended terms, and so on are just other more creative ways for a salesperson to discount your offering. I suggest that the salesperson who sells less but at full price should be rewarded more than the salesperson who spends most of their time with internal management justifying that a particular customer needs to get a discount.

We've looked at how you pay your salespeople, but we should also look at whether you've given your customers an option to buy based on value realized. In other words, do you use pay-for-performance models that allow customers to pay once value is realized for them? If not, then they might not be able to buy based on promises of potential future value. At SKF we use a few different methodologies: for large customers we might enter into a guarantee of annual cost savings. As a CEO once said to me, "I have 25 different ways to offer a discount, such as volume, competitive issues, industry, new business, etc., but I don't have a way to guarantee the value we create . . . that has to get fixed."

It's great to offer customers value, but have you offered them ways to pay for that value that fit their particular situation? Before moving on, let's be clear about what it means to get paid for value. It's not about "extracting" all the incremental value delivered to the customer in a price premium, for example. To do so would leave the customer with no incentive, or value surplus, to incentivize them to choose your option. Second, I believe most companies have a "buy my product or service at a price" option only. However, a whole set of options needs to exist based on the customer's situation and what they value. The extreme is a "buy my products at a certain list price all the way to a 100% pay-for-performance" option. Within SKF we call this integrated maintenance solutions (IMS) (see Figure 8.5). As with many outsourcing agreements, we focus on where we can drive the most immediate customer savings. So we might say, "Mr. Customer, what did you pay last year for all the parts, people, and operating expenses to run these factories?" "X." "Okay, we will do it better (measuring these deliverable KPIs and doing it for an immediate savings of Y). However, as we make you more money, we get a reward as those benchmark targets are exceeded (e.g., increased production)." I would say that outsourcing IT in general follows this model, and it can make sense. Corporate experts focused on just information technology delivery should be better at it because it's their core expertise. This is a great offering; however, a few issues could arise, and I have seen companies try this, along with other pay-for-performance agreements. If all the offsets are not listed, something that looks good (increased production, less inventory, etc.) might be a short-term win, but if assets are pillaged to do this (they were run with no proactive maintenance), actual losses – not savings – will result. Just think what a pump will really be worth in a few years if the proper maintenance isn't done. All those proposed or even realized savings will be more than offset by increased future costs. With that in mind, pay-for-performance agreements work if they are long-term so that no one is incentivized on such short time frames. However, in between these two options, other getting-paid-for-value formats should exist. A simpler version is, "Mr. Customer, although our products might have a higher average initial price of X, we guarantee an annual hard savings of X." The benefit is that the customer is getting value for paying more, and the value becomes ongoing, whereas price reductions are one-time (suppliers won't or can't offer a 5% per year incremental price savings, but they can offer a new 5% guaranteed savings in another area). As a customer, as long as the savings are hard, measurable, and don't force other costs up, I am willing to keep paying more as these savings compound and make me more sustainably profitable.

A question I've been asked by procurement professionals is, "Which is better: an acquisition price savings or ongoing annual cost savings?"

Imagine you're presented with the following choice: a 5% upfront price savings on a contract for 5 years or a 5% annual cost savings over 5 years (see Figure 8.6). Which is

Figure 8.5 Pay-for-performance options

the more valuable option? First, let's assume something that rarely happens – that the 5% price savings will actually make it to your company's bottom line and that no unintended increased costs will occur elsewhere. Let's also assume that the 5% annual TCO savings are real and measurable – lubrication savings, for example.

Given these two scenarios, some procurement people might assert that because both are 5%, they are worth the same. This analysis would be correct after year one, but not after year two. Switching to a new supplier may bring a 5% price savings, but that supplier would not offer and would not be able to deliver that incremental price savings every year thereafter.

From a TCO perspective, however, during year two an additional 5% savings would be generated by focusing on a new area of opportunity such as energy savings. The magic

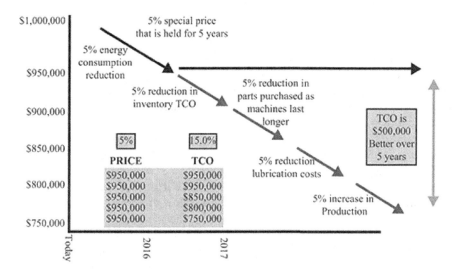

Figure 8.6 5% price versus 5% annual TCO improvements?

Source: Todd C. Snelgrove, Aberdeen Procurement Conference, March 2012, Boston, MA

of compounding and ongoing annual savings would allow a TCO annual 5% savings to be worth 15% versus the 5% price savings over a 5-year period or three times as much. Remember, we assumed the best-case scenario for the substituted product based on price.

> IACCM research shows that a focus on price concessions undermines the value achieved. For example, the probability of a poor outcome increases by more than 50%, compared with agreements that focus on performance. This translates into significant increases in cost and missed or lost revenue – at levels far exceeding the theoretical savings from the low negotiated price. SKF has provided thought-leadership in this area for more than 20 years, having successfully resisted "commoditization" by switching instead to delivering market-differentiating value.
>
> (Tim Cummins, CEO, International Association of Commercial and Contract Management, quoted in SKF, 2014: 2)

Business culture

Are you really a value company? Does your CEO talk nonstop about the value you create for your customers? Do you reward and recognize the people who create the most value or the newest ways to save customers money? Or are you just using a few buzzwords on a Power Point slide or corporate brochure? Value needs to be part of your company's DNA. Does sales get mixed messages like "Get every order and sell value"? Unless your message is clear, you will end up rewarding and motivating sales to cut prices, and volume will be the underlying dimension that's rewarded. If you're unable to prove your value you might get a short-term order based on lowest price, but over time it will not translate into more sustainable orders as someone comes along and undercuts you. We are lucky at SKF to have as our leader a CEO who continually focuses on value as our main differentiation.

Customer culture

Does procurement see you as a commodity and therefore assume you can be bought using certain tactics, or do they see your offering as strategic for them?

As a company you can do all these other things well, but if procurement sees you as a commodity, and buys your product or service as such, much effort needs to be exerted by everyone to get procurement to rethink where and why they have chosen to treat you that way. In my experience, most companies have an issue here. Let's begin with the way procurement chooses how to select suppliers and negotiate with them based on the Kraljic 4-box matrix. The Kraljic Matrix (see Figure 8.7) is a well-respected thought process introduced in 1983 in the *Harvard Business Review* article "Purchasing Must Become Supply Chain Management." Although the concept has since been modified (to a 9-box or a 36-box matrix), and procurement's implementation of it has evolved over the years, the thoughts and resulting actions of procurement still follow this concept. Too often there is a mismatch between how we perceive ourselves as sellers and how buyers perceive what we are selling, leading both sides to wonder why they cannot communicate.

A key driver of procurement is to increase spend under management (they control a higher percentage of the company's procurement dollars spent) and to buy from fewer suppliers (to increase leverage and to reduce transaction costs). When I am at a Strategic Account Management Association (SAMA.org) conference, and I ask senior global strategic account managers, "Where do you see your company on this matrix?"; in general I get the following feedback.

I get comments like "We are not the small, unimportant **Nuisance** offering, where transaction costs are the most important differentiator." However, I say, for suppliers in this realm, ease of use and ordering efficiency are the most important characteristics and decision-making criteria for procurement, with unit price being most important. When thinking about spend, we need to look at what percentage of the customer's total spend we are. In general, suppliers will focus most of their efforts on direct material spend, as that is where the most money is spent. When companies rank suppliers on spend they tend (of course) to place direct materials (all the products that go into making their primary product – steel, for example) on the right-hand side of the matrix because a small savings on a big number would seem to have a bigger effect on company profit. As

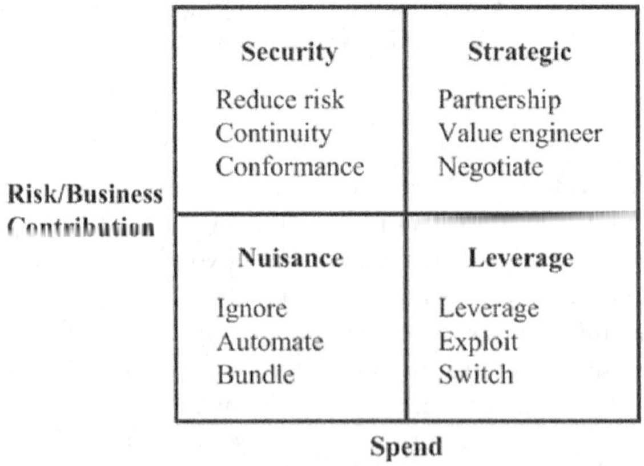

	Security	Strategic
Risk/Business Contribution	Reduce risk Continuity Conformance	Partnership Value engineer Negotiate
	Nuisance	**Leverage**
	Ignore Automate Bundle	Leverage Exploit Switch

Spend

Figure 8.7 Kraljic Matrix

we will see, the spend with a supply category is probably not the primary indicator of where efforts should be focused or the biggest hard savings and benefits can be realized. Although the y-axis represents the business contribution, if you cannot quantify the business contribution, procurement will assume that all offerings are the same and will push you into the lower two quadrants.

Most of us are not in the top left quadrant, either, at least not in the long term. This quadrant is where a supplier exists that is not a huge percentage of the customer's total spend but that has a product or service that cannot be easily substituted. Remember, the ease of substitution is based on the customer's assumptions, not ours. If you happen to have a patent on a product or service that they need or access to a chemical or raw material that no one else has, or if demand exceeds supply in a market, then you are in this position. However, in general, this is not a long-term realistic position to be in. If what you sell has an ISO specification, competitors are reasonably the same size and offering, and the perceived risk is very low or zero. I recall Robert Maguire, whose chapter appears in this volume, saying that people are confused about what an ISO standard is: "It's a conformance standard . . . not a performance standard." Yes, both products are the same size, fit the same hole, and so forth; however, that doesn't mean they'll produce the same results or perform the same way.

We suppliers want to think that we're strategic – that if the customer would really work with us, we could offer a lot of value, savings, benefits, risk reduction, and innovation. Talking with procurement professionals at numerous global conferences over the past decade, I find that they would place none or only a handful of suppliers in the top right quadrant as Strategic. However, after I discuss how often that's a mistake – that a lot of suppliers could really help their companies be more profitable by doing things differently – the standard retort is, "Then why don't they come to us and demonstrate and document how they would do that, and what the impact would be?" Sales and procurement functions both need to take responsibility for placing suppliers in the wrong quadrant and therefore not getting the possible or desired results.

The segmentations mentioned earlier are the backbone of a value-selling organization and culture; however, if the customer still perceives that the dollar spend with you is not significant (the x-axis in the Kraljic 4-box matrix) and you are not strategic enough to spend the time or effort to treat them like a partner and demonstrate the value you could bring, then much of the segmentations given earlier won't help. When you get to the procurement person or team at your customer and they are aggregating volume, threatening with low-priced offerings of competitors, contemplating the use of a reverse auction, employing some sort of benchmark pricing that shows, somewhere, one time your product price was less, asking you to explain your cost breakdown to justify a final price, then you should know that your customer sees you in one of the bottom two boxes and will focus on leveraging you. Most people forget that the x-axis label represents financial contribution, and they focus on dollars spent instead. This is a major issue that sales needs to address. Our company has made it a focus, and we have people whose job is to get customers to understand that even though the relative dollar spend might be low (versus direct spend such as raw materials), the impact can be huge. I think the x-axis should measure financial opportunity dollars (money saved using existing TCO or financial improvements Total Profit Added™). For example, supply risk might be low because other global players exist and products have an ISO specification. Dollars spent is relative. Customers might purchase $10 million of industrial parts to keep their plants running, but when their total spend is $5 billion some might assume that this "supply bucket" should be treated as non-critical or as a nuisance leverage buy (0.2% . . . not even close to 1% of total spend). However, when looking at how value can be created by reducing operating machine costs (less energy, water, lubricant, repair parts, labor, and/ or increases in machine production, throughput, or quality), one customer saw that our impact could be worth $128 million in savings. We were then moved immediately to the Strategic quadrant.

To help the market evolve, you need to do some research and work like a consulting organization that talks about the results you can impact and by how much. Don't just discuss the technical features of your widget. We need procurement around the world to challenge their assumptions. I spend a lot of time at procurement and academic conferences presenting our thoughts and methodology. This has proved very helpful in moving our market to change how they measure and choose suppliers, the most advanced being on hard value generated. A nice reference and study that I use is from Manufacturers Alliance for Productivity and Innovation (2012), a U.S.-based think tank that represents industrial manufacturers. A study they conducted with the procurement representatives of member companies found that companies that had a structured way to buy on best value were 35% more profitable than companies that had no structured methodology for measuring and understanding value.

To keep the program alive and flourishing

As I have shown in the focuses or requirements needed, a value quantification tool needs to be the output of the strategy of creating, communicating, quantifying, and getting paid for value; however, numerous other issues need to be addressed: "A fool with a tool is still a fool." For value quantification to become a company focus, a mantra, a part of who your company is and the reason for your being, other supports must be in place. Some suggestions follow.

Who will drive this program internally and externally? A program without a driving person is destined to fail. Baker and Lizou (2013) observed,

> Whenever this question is posed to a group of businesspeople – "Who's in charge of value in your company?" – someone will inevitably shout out "Everyone!" Really? If everyone owns something, no one does. Adam Smith demonstrated that the *division and specialization of labor* were a central cause of the wealth of nations; they are also the central cause of the success of a business. Not everyone can be good at everything.
>
> (p. 104; italics in original)

Will the ability to quantify the value of new products and services be part of your new product development process, so that when a new "solution" is presented to the market you can quantify its financial impact for customers?

External marketing should consistently reinforce this as part of your brand image. I'm not a fan of hearing how old a company is, or how big it is, or how many people it employs. What's in it for the customer to buy your company's offering? Spend time on the "so what is the benefit" and less on the how (the how can be discussed in face-to-face meetings). A tagline of mine is "Making Industry More Profitable." I might employ the smartest people, I might be the most knowledgeable, I might have more patents, I might have the best products, and so on; these are just things I can apply to a customer's business, with the result that I make them more profitable. Say what the result is; don't make the customer assume what those benefits will be for them. Trade shows, magazines, brochures, and company speeches should have a dedicated "section" where your company can summarize the hard value your company has delivered.

The value journey is never ending; an almost-as-good competitor will always be ready to copy your latest innovation. To stay out of the commodity game, and to make yourself and your customers more profitable, demonstrate and document when, where, why, and how you can affect how much money your customers make. It's not a zero-sum game if you can quantify your value; then you will be remunerated with an equitable portion of that value.

References

Baker, R. J. and Lizou, S. M. (2013) "Who is in charge of value? The emerging role of chief value officer," in A. Hinterhuber and S. Liozu (eds.), *Innovation in Pricing: Contemporary Theories and Best Practices* (pp. 99–118), New York: Routledge.

CEB. (2015) "Executive guidance: Building sustainable competitive advantage," *Corporate Executive Board White Paper*, Airlington County, VA.

Manufacturers Alliance for Productivity and Innovation. (2012), *Approaches Towards Purchasing on Total Cost of Ownership*, Arlington, VA: A MAPI Council Survey.

SKF. (2014) "Lowest price ≠ lowest cost: Buying on total benefit of ownership boosts profitability by bringing sustainable savings to the bottom line," *SKF White Paper*. http://cdn2.hubspot.net/hubfs/332479/SKF_TCO_TBO_White_Paper.pdf?t=1441284795161. Accessed 14 October 2015.

9 An inside look at value quantification of competitive advantages

How industry leaders prove value to their customers

Evandro, Pollono

The struggle and the benefits – forewords

Companies struggle with value quantification for two main reasons:

1. They believe it's the customers' duty to objectively quantify the value of the offering, as failure to do so would be against their interest.

This couldn't be further from the truth, as empiric research (McMurchy, 2008) shows that one of the main expectations buyers have is for vendors to quantify the financial value proposition of their solution, and – quoting an actual buyer (Gildert, 2012) – they suggest vendors to "sell your value in our numbers to get our attention."

2. Companies are over-reliant on "market-price" and "cost-plus pricing" mindsets.

As value-based pricing suggests, finding and financially expressing customer value require making assumptions and testing them with customers – a process that is not straight forward and that is based on information that is not easy to find; therefore, companies tend to rely on clear-cut information when setting their price; such readily available information is own internal cost information and publicly available price levels. Unfortunately, customers do not reason the same way: They want to improve their own bottom line; they are not willing to accept inefficiencies – in case of high production costs of the supplier – and are savvy enough to weigh many sources of value other than price – in the cases in which the vendor relies on "market price" to set its own. Nonetheless, customers do not necessarily possess all the elements to fairly judge the value of an offer. In essence, it is the duty of vendors to do the dirty work and undertake a realistic value quantification, one that is solidly based on reliable data and even endorsed by an independent third party.

At Hinterhuber & Partners, we have had the opportunity to collaborate with industry leaders and to quantify value in excess of €2 billion over the years. The following business cases want to be a proxy for other vendors to undertake the task of value quantification. The benefits of producing these business cases are: increased win–rates, as customers can easily compare one's offering with that of others while seeing the sources of value, and a lower demand for discounts, as customers – especially procurement professionals – can easily demonstrate the value proposition in terms of, for example, lower operating costs, higher productivity and risk-reduction, making the offering compelling even if the

DOI: 10.4324/9781003177937-12

purchasing price is higher than that of other suppliers. Additionally, performing value-quantification arms decision makers with reliable data giving them the confidence to walk away from unprofitable deals and to change (often increase) prices – yet changing price is not necessary, only calculating the value provided is.

Three steps to get started with value quantification

In its simplest form, value quantification can be summarized in three steps as depicted in Table 9.1.

The first step requires to identify what the customer would do without our product or service, meaning what is the market offering at the moment in terms of competition (Hinterhuber, 2004). Even if the recommendation is to not set a price based on the market price, it would be myopic to ignore it completely. This is why one must look at the market and define what is the single best option available to customers if they were not buying our offering and at what price. Usually this translates into the customer's best alternative, which is the product or service of a specific competitor that our buyer can find in the market. In less frequent scenarios the alternative can be performing the job with a completely different (maybe older) technology, in this case we would not be benchmarking ourselves against a specific product or service, yet against the "status quo"; doing manual work instead of using a machine, or being Mr. Ford selling cars to horse owners, could be examples of challenging the status quo.

Either ways, one must start with a clear option in mind. We shall call this "customer's best alternative" for simplicity.

In a second step one must list the competitive advantages offered vis-à-vis competition. This is particularly tricky as many companies tend to be influenced by product descriptions and specs when performing this activity: at Hinterhuber & Partners we call this bias the "specs-creep"; a competitive advantage is something that our vending company does better than competition, in particular better than the selected customer's best alternative. When faced with features such as size or speed, savvy managers will not simply state that their product is "100 grams lighter" or "5% faster"; they will say, "It saves X% of the costs associated with weight" and "It produces Y% more output." This indicates that a competitive advantage is better expressed in terms of benefits rather than features.

Table 9.1 Quantifying value in three steps

1	**2**	**3**
Define your reference competitor and its price	**List and select your competitive advantages**	**Quantify and document superior value**
• Identify your reference: specific competitor, industry average or status quo • Determine its price	• Decide between quantitative or qualitative advantages (or both) • Look at competitive advantages in the eyes of the consumer	• How much (€/$/£) is it convenient to choose you for the customer?

The third and last step requires assigning a financial value to the benefits listed in the previous step. As straightforward as this may seem, one should always consider the financial value for a specific customer: a machinery that saves 5% of manual cost – for example – may be of great value in a country with high labor costs; conversely it would be a less-appealing investment in a country with low labor costs. The ultimate objective of this step is being able to prove customers that not choosing the offered product or service is a costly decision for them (Hinterhuber et al., 2018). More complex assessments of company-specific value require deep customer knowledge as well as direct research, as will be shown in the next business cases.

The following sections give valuable elements to perform a value quantification: from listing competitive advantages to finding secondary data to undertake the calculation. Some visuals are created with the proprietary tool of Hinterhuber & Partners, the value quantification Tool®.

Value quantification in the information technologies industry – the case of a financial institution's back-end management system

Trigger	Price-pressure from eastern providers in requests for quotations (RFQ) setting
Solution	Finding the financial value of implicit risks for the target customer
Key benefit for the client	Deal won without price cuts; new value-based pricing methods adopted for price-setting

A large IT software solutions provider responded to the RfP of a major Nordic Financial Institution, in need of a back-end to manage a vast number of financial operations for their end-consumers. Also, an Asian company in the same industry responded to the RfP, offering an apparently similar solution at a price that was significantly lower. The financial institution asked for clarifications and invited our client to check their price.

When Hinterhuber & Partners was contacted, the team in charge of the proposal feared that the only option available was to heavily discount and match the competitor's price; some were also wondering if it would even be profitable to continue at a matched price, given their opportunity cost.

The assumption made by many managers is usually twofold: "Should the company reduce price in the uncertain hope of gaining volume or should the company maintain price and risk losing even more revenues?"; after all, aggressive competitors regularly undercut the company on price, and changing it may seem an obvious choice. Luckily there is a third option: value quantification!

Hinterhuber & Partners discussed internally with engineers, product-specialists, and marketing managers about the importance of given product and company features but also interviewed external customers to determine the main decision criteria – finding out that price was a non-critical element in the overall supplier evaluation process; what's been discovered is that there was a great potential in calculating for the customer, how much superior features and benefits meant for them, in a financial way. Features of a solution like a 1% higher up-time, or a faster response time in case of problems, servers located in the EU, and others, dramatically affect a business relying 24/7 on transactions. A financial institution missing just a few transactions, or not being able to solve a technical problem quickly, might lose tens of thousands of euros in refunds, employees time on top of the risk of losing brand equity.

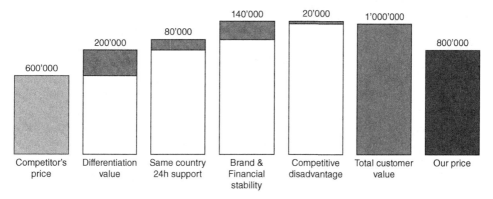

Figure 9.1 Quantifying value by breaking down competitive advantages

Source: Hinterhuber & Partners

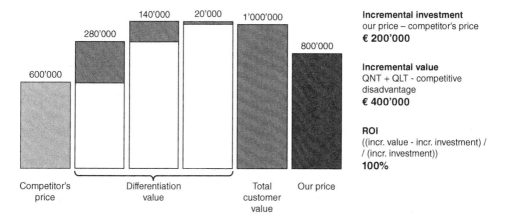

Figure 9.2 Quantifying value and showing sum of competitive advantages

Source: Hinterhuber & Partners

Hinterhuber & Partners applied value quantification to find out what the value delivered to the consumer was in financial terms.

These advantages, once translated into lower costs, lower risks, and higher performance, proved that the price premium with respect to the Asian competitor was nothing more than a small investment that would pay for itself already in the first year thanks to quantified benefits, written on the contract, that our client was delivering.

A disguised example in Figure 9.1, created with the value quantification Tool®, illustrates the principle.

Instead of submitting an underpriced offer of €600 thousand just to match the competitor considered by the buyer, our client calculated the total quantified customer value of €1 million in order to show that the purchase price it was offering, €800 thousand, was more than justified by an excess of €200 thousand in extra value. Considering that such an IT solution would last many years, the overall results would then be multiple times higher (for simplicity only the first year of quantification is presented here).

Once our client was satisfied with the calculation and could present it to its own prospecting customer, along with solid data endorsed by other existing customers to corroborate its reliability, it framed the whole message in a language that every manager can understand: return on investment, or ROI, as depicted in Figure 9.2.

It's worth noting that there is a price premium over low-cost competitors, nonetheless the main point is that an investment of €200 thousand (i.e., the price difference) leads to incremental customer benefits of €400 thousand (difference between total customer value and competitor's price), or put differently an excess of €200 thousand in extra value, thus leading to an ROI of 100% just considering the first year of operations.

In summary, our client won the contract in spite of a 50% higher purchase price, proving that the superior value offered was actually more important than an up-front lower purchase price. The company mastered value-based pricing and new prices are set based on the value delivered to their customers and not anymore on internal costs.

Value quantification in the intelligent transport systems (its) industry – the case of electronic road signage

Trigger	Superior products benchmarked against low-quality offers by customers
Solution	Quantification of maintenance costs over the product life cycle
Key benefit for the client	Increased win-rate, clients increasingly aware that "conformance" ≠ "performance" value-mindset spread throughout the organization

A global company operating in Europe, leader in the Intelligent Transport Systems industry, noticed the trend of continuous price pressure for its electronic road signage products, due to aggressive pricing from non-EU competitors. This trend threatened the growth targets that the company consistently met in the previous decade.

Hinterhuber & Partners was contacted to guarantee growth would continue and to assess on which product families' price changes could be made to ensure positive margins. Hinterhuber & Partners conducted extensive interviews, both internally and externally to customers and governmental authorities; the interviews allowed to determine precisely which benefits customers sought and what value different segments attributed to each one of them. We collected performance data from highway operators on meantime between failures: this allowed us to precisely quantify the maintenance cost of road signage signs from each provider, yielding solid and third-party approved data to prove the superior performance of our client's products.

The transition from "gut-feeling" to "structured-approach" in identifying what the company did better than competitors produced insights that were everything but obvious: for example, sales managers often reported highway authorities questioning about energy consumption; at first sight, one may think that operating wattage is a decision criteria to save money on energy bills; in reality customers were interested in the lower failure rate of components that goes hand in hand with lower wattage: low wattage is not a source of value per se, but lower failure rate definitely is a benefit sought after by customers. As a result, sales managers started calculating precisely their lower failure rates and the associated lower costs of maintenance, providing value amounts tens of times higher than "energy savings" – which remained useful but was not crucial for the decision; this new approach even taught customers the best way to compare suppliers.

Figure 9.3 represents just one of the many competitive advantages identified by our client. The company deals with detail-oriented customers and wanted to break down each

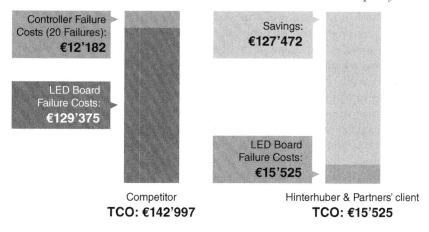

Figure 9.3 Quantifying value with TCO

Source: Hinterhuber & Partners

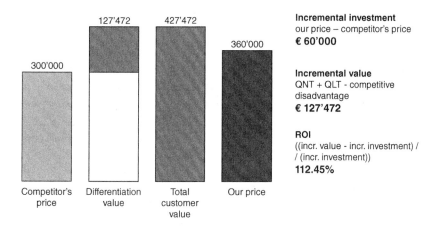

Figure 9.4 Quantifying value with economic value for consumers

Source: Hinterhuber & Partners

element in isolation to reinforce the fact that such calculation was the result of lab tests and external data.

The same saving could be reframed in terms of ROI if it was sufficient to justify a price premium (as it is in this specific case), as shown in Figure 9.4.

A vendor wanting to undertake value quantification may decide to approach the communication differently, by clustering together similar expenses and then working with customers to explain how the total is reached; clustering all value at once is usually the preferred approach if a vendor wants to give customers a memorable number to anchor to. Nonetheless, a benefit of breaking down the value delivered into its constituent parts is that different sources of value may require different explanations. In the specific example of a vendor in the ITS industry an expense like energy is ongoing and always taken into account, even by customers. On the other hand, the cost of a single item to be replaced like an LED board (note: it takes about 100 LED boards to make a full sign) tends to be considered by customers only after the warranty expires (2–4 years); our client decided to change this mindset and manifest the importance of the hidden costs connected to LED replacement taking place even under warranty periods, consisting in workers' salary (operating cost), road-closure (missed revenue) as well as workers and drivers safety (safety risk), adding up to tens of thousands of euros.

One recommendation when communicating value quantification to customers is to use Pareto efficiencies to one's own advantage: limit communication to those advantages delivering the most value. Companies overwhelm customers with too many features, but a rule of thumb concludes that 80–90% of the differentiating value can be expressed, in most cases, with 3–5 competitive advantages.

The client learned that customers were less price sensitive than expected and very open to acknowledge that "**conformance**" ≠ "**performance**" (which soon became a sort of internal motto); this in turns lowered demand for discounts immediately: the price was now a fraction of the acknowledged value received.

The communication strategy shifted away from soft advantages and onto solid, quantified, and mathematically proven competitive advantages. Recognizing that different segments assign different value to the same benefit allowed to introduce new pricing methods and develop win-win contracts that included longer warranties.

In short, the value mindset spread throughout the company, and the implications extended to customers who were receptive to value quantification.

Value quantification in complex B2B services industry – the case of compliance services for large projects

Trigger	Downward price trend, dispersing industry with volume-driven hostile pricing
Solution	Alignment of company to customers metrics, revealing true cost of "cheaper" options
Key benefit for the client	Reduced demand for discounts, creation of additional services

A European company, global leader in complex B2B services industry, witnessed a market share erosion from small providers expanding in its arena. The technical nature of the industry made it really hard to explain comparative differences among competitors, and some customers treated their services as a compliance issue to be dealt with at minimum cost. The industry volume was constant but shrunk in total value.

When Hinterhuber & Partners was called, the downward price trend was consolidated, with peaks of 5% price reductions per year. The company could rely on a solid and loyal customer base, but the outlook was far from positive.

After analyzing transactional data extensively, the immediate suggestion was the implementation of pricing policies that would normalize the assignment of discounts, a technique also called conditional discounting, which is generally appreciated by customers as they can immediately see a value in their bottom line on top of having more reliable cash flow. Conditional discounting means in fact granting discounts in exchange of a larger share of the portfolio, combining extra services not previously purchased in order to provide value to the customer, while not reducing the invoice value for the company.

Table 9.2 Quantifying value through third-party data

In the industry sub-set considered the risk of adverse outcome accounts for 15% to 22% of total project value.
Average yearly cost of avoidable risks is €750,000.
Most described projects run into at least four major issues over the course of the project itself, with varying degree of severity. Most projects (90%) take between 1 and 2 years to complete.
Due diligence reports on both suppliers and vendors ends suggest that more rigorous risk reduction services would have avoided more than half the issues experienced.

This allowed to create win-win deals and to escape the vicious spiral of indiscriminate discounting.

Second, Hinterhuber & Partners accessed risk data from third-party authorities, calculated with the company how much the risk of an issue would have costed a customer, and then compared internal data on actual occurrences against its own customers. The client was able to show that their in-depth risk reduction services were outperforming competition. Even accounting for a higher price, the return in terms of lower-risk savings granted to customers compared to the best available competitor was 3–4 times higher: a metric that is very clear and understandable by any manager. A clear ROI speaks louder than a long list of specs. This approach allowed to speak the customers language and prove it was better to be on the safe side with our client, instead of saving little money with sub-par services from the competition. Whatever the selected communication method, one recommendation is to be creative in finding sources of value and making them relevant for the customer (Hinterhuber, 2017; Hinterhuber and Liozu, 2012).

Table 9.2 lists some of the statistics coming from a third-party authority that Hinterhuber & Party used; it is meant for the reader to understand a possible source of third-party information.

Already during the course of the consulting efforts, the company was able to halt the downward price trend company-wise and revert it with key accounts and biggest customer segments. Better explanation of value to customers de-commoditized the services offered; the company also introduced more thorough services thereby generating additional sources of income. The client leveraged the knowledge developed by third-party authorities on risk costs and developed checklists to show prospecting customers how to purchase complex B2B services.

Value quantification in the electronic payment industry – the case of accounting and management solutions

Trigger	Preparing for possible future EU regulations on electronic payments fee
Solution	Creation of benefit-based packages of services
Key benefit for the client	Customer loyalty increased upon realization of value of benefits

A company in the global electronic payments industry wanted to be prepared for possible new EU regulations. The company provided accounting and management services for customers dealing with hundreds if not thousands of expenses, managing credit and debit cards of all employees. The industry as a whole relied on transaction fees on the issued credit cards to finance the services provided to customers.

An EU regulation imposing a transaction fee reduction would have compromised profitability, and the company wanted to have a contingency plan ready; Hinterhuber & Partners was contacted to help defining the best available strategy.

The consulting project started with a competitor analysis, finding out that other providers, with higher transaction fees, were offering end-of-year rebates in the form of miles, cash presents, and other form of rewards in order to compensate the lack of management and accounting services. Our client was the industry leader in terms of market share, and most customers, over the course of their professional experience, have tried more than two or three suppliers. The simple realization that most customers prefer management and accounting services over rebates is a clear indication of value, so Hinterhuber & Partners moved onto a second phase, customer interviews, to understand from customers themselves how much each service was worth.

To make one simple example, the client was offering its customer a detailed accounting report, listing all expenses, in multiple currencies, associated to the managers incurring the expense, with detailed breakdown of costs in terms of pure-product and tax (varying by country) and other useful information; compiling just one line of such a detailed report would require accountants up to 7 minutes depending on the technology used before incurring the expense; customers would have thousands of such entries each month. Accounting costs were evident to customers at least in their essence, but having a system to calculate them would provide some tangible assessment of value. Hinterhuber & Partners' client decided to do just that and give customers a system: it first clustered customers to tailor the calculation around the value they captured, and then it published a white paper on the company website detailing such benefits and how to calculate them, proving it was worth to choose them as sole service provider. Customers do not believe in empty statements, and the client provided the endorsement of current major customers to confirm the validity of the information.

Once the sources of value were identified (service A = benefit € X) Hinterhuber & Partners went ahead and suggested a few bundles of services with "accounting services" being the common denominator. Such packages would cover most needs of most customers, and their prices were set in order to always grant an honest profit to the client and a clear saving to the customer.

Being this a contingency plan not to be implemented in the market anytime soon, Hinterhuber & Partners ran a willingness-to-pay survey with 20 customer companies, inquiring about the price of these bundles. In no instance did any manager expect to get the value of any package for free, and in no instance the price suggested by interviewees was lower than the one identified by Hinterhuber & Partners and the client.

If value is clear, confirmed by the customer, and the price is lower than such value (even if it is at a premium with respect to competition) the sale should take place almost effortlessly with most customers.

Conclusion

Savvy managers already know in their guts that price is not the only factor involved in a decision to buy our product or service: providing superior post-sales support, being reliable in fulfillment, having experienced employees that understand the bottom line of the buyer are a few simple examples of factors weighted in the decision, which are not even directly connected to the product or service being sold (but still they are directly connected to the perceived value).

Armed with this knowledge, all managers can and should identify the benefits unique to them, that is, competitive advantages, and calculate the financial benefits they bring to customers. All companies can differentiate themselves on a spectrum of parameters and prove customers why choosing them is the right decision, in spite of possible price premiums.

References

Gildert, P. (2012) *Head of R&D Procurement – Astra Zeneca.* quoted in Snelgrove, T. Journal of Revenue and Pricing Management.

Hinterhuber, A. (2004) "Towards value-based pricing – An integrative framework for decision making," *Industrial Marketing Management 33*(8), 765–778.

Hinterhuber, A. (2017) "Value quantification capabilities in industrial markets," *Journal of Business Research 76*, 163–178.

Hinterhuber, A. and Liozu, S. (2012) "Is it time to rethink your pricing strategy?" *MIT Sloan Management Review 53*(4), 69–77.

Hinterhuber, A., Pollono, E. and Shafer, M. (2018) "Elevating the cost of doing nothing: An interview with Mark Shafer," *Journal of Revenue & Pricing Management 17*(1), 3–10.

McMurchy, N. (2008) "Tough times in IT: How do you exploit the opportunities?" Gartner presentation, Stamford, CT.

10 Quantifying the value of services

Snelgrove, Todd C.

For those companies in the business-to-business world that have a services offering or realize the need and benefit to build one, quantifying your value throughout the sales process and afterward is just as, or more, important to avoid the "lowest price and good enough" procurement trap. Combining service value quantification with performance-based pricing models will turn your firm into the market-leading service provider. While quantifying service value might be different than using tangible product features and benefits, it can and needs to be done. Or else your growth and profitability will suffer.

Quantifying the value of products versus services differs in two important ways. Product performance tends to be more consistent and repeatable. Just put two competing components, devices, or machines next to one another and see how they perform. That performance is usually easier to objectively measure. How fast did each run? How much energy does each need? How often did each need service? When did each need to be replaced? We quickly get to tangible customer outcomes like this machine is 3% faster or uses 2% less energy. Do the same test 100 times, and you get basically the same results.

This is not true for services. Outcomes from service delivery typically vary much more than product characteristics: services are, of course, co-produced with customers and value is jointly created. While we can objectively measure the customer outcomes, the variability in those outcomes will be higher since both the starting and ending points are more variable for services than products.

Usually, the standard response I get from people that have a services offering is, "It's impossible to quantify the value our Services deliver. . . . A product would be easy to prove value." It is not impossible but needs to follow a little different process. In a product world we can start with – our engineering data show that this "should" do something; if it does so it would be worth this for you, and hopefully we come back and measure what actually happened (this helps build our credibility next time when we say our offering uses 3% less ink or water).

In a services world it's similar.

Step 1: Benchmark the status quo: Start with the customer's existing situation (the average life of your machines, or hours to do this, or cost to do X).

Step 2: Our performance claim: Our proposal for how we can do it better (faster, less expensive, so the cost of repair is less; predict the failure so that no loss of production occurs, etc.).

Step 3: Calculate and prove the improvement: If the benefit occurs it would be worth $X, and the reason to believe you'll get $X is because only we have this, can do that, etc. At this point the customer can "buy" into your logic because of the

DOI: 10.4324/9781003177937-13

obvious improvement, your references, risk of not getting the benefits, probability of the value occurring, and your experience.

Step 4: Align your pricing model: Offer a pricing model based on the actual improvement. Since service offering performance can be more variable than products, the customer will want more of the value in order to compensate them for the additional risk. A performance-based pricing model solves this problem. This could pay a fee now and a performance fee when you deliver that improvement, or here is the full fee and we have a penalty or bonus if the improvement is missed or exceeded. It's a win-win. The performance-based price reduces the risk of service offering variability for the customer and, therefore, allows you to capture more value from your superior service.

Of course, you need to take into account other considerations, but these also exist with products. In a product world where data show 3% less energy consumption as an example, it probably is based on the person installing it properly, maintaining it, etc. So it has a potential for 3% improvement, but that will only occur if certain other conditions are met. For services, the same thing exists, BUT you may do the service and also manage the process so you are the person 100% responsible for the outcome and improvement.

Let's look at some examples.

- **Product sell** – my machines last longer because they are made with higher-quality parts, and we assume by 20% (references, technical reasoning, etc.).
- **Product and service sell** – these machines are running 3 years on average now; we think that based on our product and/or services together (our people, processes, tools, experience, etc.) we could get them to last 25% longer. We know when they fail, it costs this much dollar to fix (parts and labor BUT also downtime, other costs, loss revenue, etc.). We will do the service for a fee of $100K (using part of the benefit of the improvement as the target). If we don't hit 25% longer, we pay back $x, or if we exceed a target, we get a bonus. A lot of customers might say we believe you're right and able to do this and we will just pay the fee (getting rid of the bonus AND the penalty). If you don't want the customer to enter into a fee-at-risk agreement set the reward dollar high so it is not worth the "risk" to them.
- **Pure knowledge Service** – the billable hour is $250, and we might give you an estimate of 4 hours to do the job, or maybe we say $1,000 for the job (and hope we can do it quicker and customer is happy as the fee is known); however, we are not guaranteeing the job is done "right" but hope it is so you come back and we get referrals.
- **Pure service value based** – what we see is that people pay $1,000 on average to have this service done, BUT we have experience, people, tools, processes to do it better and achieve a better result for you. For example, we think we can do your taxes and have them lower (and you don't get audited) so we will charge you $900 plus 50% of the improvement over previous years' averages or bring in what you have, and we will check it and charge you a higher percentage or the improvement we find. I see this starting to happen in the legal world. Option one by the hour, option two is fixed fee or flat fee arrangements. *Types of Legal Services Pricing: Fixed Fee and Retainer – Find Law.* Where a fee is paid for the result, no matter how many hours or activities are required, it aligns the client and the firm interests. If you're the expert then resolve this – if it only takes an hour, I don't care but this is the result what I am

paying for. The argument from the lawyer's side might be that variables change (the other party, etc.); well, isn't that what I am paying you for lawyer is to eliminate variables and reinterpretations? If not, our incentives are misaligned. The more times the case gets re-adjudicated on issues, the more the lawyer gets to charge. If it is a flat fee, my concern would be that they would just stop responding or working, etc. (that's why a percentage of fixed fee needs to be held back).

- **Pure service NOT value based – misaligned value promises and pricing**. In some countries of the world, real estate agents charge a fee as a percentage of the selling price of the property (usually paid for by the seller and split with the buyer's agent and then both agents with their brokerage). However, in most cases the pricing model does not align with value "promised" or realized. An agent could be "incentivized" to tell the seller that they will get a great deal more for the home than other agents for selling their house; let's look at how this process doesn't align the seller and the selling agent:

  - In North America, the seller of a home pays the real estate commission from the proceeds from the sale, those commissions are split usually as 50% goes to the buyers agent and 50% to the sellers agent. Of each 50% they pay half (in general) to the broker they work for.
  - So for a sale of $100,000 that would be 6%, or $6,000 is withheld from the money the seller gets. $3,000 goes to the seller's and buyer's agents each. From that they pay approximately 50% or $1,500 to the broker they work for, keeping $1,500.
  - You are going to sell your house. You invite ten agents to come and show why they should be the listing agent, how they will sell and market the house, and at what price. Nine of the ten agents say, based on research, that the house should be listed for $300,000.
  - So the money would look like this: Commission equals 6% of $300,000 or $18,000, and the seller would gross $282,000. The commission would be then split as $9,000 for selling agent and $9,000 for the buyer's agent. They would each split this with their respective broker, meaning they each would earn $4,500.
  - One agent said that the house could sell for $400,000, and they play to the seller's emotion of how special the house is, use great comparables to justify, etc. As the seller, you are thinking, 6% commission of $400,000 is $24,000, so in this scenario I would walk away with $376,000 versus $282,000 or ($94,000 more) versus the other suggestion to list at $300,000, which sounds awesome. As a reminder, that $24,000 commission would be $12,000 for the buyer's and seller's agents, each then paying half (as an example) of it to their broker. In this scenario, selling the house for 33% more changes commission from $4,500 to $6,000.
  - However, a few weeks later the game might start and look something like this – the agent says, Well, the market has changed, new comparable house prices just came out, or feedback says you need to invest lots of money to update the house, or just drop your price. The real estate agent is now more concerned about selling the house quickly and easily, as an easy $4,500 commission when selling the house at $300K is better than never selling or working really hard and investing their own money to sell at "promised" $400K (remember that only gets them an additional $1,500 in commission). Or recommend the seller put $75K into the house to make it sellable.

If you are better, then you should offer a pricing model that is performance based. For example, at a list of $300K I will take less commission – say 5%, but as we exceed that, I want a bonus but you will be better off – say 10%

		Traditional $300,000		Performance $300,000		Performance max $400,000
Commission		6%	$18,000	5%	$15,000	
Bonus	10%	$0	$0	0%	$0	$10,000
Total commission			$18,000		$15,000	$25,000
Net benefit seller			$0		$3,000	$93,000
Net benefit to sales			$0		($3,000)	$7,000

Bias in valuations cannot be explained by heuristics alone. Different studies show the relevance of agency problems and misaligned incentives. Levitt and Syverson (2008) find that houses owned by real estate agents sell for about 3.7% more than other houses and stay on the market for 9.5 days more (Levitt and Syverson, 2008: 599). They state that this is the case because real estate agents receive only a small share of the incremental profit when a house sells for a higher value. Residential real estate contracts cause real estate agents to receive only a small proportion of the purchase price, while bearing a large share of the costs like hosting open houses, advertising, and marketing. The result is a misalignment of incentives. A potential solution would be to introduce nonlinear commission structures in contracts to improve incentives (Levitt and Syverson, 2008).

Levitt and Dubner (2005) explain the roots of misalignment. They state that it is normal in our capitalist world to assume that one (often an expert) is better informed than the other (the consumer). This phenomenon is called information asymmetry, which is highly applicable to real estate. Home-sellers are reluctant to sell their house at a low price or not at all. Appraisers are aware of this fear and often profit from it. They tend to convince sellers to accept a low-bid price, because they benefit more from a quick deal than they benefit from long-lasting negotiations. Furthermore, the consumer has a tendency to be overconfident in the skills and knowledge of the expert.

However, after discussing the idea of performance pricing with some real estate agents in North America and the National Associational of Realtors, I am told this is illegal in the United States. Not sure why to be honest. However, it is something I would propose if I was selling my home. In the interim I suggest that sellers ask for a simple metric of the agent's "accuracy in selling price versus list price" so that the one with a 95% accuracy is better than the one that is at 50% (as you know the second one will be the one that actually costs you more in the end no matter what they say the house should list at). Former colleagues have told me that in Sweden, this "accuracy percentage" is something that all real estate professionals have as a KPI, and they have put a heavy weight on these criteria when choosing a selling agent.

Value and value pricing models in financial services

- **Pure Service fee based** – in the Asset Management industry these are the fees charges for each service – currency, trades, custody, complex derivatives, etc. These are totaled up and charged.

- **Service fee based on value** – Welrex (www.welrex.com), a UK Asset Management company that I have supported, has chosen to offer its clients and Investment Relationship Managers (IRMs) a choice in how it charges for its services. One is a "traditional model," charging a fixed fee for services provided and calculated purely on the Assets under Management, that is, 1% of Assets under Management, but still explaining the value they can bring versus competitors. They also have created a performance-based pricing model, which is sometimes seen in Institutional Asset Management but is a rare occurrence in Wealth Management for High-Net-Worth Individuals (HNWI). Under this pricing structure, the client pays a lower than standard management fee, but a performance bonus is paid when exceeding certain target returns, thus, aligning incentives between the two parties.

A few takeaways: service value calculations can be done, and they are not that different from product value calculations. It is very important to track what actually happens for clients. Value calculation starts with a "we think/assume" assumption but with a promise to go back and see what was actually realized. This then becomes the evidence that 94% of people that have used our service have seen these improvements. As new outcome and performance-based business models become the norm, people that offer services will need to really be able to demonstrate value and have pricing models that align with it. I highly recommend the book *The Ends Game – How Smart Companies Stop Selling Products and Start Delivering Value* from my two professor friends Marco Bertini and Oded Koenigsberg, 2020 MIT Sloan Publishing. Finally, tying the payment model to how much and when the customer actually receives the value is a great way to reduce customer risk, show the customer you believe in the value you create versus it just being said on a PowerPoint slide or tool, and aligns the benefits and interests for both buyer and seller.

References

https://practice.findlaw.com/financing-a-law-firm/types-of-legal-services-pricing-fixed-fee-and-retainer.html

Levitt, S. D. and Dubner, S. J. (2005) *Freakonomics: A Rogue Economist Explores the Hidden Side of Everything* (1st ed.), New York: William Morrow.

Levitt, S. D. and Syverson, C. (2008) "Market distortions when agents are better informed: The value of information in real estate transactions," *The Review of Economics and Statistics* 90(4), 599–611.

11 Quantifying intangible benefits

Best practices to increase willingness
to pay while creating longer-lasting
customer relationships

Paolo, De Angeli and Evandro, Pollono

Competitive advantages and benefits – some forewords

This chapter discusses the implications and best practices around intangible benefits. Before delving into the topic, it is useful to introduce some clarifying definitions: pricing practitioners – as we authors are – often face internal challenges in explaining the difference between features, benefits, and competitive advantages. At times a given competitive advantage only applies to one segment and not to another. The terms "feature," "benefit" and "competitive advantage" are often used throughout the following text and may – at a first glance – appear interchangeable. To provide clarity they can be described as follows:

A **feature** is a mere attribute of the product or service one sells. If we think about the passenger airline industry, having 60 cm of leg space is a feature but it may be a lot or very little for different travelers; a feature is usually very precise yet it does not provide any suggestion as being something to be valued or not.

A **benefit** is something of value that a consumer enjoys. It is subjective and may vary from one segment to another and from one individual to another, yet the company can identify a benefit that it provides with approximate confidence. In the airline industry this can be a comfortable travel experience thanks to a large leg-space in the seat. If a person has problems sleeping and travels a lot, this benefit may be appreciated more than by an average traveler.

A **competitive advantage** is the result of an enduring value differential between the products and services of one organization and those of its competitors in the mind of customers. It is something a company does better than competition. An example of competitive advantage in the airline industry is having the largest leg-space in the industry providing comfortable travel.

Given the examples cited earlier one can see how all the terms are connected: a company has a given feature, like 60 cm leg-space; it realizes some customer segments appreciate it since it provides the benefit of comfort, and if the company is the only one providing it then it will be a competitive advantage, meaning something that sets said company apart from competitors and worth communicating to the relevant segments even in monetary amounts.

The funnel in Figure 11.1 shows one possible approach to understanding how companies can calculate the value of a competitive advantage for a specific segment or how pricing practitioners tackle the issue of going from feature to (quantified) competitive advantage, which then they communicate.

DOI: 10.4324/9781003177937-14

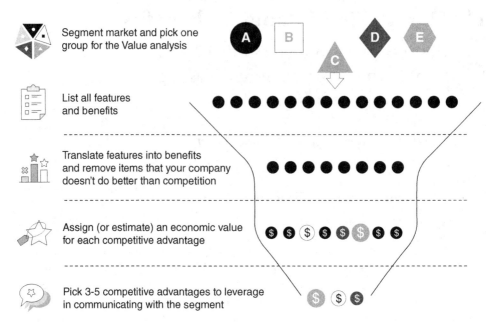

Figure 11.1 Intangible benefits: translating features into value

As straightforward as the approach may be, there is a caveat in the process: some features and benefits may be intangible, intrinsic, non-obvious. Having dealt with basic terminology it is useful to delve into the specific dynamics of intangible benefits and its associated value.

Introduction to intangible benefits and value

One capability that practitioners need to possess is to create value and make evident the value that already is present (Hinterhuber, 2004). New product development after all goes through a deep knowledge of customers and the continuous alignment of what customers want with what the company can provide. The metallurgic and the cement industry in recent years witnessed radical changes in consumer's buying behavior: customers inquire more and more about the net CO_2 cost for the environment and are willing to pay a premium to those producers that can certify the use of eco-friendly sources of energy in their production process. A cubic ton of what most believe is a "commodity" can and is already being differentiated by leading companies thanks to intangible benefits intrinsic to the product. Therefore, the practitioner of the future needs to create and make evident even the "intangible" value and benefits of an offering.

The importance of intangible benefits

The intangible elements of value are typically related to some sort of "soft" differentiators (like brand, reliability, safety, and even technical and customer service) that are recognized in the market but very seldom quantified in monetary terms, because the task is perceived as too difficult. Working with some experts and practitioners in various industries, we suggest that a company able to prove a strong differentiation in intangible elements of value helps its customers to avoid the cost of the unknown and, typically, customers are willing to pay a premium to avoid such unknown costs in the future. In practical terms to be able to quantify intangibles one needs to be curious, creative, and know very well the customer's business and problems. These prerequisites allow a practitioner to create value and make customers more willing to work with them.

2.1.1 Techniques to increase the perception of intangibles

As some practitioners suggest, one needs to engage in a form of interrogation that breaks the intangible feature into tangible components, and this takes curiosity, creativity, and a deep knowledge of the customers' business; it is then of paramount importance to quantify the financial value of such components. How to quantify, let's say, "reliability"? One should ask themselves, what does "reliability" mean for customers? It can translate into less safety stocks, less inventory, less time invested in solving problems, and lower opportunity costs since they can invest their money somewhere else and make a profit out of it, rather than building a warehouse. At a first glance it could be easy to conclude that intangibles are impossible to quantify. This is not the case, according to our experience: everything can be quantified.

2.1.2 Intangibles as a source of differentiation

Sometimes it is very difficult to perform the monetary quantification of benefits: assumptions may be stretched, and they may not be fully accepted by customers, yet everything can be quantified eventually and presented as a value argument in a value conversation. What matters is to have a solid thought process to follow, when preparing the rationale behind the quantification.

Performing value quantification, even of intangibles, has significant implications for any company; consultants always remind clients that if they are not perceived as being different, then they will be benchmarked on price! In essence, the inability to quantify value is a lost opportunity, a tax a company inflicts on itself.

2.1.3 Opportunities in value quantification of intangibles

Approaching value quantification of intangibles in a structured way yields two main advantages. First, the company is able to fully assess its own differential value proposition by paying the deserved attention to all the extra services and capabilities on which it invests time and efforts daily to differentiate itself from competition; many companies pride themselves for being reliable/easy to work with/knowledgeable in their field, yet hardly any of them calculates how it impacts customers in a financial and non-qualitative fashion. A company that investigates its own value proposition starts focusing on what really matters to customers thereby changing the approach to product development; also, it begins to identify different clusters of customers based on the differential value drivers that they recognize and are willing to pay for, thus changing the approach to market segmentation.

Second, value quantification of intangibles helps capturing the fair share of value the organization creates every day; as a matter of fact, customers look at their suppliers not only for what they sell (products or services) but also for how they sell (services and capabilities), and intangible value is often a key decision criterion in the final selection.

So why don't all companies acknowledge the monetary value of intangibles? The simple answer is that it takes effort and time. Nonetheless, once the strategic thinking revolving around finding intangibles becomes part of the company's DNA, the return on investment is typically very high and the value-mindset becomes a pivotal element in the company's strategy (Hinterhuber and Liozu, 2019).

2.1.4 *Intangible value in the purchase process*

In their experience as practitioners, we have encountered a number of intangible benefits. It would be too ambitious to list all of them and probably not relevant to the reader; nonetheless a few seem to be mentioned more frequently in intra-company conversations revolving around the topic:

- quality;
- reliability;
- safety;
- customer service;
- sustainability;
- technical service.

When a company starts considering intangible benefits, an interesting pattern emerges: more and more non-product-related elements are recognized; let's take customer service, sustainability, and technical service: these typically have post-sales effects or, in the case of sustainability, are not even connected to the fruition of the product or service in use.

One can conclude that identifying intangibles is a very holistic approach, considering not just what is being sold, but also how, and the way it impacts the environment, the community, and other possible stakeholders.

2.1.5 *Explaining tangible versus intangible value*

Competitive advantages serve a clear purpose: set a company apart from competition and allow it to gain a share of the superior value delivered to customers through a price premium (price premium being a fraction of the superior value delivered).

When it comes to tangible benefits, what we call "hard-green-money benefits," such as energy savings, the value is usually immediately recognized by customers; external endorsers or certifications may increase their credibility and are recommended, but they are not always necessary. This is not the case for intangible benefits, where it is much harder to have immediate acceptance. The reason lies in the assumptions made and the difficulty to measure them: they may relate to external effects (better for the environment) or happen somewhere in the future with no guarantee of performance. Value of intangibles is indeed less evident, nonetheless there is a silver lining for a company wanting to have an intangible benefit recognized: if the counterpart does not see the value in some of the elements of the products/services provided, the company can propose removing the contended part. In practical terms this could be a customer not seeing value in post-sales services: the company may propose removing it and providing a separate list-price for on-demand support. What happens in almost every case is that customers then ask to maintain the high service level, thereby confirming the value is there, even if it's hard to quantify.

2.1.7 Framing value

The character in a popular American TV show stated: "[I]f you don't like how the table is set, turn over the table"; in real business life the implicit cards on the table represent a possible deal based on price, and the fact of flipping the table represents changing the rules of the game quite dramatically. In a value quantification environment this translates into not even talking about the price, if not at a later stage, but to instead focus on the benefits received.

One of us encountered a company in the Intelligent Traffic Solutions industry which did just that: It found an innovative way to express value where instead of talking about the price of the product, it talks about the savings from lower maintenance customers would get if they choose it. This is what Nagle and Müller (2018) mean when they suggest to align value communication with metrics that matter to customer.

It is always very relevant to think from the customers' perspective and in terms of total cost of ownership (TCO), yet TCO should be complemented with intangible considerations. If a company can prove that – regardless of the purchase price – customers are more profitable working with them, resistance to working together should almost disappear.

One way to align with customers metric when more refined ways are available can be calculating value in annual levels instead of units, or users, or weight, since "the year" is an easily accepted unit of measure that companies and customers share. Of course, this can be translated into other units of measure that customers find more appealing, but it still stands as a general rule of thumb. Once annual sources of saving are bundled together it is easier for customers to escape from the fixation on purchase price. The automotive industry understood this concept very well after oil price surges made consumption a relevant metric: The most virtuous manufacturer started explaining customers how much money they would save on gas with their cars every year, instead of using unrelatable metrics such as mileage-per-gallon: purchase price differences between two car models became almost irrelevant once compared with benefits that would become visible only over time.

Introduce the value mindset in the company

The intuition that having a "value mindset" would benefit the company through improved value communication and new product development is a good start, but it can take time to spread throughout the company. The main prerequisite is to have a drive to be innovative and tirelessly searching for new opportunities that create unique value for customers. Second, one must not shy away from the challenge of quantifying value: it is always a daunting task, but it is also true that it gets easier with experience. It's worth noting that value quantification may happen when a product or solution is yet to be developed: one must think strategically, build realistic assumptions around the additional value (and profits) that the solution may deliver to customers and then get to a number, then see how this may be better than before or better than competition. When all stakeholders are involved in the process and can already imagine the superior value customers will enjoy, the fear of product rejection (or value rejection) fades away, making them more eager and exited in what they are doing.

In summary, a company wants to quantify value to improve its profit position, but to spread the value mindset throughout the organization it must be efficient in explaining stakeholders that it will improve their professional life as well. Let's take the sales force for example: it gets enormously facilitated in its job when the value mindset is part of the corporate DNA, as value is ultimately the only thing customers are interested in; therefore having better value-based argumentations than competition gives the sales force a great advantage.

2.2.1 Value mindset and the sales force

As said before, having a value mindset makes stakeholders very passionate and creative about finding new elements of value that generate win/win solutions for the company and customers alike. The value mindset gives a sense of "awareness" of the product, and this is transmitted all the way down to the customer-facing side of the company: the sales force. Having the capability to find, calculate, and explain value (Hinterhuber, 2017) also provides a dramatic change in the way the sales force approaches customers: instead of claiming "we are better than our competitors," or "the quality of our products is better," sales managers are able to explain why the company or solution is better, they are able to collaborate with customers and focus on the aspects that are more relevant to them, they are also able to state by how much the company or solution is better, while proving customers the ability to deliver on promises.

In essence, the simple fact of looking for value, even intangible one, inside the company, spreads the value mindset among all stakeholders and through a trickle-down effect it ends up improving the relationship with customers.

A business case of intangible benefits: Sharing the value created

In a previous section, sustainability was presented as an illustration of intangible benefits. In our experience, many companies use sustainability as something of value they can deliver, but they do so in a qualitative manner, thus expressing it in terms of percentage reduction of emissions, lower energy consumption in their facilities with respect to previous years, and fighting deforestation through the plantation of acres of forest. These activities are all commendable, but their communication can be improved in order to create the incentive for both buyers and sellers to fight for a common cause. If customers consider giving their business to virtuous suppliers, they may be tempted to choose – given the option – the supplier that reduced consumptions more in the past decade, without considering that it may have a less efficient facility to begin with. It is hard to measure comparative effects when there is no common starting point or reference. Legislators and independent institutions have taken a step forward and estimated the environmental cost of CO_2 per ton (for example. USD 200). A price/unit formula gives the benchmark that was lacking a few years ago. Today companies have the ability to demonstrate how much better than competition they are, in a financial way, also when it comes to sustainability.

In the base chemicals industry, a virtuous company has invested heavily in R&D to create products that improve customers processes by reducing CO_2 emissions. In terms of operating cost, the customer is virtually indifferent between choosing that product and continuing with the old one, but in terms of purchase cost there is a price difference of

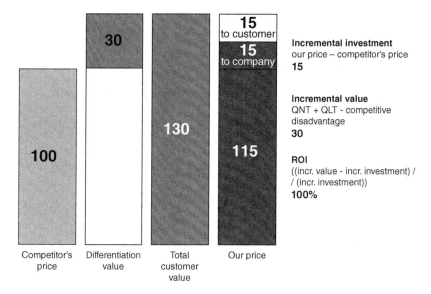

Figure 11.2 Quantifying intangibles
Source: Hinterhuber & Partners

about 15%. Figure 11.2, developed with Hinterhuber & Partners' Value Quantification Tool®, shows how the company has been able to both deliver extra value to consumers and retain a margin for itself to repay the R&D expenses incurred, thus sharing value with customers.

The future will see more and more countries developing "carbon credits," and calculation of intangibles like sustainability is meant to become the norm. Savvy managers should anticipate the trend and include other sources of intangible value in their calculation.

Closing remarks

Reaching the maturity to quantify intangible benefits is a journey that starts with value quantification; it can seem difficult at times, but it is an effort worth taking. Companies that want to compete successfully often develop unique ways of serving their customers and are really able to differentiate themselves both with their products, as well as with their services and capabilities. Yet they might be so busy in running and fighting for volume that they neglect to stop and quantify their differential value and challenge if what they are doing is really helping their customers being more profitable. In our experience as pricing practitioners, it is very beneficial (and very well accepted by customers) to have company-wide workshops around the topics of value, value quantification, and intangible benefits. This creates the conditions to identify concrete areas for value creation and profitable collaboration with customers.

Especially when dealing with intangible benefits, the advice to those not finding them or not being able to quantifying them is to quote Picasso which believed that "[i]nspiration exists, but it has to find you working"; this applies also to intangible benefits or competitive advantages in general: if you work on them, you'll find them.

References

Hinterhuber, A. (2004) "Towards value-based pricing – An integrative framework for decision making," *Industrial Marketing Management 33*(8), 765–778.

Hinterhuber, A. (2017) "Value quantification capabilities in industrial markets," *Journal of Business Research 76*, 163–178.

Hinterhuber, A. and Liozu, S. (eds.). (2019) *Pricing Strategy Implementation: Translating Pricing Strategy into Results*, Abingdon, UK: Routledge.

Nagle, T. and Müller, G. (2018) *The Strategy and Tactics of Pricing: A Guide to Growing More Profitably* (6th ed.), New York, NY: Routledge.

12 Toward a shared understanding of value in B2B exchange

Discovering, selecting, quantifying, and sharing value

Pekka, Töytäri and Rajala, Risto

Introduction

Creating value for customers and other stakeholders is fundamental for any business. The ability to provide quantified evidence of customer value is expressly important for new offerings and innovations. Launched successfully, new services aid companies to grow, prosper, and differentiate. However, the business impact of novel offerings and innovations is often unknown and challenging for customers to evaluate. Hence, assessing the value of an offering requires an active participation of suppliers and their customers.

> We need to provide the tools to support our value articulation because our customer doesn't understand the true value of [our service]. It's that simple.

A convincing evidence of an offering's value creation opportunity has implications beyond immediate service and product sales. The possibility of creating and gaining value motivates companies and customers to evaluate the value of their capabilities, pursue changes in their businesses, and help them focus on their core capabilities and resources. Eventually, it may lead to new collaborative arrangements concerning higher value creation at the levels of business ecosystems and networks.

Value quantification is an important step in a comprehensive and iterative process, which often begins with acquiring customer insight and ends with value verification, leading to the next round of learning and influencing by value. We present and discuss the key concepts and process in detail.

The value process includes the elements of identifying, selecting, formulating, quantifying, pricing, and verifying the shared conception of value. The value conception contains all the benefits and sacrifices that all stakeholders acknowledge as relevant decision influence. Much of the realization of the potential value depends on the jointly known, accepted, and implementable value conception. The greater the shared conception of value, the greater the potential for value creation. However, realizing the value creation potential involves overcoming profound challenges for all stakeholders. On the basis of the findings from our cases, we discuss some of the challenges pertaining to the implementation of the transformation toward a better value creation system and conclude by delineating the challenges and opportunities for value implementation.

DOI: 10.4324/9781003177937-15

Underlying research

This chapter is based on research projects that the authors have conducted during 2009–2021, involving dozens of globally operating industrial and ICT companies and hundreds of informants in different specialist and managerial positions. The research has focused on exploring the organizational capabilities and business norms that guide value quantification as required by value-based selling and value-based pricing.

The concept of value

Research has identified several characteristics of value. Value is considered subjective, contextual, dynamic, and based on the individual evaluators' past experiences and preferences. The attributes of value have a profound impact on the shared understanding of value. We present and discuss an actor's cognitive process of arriving at a value perception to illustrate how the attributes of value affect the outcome.

Value has an internal structure. It is often defined as the difference between the customer perceived benefits and sacrifices.

> Value is what you get for what you give.
>
> (Zeithaml, 1988)

Further, both benefits and sacrifices are multidimensional concepts. Benefits include (short-term) operational gains and (longer-term) change and cooperation-related gains. Sacrifices include different costs and risks during the life cycle of the value creation. A multidimensional conceptualization of customer value is provided by Rajala et al. (2015). A slightly adapted version of the conceptualization of value hierarchy is illustrated in Figure 12.1.

The **operational benefits** primarily relate to the current or future operational performance of a company. Operational benefits typically relate to business process improvements such as reducing process downtime, improving output quality, improving process performance, improving process resource efficiency, and the like. Rajala et al. (2015) denote these benefits as process-related value elements. These benefits can be achieved even in relatively transactional relationships. The set of interaction-related benefits relate to the relationship performance and how effectively the organizations work together. These benefits reduce relationship governance cost, improve information exchange, and

Figure 12.1 Dimensions of customer value (adapted from Rajala et al., 2015)

reduce the risk of failing to create the expected value. The interaction-related benefits also contribute to the operational benefits by facilitating the discovery of opportunities to re-allocate activities, resources, and capabilities between the organizations to find the best activity-to-organization match.

Another domain of benefits relates to change, adaptation, and learning. These **strategic benefits** can be divided into three value dimensions, named resource-access, capability, and partner network. The resource-based view suggests that a company's competitiveness resides in its capabilities and resources. Critical value creating resources may reside outside of the firm boundaries, in its relationships with other companies, as complementary resources and capabilities. The capability-related value builds on the strengths of a service supplier to develop and leverage the abilities of the customer organization. Learning, service supplier know-how, and innovation improve the customer's ability to develop new capabilities, leverage existing ones, and absorb them from the external environment, hence supporting future innovation. Many researchers endorse a service supplier's ability to innovate as a method of creating value for customers. Instead of creating non-differentiated offerings, service suppliers can support the invention of new offerings that improve value creation. Further, continuous and incremental innovations are necessary for the service supplier to maintain the customer's competitiveness. Hence, supplier know-how, technical competence, and the ability to reduce the customer's time to market can provide the customers with substantial strategic value.

Long-term relationships can create partnership-related value. Safety, security, credibility, and continuity build trust, and trust is conducive to long-term relationships. Trust is vital in inter-organizational relationships because it enables both parties to focus on achieving long-term benefits. Strategic goals should drive a long-term relationship or partnership. The very reason for investing in relationships is to gain a competitive advantage, strengthen core competencies, and improve market position. However, partnering and setting mutual long-term goals and objectives are risky; this reinforces the need for a trust-based relationship. Moreover, being associated with a highly esteemed business network can improve a company's image and its reference value in business markets. Either party's relationship and reputation may improve either party's internal motivation and external prestige, hence improving legitimacy, productivity, market access, and brand recognition. We label these partnership-related value elements as symbolic (internally oriented) and social (externally oriented) value.

Previous research identifies different categories of sacrifices that should be considered when assessing the operational and strategic benefits. The total costs of operation (e.g., Wouters, 2007) define a broad category of costs related to the search, acquisition, implementation, adaption, and operational activities related with a service. The future orientation of value, relationships, and business engagements involve risks associated with failures, delays, reputation, profitability, and other similar factors. Strategically significant sacrifices may also include risks of potentially unhealthy dependencies, erosion of absorptive capacity and current capabilities, and intellectual property and knowledge leaking. A rather obvious category of sacrifices contains costs related to change (such as structural, capability, and identity change) that are required to realize the benefits.

From value conception to value perception

Different organizational actors may have diverging conceptions of value, thereby a varied understanding of the value potential in the B2B exchange due to the subjective, dynamic, and contextual nature of value. For example, either suppliers or customers may hold an excessively narrow conception of value, which potentially greatly limits the discovery of mutually acceptable value creation opportunities. For instance, industrial procurement often focuses on only few elements of the life-cycle costs when making purchase decisions. However, the initial purchase price of a truck, for instance, represents only about 12% of the life-cycle costs of operating the truck (e.g., Snelgrove, 2012). Clearly, a purchase decision based on the initial acquisition cost may be unwise. To understand how individual actors process value, we suggest a cognitive model of three stages from value conception to value preference to value perception. Figure 12.2 illustrates the relationship between these concepts.

First, we define **value conception** as the scope of a value definition, what value dimensions the actor recognizes as relevant and is willing to consider as having value creation potential. For instance, a car's potential value dimensions include performance, comfort, social, symbolic, ownership cost, environmental, and similar dimensions and sub-dimensions. An individual actor's value conception may consist of any combination of these, depending on their "value awareness." Then, individuals make a *value selection* from their value conception to arrive at their **value preference**. Value preference identifies those value dimensions that the actor finds relevant in the current decision-making situation. An individual may be aware of a powerful engine's potential benefits in a vehicle but may decide that the performance is not relevant decision criteria in their specific situation. Finally, **value perception** is formed by *value assessment* of the value preference to estimate how much value can be created.

A broad and holistic value conception brings all the relevant dimensions of value into the value preference evaluation. Similarly, understanding the value creation potential of all the appropriate value dimensions can result in a comprehensive value preference. Finally, the ability to quantify the value potential of each of the value dimensions included in the value preference provides the best measure for the value creation. Therefore, successful value creation requires that the parties involved in the value creation system analyze and expand first their individual and then their shared value conceptions and value preferences to ensure that all relevant value creation opportunities are considered. Any benefits or sacrifices falling outside of the actor's value conception or excluded from the value preference as irrelevant represent a lost value creation opportunity or potential for positive or negative surprises for the involved stakeholders.

Both the value conception and value preference are greatly influenced by the actors' and organizations' absorptive capacity (Fabrizio, 2009) to identify, evaluate, and implement the emerging value creation opportunities. In addition to the (primarily) cognitive awareness of value creation opportunities, the institutional influences also greatly modify

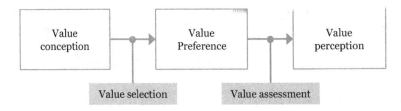

Figure 12.2 The relationship between customer's value conception, value preference, and value perception

especially the value preference. Some value creation opportunities can be deemed unacceptable by the actors, going against their beliefs, norms, and rules about proper ways of doing business (Thornton et al., 2012). Firm identity may rule out otherwise promising value creation opportunities that would require either firm to change their perceived identity. Ultimately legal rules limit how different resources can be utilized or what agreements are acceptable. Often two organizations have only a partially overlapping beliefs about proper ways of cooperating (Besharov and Smith, 2014), limiting the joint value creation opportunities by exclusion. Hence, suppliers and customer have often greatly differing value conceptions and preferences due to their idiosyncratic histories and culture. The different domains of supplier and customer value conceptions are illustrated in Figure 12.3. Figure 12.3 could be complemented by presenting the corresponding sets of supplier and customer value preferences, which would further constrain the available value creation opportunities. It is also important to note that there likely exist value creation opportunities outside of the supplier and customer value conceptions in $C \cap (A \cup B)$.

In summary:

1. The suppliers and customers should openly explore their value conceptions to arrive at a broad shared value conception $A \cap B$.
2. Then, the parties influence the mutually shared value preference. Suppliers strive to include their differentiators into the shared value preference and vice versa. For instance, if a car is differentiated by a low insurance premium or high resale value, the seller likely influences the customer to include those value dimensions into the shared value preference. Value quantification is an important tool in demonstrating the value creating potential of a particular dimension of value.
3. Finally, the parties should first pursue a joint qualitative assessment of value creation potential along the value dimensions included in the value preference, and then quantitative evaluation is performed for those value dimensions that allow numerical quantification. Then, participants should contribute to the combination and aggregation of those quantified measures of value that can be expressed in terms of commensurate key performance indicators such as cost savings, revenue improvements, and risk mitigation. These steps suggest that customer's value perception is influenced by a combination of qualitative and quantitative evidence of value. Currently, the

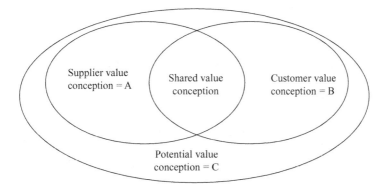

Figure 12.3 Domains of value conception (Rajala et al., 2015)

observed industrial value propositions emphasize those value dimensions, for which convincing numerical evidence can be generated, whereas the "softer" symbolic, social, and strategic dimensions of value are less explicitly communicated by using anecdotal evidence, reference stories, and the like.

Framework for discovering, selecting, quantifying, and sharing value

Figure 12.4 suggests a framework for a value process. The framework includes three stages from gaining customer insight to value sharing and consists of six groups of actions.

Customer insight

Gaining customer insight, or customer value research, seeks to understand and analyze customer activities to identify opportunities for improvement. In most areas of industrial activity, gaining customer insight focuses on (a) understanding and mapping customer's business processes and (b) customer's business drivers and associated performance metrics. Practical techniques for understanding and mapping customer's business processes and value preferences include customer value audits (e.g., Ulaga and Chacour, 2001), customer value analysis (e.g., Miles, 1972), and customer value research (Anderson et al., 2007; Bettencourt and Ulwick, 2008). The case companies describe their activities as follows:

> Having identified key stakeholder groups, we set out to analyze the individual stakeholder processes, building an intranet resource of stakeholder processes, and describing stakeholder goals and challenges to guide segment specific value proposition development.
>
> (Industry Manager)

> We are trying to holistically understand our customer's processes, the different flows of material and money, to understand how our products affect their business performance in different economic cycles.
>
> (Industry Manager)

> We are continuously researching the cargo-handling process for improvement opportunities.
>
> (Industry Manager)

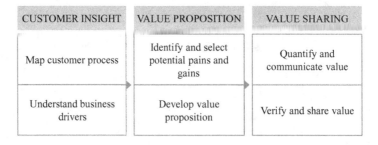

CUSTOMER INSIGHT	VALUE PROPOSITION	VALUE SHARING
Map customer process	Identify and select potential pains and gains	Quantify and communicate value
Understand business drivers	Develop value proposition	Verify and share value

Figure 12.4 From customer insight to value proposition communication

To gain management attention, value communication needs to address timely and salient business drivers and key performance indicators. Most case companies evaluate value creation opportunities in terms of (a) revenue impact, (b) cost impact, (c) impact on asset efficiency (or return on capital employed), and (d) risk impact. Salient business drivers and associated KPIs change across market cycles and decision maker profiles, and hence value communication needs to be adapted to different market, customer, and decision maker situations.

Value proposition

The research on customer's business processes and business drivers facilitates building effective value propositions. We define value propositions as communication tools that suggest how the parties could create value by leveraging their combined capabilities and resources. Previous research has established that value propositions are *bundles of benefits* that address *business goals* of *specific target groups* and offer *significant value* for the customer. For a supplier, value propositions must help in *differentiating* from alternatives (e.g., Anderson et al., 2006, 2007; Lindgreen and Wynstra, 2005).

Once a sufficient understanding on a customer's situation, business processes, and drivers have been acquired, the next step in the process is to identify improvement opportunities. The case companies analyze their customer's business processes to identify "pains" and "gains," that is, opportunities to remove problems and implement improvements that offer potential for value creation. Value research typically yields a number of improvement opportunities along the different value dimensions included in the value conception.

> When we use separate value sources, we are actually telling the customer that "you are getting benefits in all these places."

In industrial setting, the value creation opportunities often relate to changes in business process, resulting in improvements in processes performance. Examples of such improvements include reduced energy consumption, higher production volume, improved resource efficiency, improved quality, reduced planned and unplanned production stops, improved safety, lower environmental impact, and the like. The improvement opportunities identified form the set of value dimensions to choose the "bundle of benefits"

Table 12.1 Value enhanced through change in a construction system

---

CASE: Value research by global elevator and escalator supplier

---

A global supplier of elevators and escalators conducted research on their key stakeholder's business processes. One of the stakeholder segments is constructors. Constructors typically install temporary construction time elevators to move builders and materials in and out of the building. Those elevators are attached on the building walls outside of the building using exterior hoists. The value research process led to a discovery that the permanent elevators of a building could be used already during the construction time, appropriately protected. The value research process revealed several important benefits: The final, permanent elevators are faster, safer, more energy efficient, and more reliable, meaning lower energy cost and less waiting time at both ends of the worker shifts, and hence improved construction efficiency, and shorter construction time. Also importantly, there is no need to keep the façade of the building open for the temporary solution; the façade can be closed and the interior work started earlier, further reducing the construction time. Earlier delivery of the building kicks off the revenue streams earlier, adding to the life cycle revenues of the building.

---

included in the value proposition. The selection is guided by three selection criteria, each creating a priority order among the improvement opportunities.

Impact on goal: Rather obviously, large financial rewards are more interesting than small. Suppliers and customers need to apply value quantification for each identified value dimension to determine the potential (financial) impact on business KPIs. Those value elements that have biggest potential impact on business goals are then included in the value proposition.

Supplier differentiation: Suppliers likely have differing capabilities and resources to create value. Suppliers should incorporate those value dimensions in their value propositions that differentiate them from competition (Anderson et al., 2006).

Saliency: As already discussed, some value creating dimensions may be ruled out as unacceptable by either party, going against their beliefs, norms, and rules about legitimate ways of doing business (Töytäri et al., 2018). Due to industrial imitation and benchmarking, the stakeholders are likely more receptive to some value creation opportunities than others.

The *value selection* described earlier generates the "bundle of benefits" of the value proposition. The "bundle of benefits" consists of a number of impactful, differentiating, and appealing changes to the target customer's existing situation. The value proposition is then designed around the bundle of benefits by documenting (a) the supplier's solution that implements the bundle of benefits, (b) the bundle of benefits, and (c) the impact of the bundle of benefits on the customer's business goal.

Value sharing

The remaining steps of the value process involve adapting, quantifying, communicating, verifying, and sharing value. Each of these steps is discussed here.

Figure 12.5 Elements of a value proposition

Table 12.2 Value proposition example for a running shoe

CASE Running shoe for a professional marathon runner
A marathon runner recently succeeded in breaking the 2-hour limit on a full distance marathon. The runner was using an innovative running shoe that features a carbon-fiber plate to improve the preserving and releasing of energy during the running motion. The shoe manufacturer's value proposition says that "the shoe reduces the energy needed to run at given speed by 4% and helps reducing muscle fatigue." The bundle of benefits includes two improvements over the existing alternatives and quantifies the impact of those improvements on customer's goal.

Adapting value proposition: Designing a value proposition is an optimization exercise between impact and scope (Töytäri and Rajala, 2015). An impactful value proposition matches the recipient's value views. However, the subjective nature of customer value renders the task of designing stakeholder-specific value propositions impractical; the pre-designed value propositions are scoped to address broad-enough stakeholder segments, hence potentially leaving a gap between the value proposition scope and individual stakeholder perceptions. This gap can be filled in two obvious ways; either the value proposition communication tools and practices allow adapting the value proposition to match individual views and/or the value proposition communication is impactful enough to change the stakeholders' views with the pre-designed value proposition. One identified practice to adapt the value proposition involves building value selection functionality into the value calculation tools so that the customer may choose the salient value dimensions to include in the calculation. Hence, the "bundle of benefits" is built individually for a stakeholder.

Quantifying value proposition: Value proposition quantification is implemented through the following steps:

1. For each element in the "bundle of benefits" the supplier and the customer need to determine the improvement potential. That is, what is the difference between current performance and achievable performance along each value dimension. For instance, in the running example cited earlier the improvement in running energy consumption was 4%.
2. Then, each improvement needs to be translated into a salient measure of value (such as revenue increase or cost reduction) by identifying an appropriate value function to calculate the monetary value of energy savings, production increase, and the like.
3. Finally, the individual improvements are aggregated into an overall measure of value impact on customer's goal.

The quantification steps mentioned earlier include a number of challenges for practical implementation. The current state performance is often difficult to determine. The growing digitalization of industry is helping to remedy the problem by creating volumes of component, equipment, process, and plan-level production data, but often the lack of information poses a challenge. Suppliers also need to determine what is possible to achieve, and what level of risk in committing to the results is acceptable. Suppliers are actively building databases of success cases and verifying the results achieved together with their customers. However, goals involve risk, and risk sharing between the parties is a profound new business model–related topic on the agenda. Finally, the value function that translates the operational changes into (monetary) KPIs is often difficult to determine. In simple cases the industrial process can simply be modified to reveal the impact of the changes, but often the value creating changes have delayed effects on the KPIs, or there may be other uncontrollable variables also influencing the KPIs. Hence, the equation between the value creating changes and the resulting KPIs may be difficult to determine and convincingly demonstrate.

Communicating value proposition: Value propositions are translated to and communicated by marketing messages, reference stories, and value calculators in an increasing order of customer specificity and accuracy of value evidence. These value communication means greatly improve the impact and efficiency of value communication by leveraging wider organizational knowledge that is then orchestrated by the marketing and sales

Table 12.3 Value derived from process improvement

CASE: *Process equipment modernization of value assessment*
A global supplier of mining and metals processing equipment, services, and processes has innovated an improved solution for their flotation copper extraction unit. Compared with their older equipment, the new solution improves minerals recovery percentage, reduces energy consumption, and lowers maintenance cost. While the actual revenue improvement and cost saving are site-specific, in an example case an achievable two percentage unit improvement equaled to 2 million euros in additional revenue. Correspondingly, a 50% reduction in energy cost equaled to EUR 100,000 savings, and a 50% decrease in maintenance costs, which equaled to EUR 50,000 yearly saving in maintenance expenditure.

forces. Traditionally, the industrial marketing messages have been highly product-focused. However, all the case companies we studied are actively developing databases of success stories to influence their customers at the different stages of the decision-making processes, to create urgency to act by demonstrating value creation opportunities and outcomes and to build credibility during buyer-seller interactions. Then, value calculators are tools for analyzing the value creation potential in a specific customer situation. The case companies are increasingly building visually and technically sophisticated tools to help the sales force to conduct structured and fact-finding oriented conversations, for instance, by simulating the value impact of different solution alternatives and scenarios. In any case, impactful value proposition communication requires powerful IT tools, which hide computational complications, connect to reference information databases, and present the results visually appealingly.

Verifying value created: Value verification is a post-implementation activity, which seeks to, indeed, verify the value promises made and possibly committed to during the earlier stages of the process. Value verification is essential for value-based pricing. Value verification has also differentiating power among suppliers. Those suppliers that dare to accept and manage the risk associated with value guarantees likely win in competition against those suppliers that cannot commit to value creation.

> Committing to the value makes us a really strong business case. Value verification is steering our product, software and process development, to continuously improve the earning potential of our customers.

Sharing value: Finally, one of the key goals of the entire value quantification exercise is to tie pricing to value created (Hinterhuber, 2004; Liozu et al., 2012). All the steps related to value quantification require significant upfront investment are very demanding and costly to implement and require significant new capabilities and resources. To justify this investment, value quantification should pay off in terms of improved margins. Figure 12.5 illustrates the value-based and cost-based pricing logics. Both parties capture a share of the value created if the price is anywhere between the supplier cost and value created (Kortge and Okonkwo, 1993; Töytäri et al., 2015). In essence, price determines how the value created is split between the supplier and the customer. A price close to the supplier cost (cost-based pricing) favors the customer, and a price close to the value created favors the supplier, correspondingly.

There is emerging evidence among the case companies that their win-rates and profitability actually improved as a result of value quantification (Aberdeen Group, 2011). Convincingly demonstrating the value creation potential may allow tying the price to

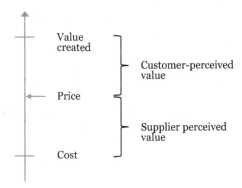

Figure 12.6 Price in relation with value created and supplier cost (Töytäri and Rajala, 2015)

the realized value, instead of applying the prevailing cost-based pricing logic, and hence improve profitability. However, value-based pricing and value-based customer approach are challenging strategies to implement for a number of reasons. The challenges associated with becoming a value-focused organization are discussed next.

Transition challenges and opportunities in value-based exchange

A convincing demonstration of value creation opportunities by the supplier motivates customers to transform their buying behaviors toward value-based exchange. However, research has identified a number of challenges faced by the suppliers to actually benefit from the value-based approach to inter-organizational exchange (Töytäri et al., 2015). The first category of challenges relates to the differing value conceptions held by the parties. In particular, if the customer recognizes and appreciates only a very limited set of benefits, innovative suppliers, whose value creation potential resides outside of the customer's value conception, are likely to fail in impressing the customer. Such failures can result in a significant loss of value creation opportunity. Hence, suppliers need to influence and broaden their customer's value conception in order to help them to recognize and evaluate the opportunities for value creation. One way to achieve this objective is to leverage the reference cases to illustrate how (a) critical business challenges are (b) solved by specific solutions to (c) achieve significant business results. Such a "reference marketing" has been found to be effective means to influence perceptions (Jalkala and Salminen, 2010).

The second category of challenges in leveraging value for the customers pertains to the inability of the suppliers to quantify value convincingly. Among the identified reasons for this inability (Töytäri et al., 2015) are the lack of current performance data, lack of access to key decision makers to influence decision making, lack of trust in sharing confidential information, customer's reluctance to engage in the value quantification exercise to avoid the possibility of weakening own negotiation position, and, finally, inability to calculate value.

Finally, quantifying and demonstrating value do not guarantee that a supplier actually benefits from the value created. Value sharing is largely determined by the relative negotiation positions (Brandenburger and Stuart, 1996) of the exchanging parties. The prevailing industrial practices are deeply rooted in the procurement of commoditized products, favoring aggressive procurement practices (including cost-based pricing) to strengthen the customer's value capturing power to maximize their short-term gain. To benefit from value created the suppliers need to differentiate, to achieve a position of preference based on highest value creation potential, uniqueness of the solution, uniqueness of the relationship, or an attractive business model including risk and resource sharing.

If implemented successfully, value-based exchange holds a potential of enabling much improved value creation by helping companies to evaluate relationships and business opportunities for their value creation potential, benchmark value creation performance to inform make-or-buy (i.e., outsourcing) decisions. Also, it permits firms to focus on their core competencies.

Acknowledgments

The authors are grateful for the financial support received for this research project from the Finnish Funding Agency for Innovation through the DIMECC research program [2470/31/2010].

References

Aberdeen Group. (2011) "Value-based selling: Building a best-in-class capability for sales effectiveness," www.zsassociates.com/publications/whitepapers/aberdeen-study-value-based-selling.aspx

Anderson, J. C., Kumar, N. and Narus, J. A. (2007) *Value Merchants: Demonstrating and Documenting Superior Customer Value in Business Markets*, Boston, MA: Harvard Business School Press.

Anderson, J. C., Narus, J. A. and van Rossum, W. (2006) "Customer value propositions in business markets," *Harvard Business Review 84*(3), 1–10. www.ncbi.nlm.nih.gov/pubmed/16515158

Besharov, M. L. and Smith, W. K. (2014) "Multiple institutional logics in organizations: Explaining their varied nature and implications," *Academy of Management Review 39*(3), 364–381. https://doi.org/10.5465/amr.2011.0431

Bettencourt, L. A. and Ulwick, A. W. (2008) "The customer-centered innovation map," *Harvard Business Review 86*(5), 109–114, 130. www.ncbi.nlm.nih.gov/pubmed/18543812

Brandenburger, A. M. and Stuart, H. W. (1996) "Value-based business strategy," *Journal of Economics & Management Strategy 5*(1), 5–24. http://onlinelibrary.wiley.com/doi/10.1111/j.1430-9134.1996.00005.x/abstract

Fabrizio, K. R. (2009) "Absorptive capacity and the search for innovation," *Research Policy 38*(2), 255–267. https://doi.org/10.1016/j.respol.2008.10.023

Hinterhuber, A. (2004) "Towards value-based pricing – An integrative framework for decision making," *Industrial Marketing Management 33*(8), 765–778. https://doi.org/10.1016/j.indmarman.2003.10.006

Jalkala, A. and Salminen, R. T. (2010) "Practices and functions of customer reference marketing – Leveraging customer references as marketing assets," *Industrial Marketing Management 39*(6), 975–985. https://doi.org/10.1016/j.indmarman.2010.06.017

Kortge, G. D. and Okonkwo, P. A. (1993) "Perceived value approach to pricing," *Industrial Marketing Management 22*(2), 133–140.

Lindgreen, A. and Wynstra, F. (2005) "Value in business markets: What do we know? Where are we going?" *Industrial Marketing Management 34*(7), 732–748. https://doi.org/10.1016/j.indmarman.2005.01.001

Liozu, S. M., Hinterhuber, A., Boland, R. and Perelli, S. (2012) "The conceptualization of value-based pricing in industrial firms," *Journal of Revenue and Pricing Management 11*(1), 12–34. https://doi.org/10.1057/rpm.2011.34

Miles, L. (1972) "Techniques of value analysis and engineering," www.irantransport.org/upload/ghavanin/filepicker_users/d7955a513f-62/3.pdf

Rajala, R., Töytäri, P. and Hervonen, T. (2015) "Assessing customer-perceived value in industrial service systems," *Service Science* 7(3), 210–226. https://doi.org/10.1287/serv.2015.0108

Snelgrove, T. (2012) "How and why to negotiate on total cost of ownership," The Chief Procurement Officer Summit, Boston, MA.

Thornton, P. H., Ocasio, W. and Lounsbury, M. (2012) *The Institutional Logics Perspective: A New Approach to Culture, Structure, and Process*, Oxford, UK: Oxford University Press.

Töytäri, P. and Rajala, R. (2015) "Value-based selling: An organizational capability perspective," *Industrial Marketing Management 45*, 101–112.

Töytäri, P., Rajala, R., Alejandro, T. B. and Brashear Alejandro, T. (2015) "Organizational and institutional barriers to value-based pricing in industrial relationships," *Industrial Marketing Management 47*, 53–64.

Töytäri, P., Turunen, T., Klein, M., Eloranta, V., Biehl, S. and Rajala, R. (2018) "Aligning the mindset and capabilities within a business network for successful adoption of smart services," *Journal of Product Innovation Management 35*(5), 763–779. https://doi.org/10.1111/jpim.12462

Ulaga, W. and Chacour, S. (2001) "Measuring customer-perceived value in business markets," *Industrial Marketing Management 30*(6), 525–540. https://doi.org/10.1016/S0019-8501(99)00122-4

Wouters, M. (2007) "Beyond the acquisition price – Total cost of ownership for supporting purchase decisions," *Wbiconpro.Com*, 1–10. www.wbiconpro.com/601-Wouters,M.pdf

Zeithaml, V. (1988) "Consumer perceptions of price, quality, and value: A means-end model and synthesis of evidence," *The Journal of Marketing 52*(3), 2–22. www.jstor.org/stable/10.2307/1251446

Part IV

Buying on value – value quantification and B2B purchasing

13 Value first, cost later

Total value contribution as a new approach to sourcing decisions

Gray, John V., Helper, Susan, and Osborn, Beverly

Introduction

Imagine you are a manager at a firm located in a high-wage country tasked with sourcing a major component or service. You have quotes from an offshore supplier and from a nearby supplier with a higher per-unit price. Which supplier should you choose? If motivated only by the siren song of low per-unit price, you may choose the offshore supplier. Such an approach has been a driver of the nearly 40-year slide in manufacturing in high-wage countries.

If you are sourcing a physical good and have a sophisticated understanding of logistics and international trade compliance costs, you may build a detailed "total landed cost" (TLC) model that adds those costs to the offshore supplier's quote. As the resulting TLC model involves several interconnected sheets in a huge Excel workbook, you could be rightly proud of your thoroughness.

If you recognize that these decisions can also affect hard-to-measure factors important to your company, you may perform a "total cost of ownership" (TCO) analysis (Ellram and Siferd, 1993). The best of TCO analyses include dozens of factors such as increased disruption risk as supply chains get longer (Siegfried, 2013; Reshoring Initiative, 2020).

We suggest an alternative to TCO that we call "total value contribution" (TVC). TVC is a structured approach to sourcing decisions designed to maximize the firm's long-term value. Our approach provides a process designed to counter firms' entrenched tendency to focus on easily measurable costs. TVC starts with the question, "What do our customers, current and future, value about our products?" The TVC approach is designed to counteract common biases through careful incorporation of the individual and group decision-making literature; we believe that these biases have worked against the widespread adoption of earlier efforts to combat purchasing's tendency to focus too heavily on cost. In addition to our improved process, we argue that the term "TVC" improves upon "TCO" in two ways. First, by replacing "cost" with "value," TVC anchors decision makers on value, not cost. This is important because cost is the factor to which decision makers in global sourcing typically gravitate due to its easy measurability and internal incentives that reward managers for cost reductions. In addition, TVC replaces "ownership" with the more appropriate "contribution," thus avoiding any narrowing of consideration of when during its life cycle the activity being sourced may affect value.[1]

We are not the first to argue that sourcing decision makers should place value at the center of their buying decisions (e.g., Vitasek et al., 2012; Wouters et al., 2005; Ellram and Feitzinger, 1997) as well as the first edition of this book (Hinterhuber and Snelgrove, 2017). TVC differs from these solutions by explicitly addressing the behavioral issues

DOI: 10.4324/9781003177937-17

(including cognitive biases and piece-price-based incentives) that, we believe, have made excessive cost focus so persistent in practice.

Decision factors considered in sourcing

There are many factors to consider in supplier selection, and many are difficult to quantify. Dickson's (1966) seminal article lists 23 factors that managers reported considering in their supplier selection decisions. Modern lists are no less extensive; the Reshoring Initiative's Total Cost of Ownership Estimator currently lists 36 factors. The meaning and importance of each decision factor are context dependent (e.g., a buyer might be interested in capacity to meet fluctuations in current demands or in capacity for future growth), further adding to the complexity of the sourcing decision. Many of these factors are interconnected, such as cycle time (Sharland et al., 2003), which affects logistics and inventory costs as well as the pace of innovation. Softer factors, such as reputation (Lienland et al., 2013), and relationship characteristics such as openness of communication (Choi and Hartley, 1996), can arguably connect to every dimension of supplier performance.

Further, the linkages among production, markets, supply sources, and product development can be critical. Ketokivi et al. (2017) studied 35 production location decisions. For each decision, they examined how production was linked to supply, product development, and the market. For each linkage, they considered coupling, formalization, and specificity (respectively, the extent of the interdependence, the codifiability of activities, and how easily a node in the dyad could be replaced). They observed that locating production in a high-cost country was always associated with at least one of a high level of coupling or specificity or a low level of formalization (Ketokivi et al., 2017). As firms outsource more strategic activities, firms' abilities to consider multidimensional objectives through sourcing has become even more important to firm value, but also more complex.

A common omission from lists of factors to be considered in sourcing decisions is the impact of suppliers on revenues. TCO models can theoretically include any factor, but few, if any, give as much attention to revenues as costs.[2] If one thinks of revenues as negative costs, the lack of attention to revenues might seem unimportant. However, considering revenues explicitly ensures they are given full consideration beyond simply, for example, lost sales due to disruptions. Excellent suppliers may allow the firm to increase its prices and/or the quantity it sells; the sourcing decision process should explicitly elicit these impacts. Thus, it is often useful to include a buyer's marketing and product design experts in sourcing decisions to understand these revenue-side implications; such inclusion is far more likely in a TVC process than in cost-based processes.

Decision-making approaches used in sourcing

We can see from the prior section that sourcing has long involved multidimensional decision making. In the following section, we briefly discuss some common purchasing methods and describe how each one handles this complexity, before introducing the TVC process. Table 13.1 offers a summary.

Unit-price-based procurement

Rather than disregarding non-price factors entirely, firms often combine the unit-price-based approach with some form of pre-qualification, however, in this case. Potential

Table 13.1 Overview of sourcing approaches

Approach	Factors considered	Advantages	Disadvantages
Piece-price/ lowest quote	Unit price	Very easy to understand Very easy to implement Requires little data Objective: clear incentives for decision makers	Does not consider non-price cost elements[3] Does not consider revenue-generating factors Does not consider risks
Total landed cost (TLC)	As earlier, plus: shipping and handling costs; trade compliance costs; inventory costs	Easy to understand Conceptually easy to implement (can be tedious) Considers more cost elements than piece-price Objective: clear incentives for decision makers	Does not consider all non-price cost elements Does not consider revenue-generating factors Does not consider risks
Total cost of ownership (TCO)[4]	As earlier, plus: design and development costs; start-up/switching costs; training costs; operating costs; software costs; governance costs (e.g., monitoring); supply chain support costs; retirement/ disposal costs	Provides a framework for identifying relevant factors Tends to result in lower total costs than piece-price, TLC Information gathered has secondary uses	Anchors decision makers on cost Does not explicitly consider revenue-generating factors or factors related to risk Difficult and time-consuming to fully implement
Total value contribution (TVC)	As earlier, plus risk: costs of shortages, disruptions, and downtime; risk of brand damage; risk of loss of IP As earlier, plus revenue: social/environmental performance; product and service quality; other factors affecting demand/ willingness to pay As earlier, plus the value of options: capacity for future growth; innovation capabilities; the potential to learn from suppliers; factors that affect the firm's social license to operate As earlier, plus to the potential to identify factors not listed here through a cross-functional process	Conceptually correct TVC process anchors on customer value, not cost Provides a framework for identifying relevant factors and an implementation process Information gathered has secondary uses	Subjectivity in the decision factors considered Difficult to quantify differences between options Difficult and time-consuming to fully implement

suppliers do not gain any advantage by exceeding the minimum standards on non-price dimensions. One incarnation of unit-price-based procurement is the price-only online reverse auction, in which suppliers bid for the right to supply a customer's needs and the winner is chosen based on low price (Jap, 2002), even in cases where a slightly higher-priced supplier might offer greater quality or reliability (Helper and MacDuffie, 2003).

Total landed costs

TLC models add measurable transportation, packaging, and storage costs to the unit prices. This distinction is most relevant when buyers are considering options in distant locations as sources for physical goods. TLC analyses can be very extensive and complex (e.g., Erhun and Tayur, 2003; Young et al., 2009). Thorough analyses require not only a deep understanding of transportation costs but also customs, duties, tariffs, and trade compliance costs if global sources are under consideration.

Total cost of ownership

The most widely recommended sourcing decision framework today is TCO. TCO "implies that all costs associated with the acquisition, use and maintenance of an item be considered in evaluating that item and not just the purchase price" (Ellram and Siferd, 1993). Under the guise of TCO, managers can (and some do) consider a very broad set of factors in strategic sourcing decisions. Attesting to TCO's credibility, the U.S. Department of Commerce included a referral to the Reshoring Initiative's "Total Cost of Ownership Estimator" in the "toolbox" on its "Assess Costs Everywhere" website.

As highlighted, sourcing approaches have evolved to use an expanding pool of information. More extensive information search and analysis are characteristics of rational procedures, which are associated with better performance outcomes of supplier selection decisions (e.g., in terms of costs, defects, and delivery; Riedl et al., 2013).

The total value contribution (TVC) approach

Our hope is that TVC will make it easier for forward-thinking managers to make sourcing decisions based on value. We also hope TVC will spur managers who would otherwise have relied on cost-centered heuristics (Gray et al., 2017) to source based on value instead. We outline our proposed TVC approach in the next section. As shown in Table 13.2, the features of this approach have a theoretical basis in the individual and group decision-making literature.

Setting the objectives

The first step of TVC-based sourcing, and arguably any sourcing decision, is to clearly *define which activity*[5] *is under consideration.* As Figure 13.1 shows, the TVC approach then starts with two key questions about the goods or services affected by the activities under consideration:

> What do our customers, current or future, value about our products? How can this sourcing decision affect those values?

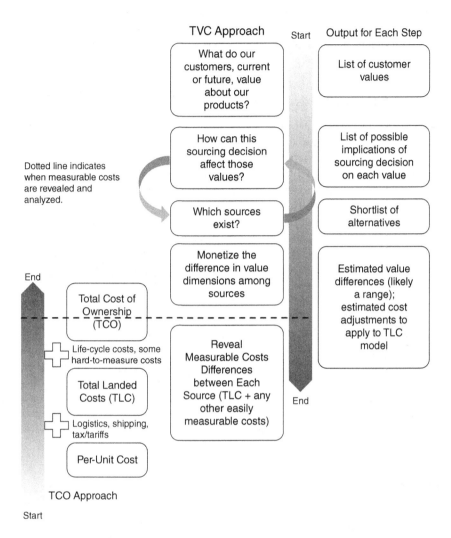

These questions require decision makers to listen to gather information from customers and those who work with them on what customers value in the product or service and link the sourcing decision to those value drivers. Answering the question well requires cross-functional expertise, because information about customers and how sourcing decisions affect what they value is distributed across the organization. Generally, the decision should involve people with a strong understanding of customer requirements, technical requirements, and supplier capabilities (e.g., in a manufacturing context, at least marketing, engineering, operations, and procurement). In some cases, value creation could be almost entirely based on obtaining the item for a low price, making the TVC choice the same as that obtained by employing TCO, TLC, or even piece price. In other cases, the answers could include factors such as consistent quality, protection of intellectual property, fast delivery, social responsibility, or a specific technological capability. A customer may value having a partner with the capability to participate in co-developing new products; considerations such as this one require evaluation of alternatives at the supplier or relationship level, as well as at the product level.

Determining the alternatives

The second step in the TVC approach is to identify alternative sources. We do not prescribe how a firm should go about identifying alternatives: Potential supply bases are typically quite activity-specific. It is possible that, as decision makers refocus on what customers value, they will identify a need to search for new alternatives that are more closely aligned with these priorities. Figure 13.1 shows feedback loops for these reasons. For example, recognizing customers' need for responsiveness may lead buyers to seek sources capable of implementing *seru*, a manufacturing approach using reconfigurable cells that allow fast product changeovers (Yin et al., 2017). Further, after thinking through these issues for a specific activity under consideration, the firm may find it useful to bring related activities into consideration, or the firm may find unexpected performance differences between alternative suppliers. For example, when two separate components work together to provide an attribute that customers value, it may make sense to use a single provider for both products. Using a single provider for both time-sensitive and insensitive products can also be profitable, as it can allow better use of capacity buffers (De Treville et al., 2017).

It will sometimes be appropriate to pre-qualify potential suppliers so that only viable options are considered in the next step in TVC analysis. This decision, too, should be driven by customer values. Some factors may be non-compensatory: a failure to achieve a certain level of performance in one factor (e.g., provision of a safe workplace) may disqualify a supplier from further consideration, regardless of how well it performs on other factors.

Evaluating the differences

The hardest part of TVC comes next: assigning a rough monetary value to the differences between the alternatives on the identified values. This may be even more challenging for those sourcing components or backend services, rather than finished goods. To simplify this step, we recommend focusing only on value drivers with significant differences in customer value between options under consideration (as in Wouters et al., 2009; Wynstra et al., 2012). TVC allows for any method of calculating value differences: No functional form is prescribed. It is acceptable to have a wide range for some values, if necessary.

As value differences are uncovered, the TVC approach may lead decision makers to identify safeguards that the firm can implement to reduce differences between options. For example, the team may see that one potential source has higher disruption risk and that a disruption at a peak time may result in millions of dollars of lost revenue and goodwill. One option is to roughly quantify that lost value (e.g., an x-y% higher likelihood of complete disruption, which would result in $X-$Y lost sales, and lost goodwill valued at $W-$Z). But a better option may be to implement safeguards such as higher inventory or flexible capacity buffers during the peak season. The TVC team should note the need for these safeguards, which must then be included as adjustments to the cost model associated with the suppliers for which they are required. Often, estimating the costs of implementing these safeguards requires knowing the supplier's unit costs: Such calculations should not be performed until the value differences have been fully determined[6] so that knowledge of unit costs cannot unduly influence value estimates (DeKay et al., 2014). Dekel and Schurr (2014) provide evidence in favor of this "value first" approach.[7] They performed an experiment with government procurement managers. They found that when managers knew the lower bidder, they inflated non-cost values in favor of that bidder, relative to when they did not know bids. Dekel and Schurr (2014) labeled this "lower-bid bias."

So how does a TVC team come up with value differences? It is often impossible to be very accurate. As a preliminary step, the team should agree on the categories of revenue and profit that the sourcing decision may affect. After this, the goal is to get some agreement as to the rough magnitude and likelihood of value differences between sources. In some cases, the decision makers may have the in-depth knowledge needed to define a distribution of potential value differences for each value driver, allowing a formal assessment of risk differences using Monte Carlo or similar ones. More often, they will not. In this case, one shortcut is to consider best-case, worst-case, and most-likely scenarios (as is common in risk management; e.g., Barreras, 2011). As risk managers do, the team can benefit from paying special attention to the inter-relatedness of potential outcomes and trigger events (Kleindorfer and Saad, 2005; Kern et al., 2012). For example, the probability distribution for increased sales associated with greener production at a supplier is likely not independent of that for decreased brand risk associated with the same supplier's ethical labor practices. In some cases, decision makers may find it helpful to think about the value generated by one of the alternatives, but with and without a particular feature (e.g., an option for future expansion) in order to arrive at an estimated value for that value driver. Beyond value drivers that affect revenue or risk, this discussion also forces the firm to decide how much, if at all, they truly value social issues, such as supplier pollution levels and compliance with rigorous safety or worker-protection programs.

Revealing the costs

Measurable cost differences finally enter the equation only after hard-to-measure value differences between options have been articulated. These cost differences are, roughly, the same as those captured in a TLC model. The person in charge of the cost model should add the costs of any safeguards identified during the estimation of value differences (e.g., carrying additional inventory for a distant option to offset increased disruption risk or additional oversight for an offshore supplier). The participation on the TVC team of the person responsible for creating the cost model is critical to be sure that the same factors are not double-counted through inclusion in both the value model and the cost model. The team should also be vigilant in avoiding double-counting across alternative sources: the same difference was almost included twice – as an advantage of one source and a disadvantage of another – in one early application of TVC to the sourcing of a medical product.[8] Only when both the value differences and the cost differences are revealed will the decision makers finally see the full picture. We expect that, in general, cost differences revealed in this step will not seem as large as they would have if introduced at the beginning, leading to decisions based more on value.[9]

Learning from experience

Adhering to this process, and documenting the values articulated, will lead to learning and refinement of what the firm values. After a decision has been made and implemented, one final step remains. Just as forecasters should assess the accuracy and bias of their forecasts, decision makers using TVC should document the values they quantified and attempt to compare the outcomes of their decisions to their original expectations. In so doing, they will learn to improve their estimates of value differences in future decisions. A recent application of TVC to a raw materials sourcing decision resulted in a change from an incumbent supplier.[10] After the decision was made to switch from the incumbent, the incumbent initially committed to continuity of supply during the transition. The incumbent later halted deliveries before the replacement had ramped up production, resulting in unforeseen costs for the focal firm. The TVC team intends to take these learnings to future sourcing decisions by considering risks to continuity of supply caused by incumbent behavior when switching suppliers is an option.

Learning from experience can be difficult, not only because realized value will be hard to measure, but also because information on the performance of discarded options will not be available. Nonetheless, we encourage purchasing staff to ask: "Did we identify the most important hidden costs and risks? Did we realize the expected revenue? Were our estimates reasonable? Why did we miss the things we missed?" Better sourcing decisions, and better firm performance, will result.

Implementation issues

We recognize that focusing on value in sourcing is easier said than done. We believe that estimating value differences before analyzing costs is one key to success. Forcing consensus on subjective value differences *before* the team knows easy-to-measure costs makes estimates more credible and harder to attribute to biased preferences such as Dekel and Schurr's (2014) lower-bid bias. Experiments show that purchasing managers do not treat value and price as equivalent, even when value is monetarily quantified (Anderson et al., 2000). Instead, managers doubt whether the benefits of higher value, higher-cost purchases that their suppliers promise, will truly be realized. TVC partially addresses this potential bias because the values analyzed come not from suppliers, but rather from an internal assessment of what the firm's customers value. Anderson and Wynstra (2010) showed that confirmatory data from reference customers and pilot programs can be effective for reducing ambiguity about superior value. We encourage TVC adopters to incorporate these techniques to improve the precision of their estimates when appropriate.

For TVC to be successful, firms also need to align purchasing agents' incentives with adherence to the TVC approach and downplay incentives based on piece price. Kerr (1975) vividly describes "the folly of rewarding A, while hoping for B." In our setting, A is often negotiating price cuts, while B is increasing long term firm value. Of course, measuring B directly is generally not a realistic alternative. The "informativeness principle" (Holmstrom, 1979; Milgrom and Roberts, 1992) says that the cost of providing incentives increases as the error in measuring performance increases. Although TVC complicates the measurement of purchasing managers' performance (due to consideration of value instead of cost), it also makes accurate monitoring of behaviors more feasible due, for example, to observation of efforts to follow TVC by the cross-functional team (Helper et al., 2000). Subjective performance measures can improve upon, or complement,

Table 13.2 Theoretical grounding of TVC

Feature of TVC	Explanation
Value first	Anchoring and insufficient adjustment can lead to undue influence of quoted prices on other estimates when decision makers start with costs (Tversky and Kahneman, 1974; Epley and Gilovich, 2006; DeKay et al., 2014; Dekel and Schurr, 2014). Dekel and Schurr (2014) show that government procurement officers give biased assessments of non-cost value to favor the low-cost bid when both types of information are available at once; assessing value first avoids this. Separating cost analysis from value analysis is a way of decomposing the decision, which is an effective debiasing strategy for sourcing decisions (Kaufmann et al., 2009, 2010). When faced with multiple variables, managers tend to focus more on the most easily measurable factors (Holmstrom and Milgrom, 1991); since cost is typically the most easily measurable, beginning with value instead may counteract this bias.
Customer-driven objectives	Value has many meanings, even within supply management (Lindgreen and Wynstra, 2005); beginning with a search for objectives ensures focus on what matters in context (Das and Teng, 1999). This search also encourages adoption of another viewpoint (i.e., the customer's) which is an effective debiasing strategy (Kaufmann et al., 2009, 2010). Starting with a seemingly complete list instead may make it harder to see what is missing (Fischhoff et al., 1978), and weight attributes consistently (Morssinkhof et al., 2011). Buyers are skeptical of suppliers' claims of better value (Anderson et al., 2000; Anderson and Wynstra, 2010); internally generated comparisons are likely to be viewed as more credible.
Shared goals	Managers need to do more than merely make high-quality decisions – they must also build consensus to facilitate decision implementation (Roberto, 2004). Having shared goals is associated with more cross-functional cooperation and better task and psychosocial outcomes in cross-functional group decision making (Pinto et al., 1993) and with less negative influence of functional politics in sourcing decisions (Stanczyk et al., 2015). More broadly, consensus on strategic priorities is associated with better organizational performance (Kellermanns et al., 2011). TVC requires managers to "establish well-defined and stable decision criteria prior to analyzing and debating alternative courses of action" in terms of customer values, a process associated with higher efficiency and consensus (Roberto, 2004: 640) that still encourages goal discovery (Anderson, 1983) regarding the factors that affect these values.
Rational procedure	Procedural rationality is "the effectiveness, in light of human cognitive powers and limitations, of the procedures used to choose actions" (Simon, 1978: 9). Extensive search for information and quantitative analysis are characteristics of rational procedures (Dean and Sharfman, 1993); studies have shown financial and non-financial performance benefits from using such procedures in sourcing (Riedl et al., 2013; Kaufmann et al., 2014, 2017).
Monetary quantification of differences	Quantifying differences and adding them up, as opposed to quantifying totals (total enumeration) and then comparing them, are associated with lower uncertainty and other performance benefits (Wouters et al., 2009; Wynstra et al., 2012).
Cross-functional process	Combining multiple pools of relevant information and encouraging attention to non-shared information make it likely for group decision quality to exceed individual decision quality (Brodbeck et al., 2007). Rules and procedures are associated with more cooperation and better task outcomes in cross-functional decision making (Pinto et al., 1993). Processes characterized by high information quality, procedural quality, alignment quality, and constructive engagement across functions can perform well even when functional incentives diverge (Oliva and Watson, 2011).

distortionary objective measures. This focus on rewarding adherence to procedures avoids the difficulties of trying to measure value added by individual employees in a collaborative workplace. Although TVC is a cross-functional process, the purchasing agent's incentives are especially relevant if she is responsible for initiating it and ensuring appropriate functional representatives are involved. Executive-level performance metrics should also recognize the potential for broad contributions from purchasing departments. Ericksen (2020) suggested that including customer fill rate as a metric for executives in several departments would build shared goals. We, of course, agree. TVC teams may identify factors other than on-time fill rate as an appropriate metric to build shared goals.

Limitations

While different decision-making processes tend to be vulnerable to different biases, none are immune. By anchoring on value, TVC may underemphasize cost reduction. By putting customers first, TVC may underemphasize the concerns of other stakeholders, for example, employees. TVC does not guarantee a globally optimal solution. Instead, it uses a conceptually simple procedural heuristic of starting with what customers value. Human use of heuristics to make decisions can be a successful strategy (Gigerenzer and Goldstein, 1996; Marewski et al., 2010) as well as a source of systematic errors and biases (Tversky and Kahneman, 1974, 1981).

Conclusion

The simplest argument that TVC is superior to TCO is that *firms do not compete on cost – they compete on value.* Increased outsourcing and offshoring of more strategic activities means that sourcing decisions have a greater effect on all dimensions of value then they did in the past. Firms that focus on increasing shareholder value have three options: cutting cost, increasing revenue, or lowering risk in ways that shareholders themselves cannot do by diversifying. TCO encourages a focus on just the first one of these. Any values beyond shareholder value – such as sustainability – are even further removed from a cost-first decision-making process. A majority of costs for most companies comes from purchased inputs (Mahoney and Helper, 2017). It is time that the purchasing function be managed like the strategic function that it is. We believe that TVC is powerful enough that simply changing the language of sourcing will provide some benefit. But the most benefits will result from implementing the TVC process, which anchors managers on what matters – what customers value.

Acknowledgment

Adapted, with permission, from the article: Gray, J. V., S. Helper, B. Osborn. 2020. "Value First, Cost Later: Total Value Contribution as a New Approach to Sourcing Decisions Journal of Operations Management" 66:6, 735–750, https://doi.org/10.1002/joom.1113. Copyright Wiley 2020. All rights reserved.

Notes

1 The term "TCO" originated in the context of equipment procurement, notably information technology (Mieritz and Kirwin, 2005), where the "ownership" term made sense. A TCO analysis of

a capital purchase would capture (for example) ongoing maintenance and downtime, operating costs, and material and energy use (Johnson et al., 2011: 297), as well as salvage costs. But when the decision involves a direct material, the buying firm may only own the part for a short period of time, while its circle of concern includes many aspects from the product's or service's life – from its creation by the provider (including actions by the provider's providers) to its use by customers and everything in between. Impacts that occur before and after the buying firm owns the product, such as lifetime CO_2 emissions, are relevant in many of today's transactions, regardless of product category.

2   The Reshoring Initiative's (2020) Total Cost of Ownership Estimator, a particularly complete list of factors, offers the following that pertain to supplier impact on revenues: "impact on product differentiation/mass customization, % of price," "innovation loss, expected % of price," and "opportunity cost due to delivery and quality: lost orders, slow response, lost customers, % of price." Each addresses a very broad issue in contrast to the detailed breakdown of potential costs (including items such as prototype costs and travel expenses for site visits). By focusing attention on what customers value, the TVC process can help guide firms to focus appropriately heavily on those aspects of product differentiation and innovation that would have the most impact in a particular application.

3   Any factors not included in the selection stage may be included in a pre-qualification stage on a pass/fail basis; this applies to all factors and all approaches.

4   We acknowledge that best-in-class TCO models can include some risk and value factors, as well as the cost categories listed here.

5   Referring to sourcing decisions as choices about an activity is common in the make-buy literature. The term "activity" allows consideration of the sourcing of goods and services. It also can be defined narrowly (providing the manufacture of a single part number) or broadly (providing design, manufacturing, and logistics for a whole class of related products and services). The definition of the activity under consideration is itself a key strategic choice; see "Implementation issues" later in this chapter.

6   Note that the value of the safeguard depends in part on what the customer wants. If a key part of the customer's value comes from an ability to quickly make changes in the product, carrying extra inventory may not be a good option. This example illustrates how the TVC method allows a firm to consider interdependent costs. It is arguably more difficult to consider interdependence when using methods such as TCO, which often depend on working through long checklists where costs are presented as independent of each other.

7   See Table 13.2 for additional evidence.

8   The authors are grateful to the procurement personnel involved for allowing us to observe and learn from their application of TVC.

9   Table 13.2 provides a variety of evidence for this claim. For example, experiments show that managers tend to insufficiently adjust from the first number introduced into their analysis; this number serves as an "anchor" for the rest of their analysis (Epley and Gilovich, 2006).

10   The authors are grateful to the procurement personnel involved for allowing us to observe and learn from their application of TVC.

References

Anderson, J. C., Thomson, J. B. and Wynstra, F. (2000) "Combining value and price to make purchase decisions in business markets," *International Journal of Research in Marketing* 17(4), 307–329.

Anderson, J. C. and Wynstra, F. (2010) "Purchasing higher-value, higher-price offerings in business markets," *Journal of Business-to-Business Marketing* 17(1), 29–61.

Anderson, P. A. (1983) "Decision making by objection and the Cuban missile crisis," *Administrative Science Quarterly* 201–222.

Barreras, A. J. (2011) "Risk management: Monte Carlo simulation in cost estimating," Paper presented at PMI® Global Congress 2011 – North America, Dallas, TX. Newtown Square, PA: Project Management Institute. www.pmi.org/learning/library/monte-carlo-simulation-cost-estimating-6195

Brodbeck, F. C., Kerschreiter, R., Mojzisch, A. and Schulz-Hardt, S. (2007) "Group decision making under conditions of distributed knowledge: The information asymmetries model," *Academy of Management Review* 32(2), 459–479.

Choi, T. Y. and Hartley, J. L. (1996) "An exploration of supplier selection practices across the supply chain," *Journal of Operations Management 14*(4), 333–343.

Das, T. K. and Teng, B.-S. (1999) "Cognitive biases and strategic decision processes: An integrative perspective," *Journal of Management Studies 36*(6), 757–778.

Dean, J. W., Jr. and Sharfman, M. P. (1993) "Procedural rationality in the strategic decision-making process," *Journal of Management Studies 30*(4), 587–610.

DeKay, M. L., Miller, S. A., Schley, D. R. and Erford, B. M. (2014) "Proleader and antitrailer information distortion and their effects on choice and postchoice memory," *Organizational Behavior and Human Decision Processes 125*(2), 134–150.

Dekel, O. and Schurr, A. (2014) "Cognitive biases in government procurement – An experimental study," *Review of Law & Economics 10*(2), 169–200.

De Treville, S., Cattani, K. and Saarinen, L. (2017) "Technical note: Option-based costing and the volatility portfolio," *Journal of Operations Management 49*(1), 77–81.

Dickson, G. W. (1966) "An analysis of vendor selection systems and decisions," *Journal of Purchasing 2*(1), 5–17.

Ellram, L. M. and Feitzinger, E. (1997) "Using total profit analysis to model supply chain decisions," *Journal of Cost Management 11*(4), 12–21.

Ellram, L. M. and Siferd, S. P. (1993) "Purchasing: The cornerstone of the total cost of ownership concept," *Journal of Business Logistics 14*(1), 163–184.

Epley, N. and Gilovich, T. (2006) "The anchoring-and-adjustment heuristic: Why the adjustments are insufficient," *Psychological Science 17*(4), 311–318.

Erhun, F. and Tayur, S. (2003) "Enterprise-wide optimization of total landed cost at a grocery retailer," *Operations Research 51*(3), 343–353.

Ericksen, P. (2020) "Purchasing's hidden potential: Strategy over short-term gains," *Industry Week*. www.industryweek.com/supply-chain/supply-chain-initiative/article/21133374/purchasings-hidden-potential-strategy-over-shortterm-gains. Accessed 8 June 2020

Fischhoff, B., Slovic, P. and Lichtenstein, S. (1978) "Fault trees: Sensitivity of estimated failure probabilities to problem representation," *Journal of Experimental Psychology: Human Perception and Performance 4*(2), 330–344.

Gigerenzer, G. and Goldstein, D. G. (1996) "Reasoning the fast and frugal way: Models of bounded rationality," *Psychological Review 103*(4), 650–669.

Gray, J. V., Esenduran, G., Rungtusanatham, M. J. and Skowronski, K. (2017) "Why in the world did they reshore? Examining small to medium-sized manufacturer decisions," *Journal of Operations Management 49–51*(1), 37–51.

Gray, J. V., Helper, S. and Osborn, B. (2020) "Value first, cost later: Total value contribution as a new approach to sourcing decisions," *Journal of Operations Management 66*(6), 735–750.

Helper, S. and MacDuffie, J. P. (2003) "Suppliers and intermediaries," in B. Kogut (ed.), *The Global Internet Economy* (pp. 331–380), Boston, MA: The MIT Press.

Helper, S., MacDuffie, J. P. and Sabel, C. (2000) "Pragmatic collaborations: Advancing knowledge while controlling opportunism," *Industrial and Corporate Change 9*(3), 443–488.

Hinterhuber, A. and Snelgrove, T. C. (2017) *Value First then Price: Quantifying Value in Business to Business Markets from the Perspective of Both Buyers and Sellers*, Abingdon, UK: Taylor & Francis.

Holmstrom, B. (1979) "Moral hazard and observability," *Bell Journal of Economics 10*(1), 74–91.

Holmstrom, B. and Milgrom, P. (1991) "Multitask principal-agent analyses: Incentive contracts, asset ownership, and job design," *Journal of Law, Economics and Organization 7*, 24–52.

Jap, S. D. (2002) "Online reverse auctions: Issues, themes, and prospects for the future," *Journal of the Academy of Marketing Science 30*(4), 506–525.

Johnson, P. F., Leenders, M. R. and Flynn, A. E. (2011) *Purchasing and Supply Management* (14th ed.), New York: McGraw-Hill Higher Education.

Kaufmann, L., Carter, C. R. and Buhrmann, C. (2010) "Debiasing the supplier selection decision: A taxonomy and conceptualization," *International Journal of Physical Distribution & Logistics Management 40*(10), 792–821.

Kaufmann, L., Meschnig, G. and Reimann, F. (2014) "Rational and intuitive decision-making in sourcing teams: Effects on decision outcomes," *Journal of Purchasing and Supply Management 20*(2), 104–112.

Kaufmann, L., Michel, A. and Carter, C. R. (2009) "Debiasing strategies in supply management decision-making," *Journal of Business Logistics 30*(1), 85–106.

Kaufmann, L., Wagner, C. M. and Carter, C. R. (2017) "Individual modes and patterns of rational and intuitive decision-making by purchasing managers," *Journal of Purchasing and Supply Management 23*(2), 82–93.

Kellermanns, F. W., Walter, J., Floyd, S. W., Lechner, C. and Shaw, J. C. (2011) "To agree or not to agree? A meta-analytical review of strategic consensus and organizational performance," *Journal of Business Research 64*(2), 126–133.

Kern, D., Moser, R., Hartmann, E. and Moder, M. (2012) "Supply risk management: Model development and empirical analysis," *International Journal of Physical Distribution & Logistics Management 42*(1), 60–82.

Kerr, S. (1975) "On the folly of rewarding A, while hoping for B," *Academy of Management Journal 18*(4), 769–783.

Ketokivi, M., Turkulainen, V., Seppälä, T., Rouvinen, P. and Ali-Yrkkö, J. (2017) "Why locate manufacturing in a high-cost country? A case study of 35 production location decisions," *Journal of Operations Management 49*, 20–30.

Kleindorfer, P. R. and Saad, G. H. (2005) "Managing disruption risks in supply chains," *Production and Operations Management 14*(1), 53–68.

Lienland, B., Baumgartner, A. and Knubben, E. (2013) "The undervaluation of corporate reputation as a supplier selection factor: An analysis of ingredient branding of complex products in the manufacturing industry," *Journal of Purchasing and Supply Management 19*(2), 84–97.

Lindgreen, A. and Wynstra, F. (2005) "Value in business markets: What do we know? Where are we going?" *Industrial marketing management 34*(7), 732–748.

Mahoney, T. C. and Helper, S. (2017) *Ensuring American Manufacturing Leadership Through Next-Generation Supply Chains*, Ann Arbor: Mforesight: Alliance for Manufacturing Foresight. https://deepblue.lib.umich.edu/bitstream/handle/2027.42/145153/SupplyChainReport_Digital_FINAL_reduced.pdf?sequence=1

Marewski, J. N., Gaissmaier, W. and Gigerenzer, G. (2010) "Good judgments do not require complex cognition," *Cognitive Processing 11*(2), 103–121.

Mieritz, L. and Kirwin, B. (2005) "Defining garter total cost of ownership," Gartner Research. ID Number: G00131837. Publication Date: 8 December 2005.

Milgrom, P. R. and Roberts, J. D. (1992) *Economics, Organization and Management*. Englewood Cliffs, NJ: Prentice Hall.

Morssinkhof, S., Wouters, M. and Warlop, L. (2011) "Effects of providing total cost of ownership information on attribute weights in purchasing decisions," *Journal of Purchasing and Supply Management 17*(2), 132–142.

Oliva, R. and Watson, N. (2011) "Cross-functional alignment in supply chain planning: A case study of sales and operations planning," *Journal of Operations Management 29*(5), 434–448.

Pinto, M. B., Pinto, J. K. and Prescott, J. E. (1993) "Antecedents and consequences of project team cross-functional cooperation," *Management Science 39*(10), 1281–1297.

Reshoring Initiative. (2020) "Total cost of ownership estimator," reshorenow.org/TCO_Estimator.cfm

Riedl, D. R., Kaufmann, L., Zimmermann, C. and Perols, J. L. (2013) "Reducing uncertainty in supplier selection decisions: Antecedents and outcomes of procedural rationality," *Journal of Operations Management* (31), 24–36.

Roberto, M. A. (2004) "Strategic decision-making processes: Beyond the efficiency-consensus trade-off," *Group & Organization Management 29*(6), 625–658.

Sharland, A., Eltantawy, R. A. and Giunipero, L. C. (2003) "The impact of cycle time on supplier selection and subsequent performance outcomes," *Journal of Supply Chain Management 39*(3), 4–12.

Siegfried, M. (2013) "Supply management organizations are moving from a low-cost-country strategy to a best sourcing plan that focuses on value, total cost of ownership and a changing world," *Inside Supply Management 24*(2), 26–27.

Simon, H. A. (1978) "Rationality as process and as product of thought," *The American Economic Review* 68(2), 1–16.

Stanczyk, A., Foerstl, K., Busse, C. and Blome, C. (2015) "Global sourcing decision-making processes: Politics, intuition, and procedural rationality," *Journal of Business Logistics 36*(2), 160–181.

Tversky, A. and Kahneman, D. (1974) "Judgment under uncertainty: Heuristics and biases," *Science 185*(4157), 1124–1131.

Tversky, A. and Kahneman, D. (1981) "The framing of decisions and the psychology of choice," *Science 211*(4481), 453–458.

Vitasek, K., Rijt, J. V., Snelgrove, T., Tiura, D., Tate, W., Keith, B., Holliman, S. and Coquis, M. (2012) "Unpacking Best Value: Understanding and Embracing Value Based Approaches for Procurement," *White Paper by the University of Tennessee and Sourcing Interests Group*. http://www.theforefrontgroup.com/pdf/unpacking-best-value.pdf. Accessed 15 October 2015.

Wynstra, F., Anderson, J. C., Narus, J. A. and Wouters, M. (2012) "Supplier development responsibility and NPD project outcomes: The roles of monetary quantification of differences and supporting-detail gathering," *Journal of Product Innovation Management 29*(S1), 103–123.

Wouters, M., Anderson, J. C., Narus, J. A. and Wynstra, F. (2009) "Improving sourcing decisions in NPD projects: Monetary quantification of points of difference," *Journal of Operations Management 27*(1), 64–77.

Wouters, M., Anderson, J. C. and Wynstra, F. (2005) "The adoption of total cost of ownership for sourcing decisions-a structural equations analysis," *Accounting, Organizations and Society 30*(2), 167–191.

Yin, Y., Stecke, K. E., Swink, M. and Kaku, I. (2017) "Lessons from *seru* production on manufacturing competitively in a high cost environment," *Journal of Operations Management 49*(1), 67–76.

Young, R. R., Swan, P. F., Thomchick, E. A. and Ruamsook, K. (2009) "Extending landed cost models to improve offshore sourcing decisions," *International Journal of Physical Distribution & Logistics Management 39*(4), 320–333.

14 Interview

Selling value to purchasing

Snelgrove, Todd C. and Stensson, Bo-Inge

TODD C. SNELGROVE: How has procurement evolved over the years at SKF?

BO-INGE STENSSON: Over the last three to four years we've undergone a procurement transformation at SKF. From what was a totally decentralized setup, all procurement at SKF is 100% centralized today. By applying leading purchasing and supply chain management practices, we've also gone from a price/delivery/meet-basic-quality mind-set to a buying mind-set of total-cost/value-buying strategic mind-set. By developing a strategic supplier base, we've also enabled value generation through supplier co-innovation programs and risk mitigation through our Responsible Sourcing Program.

TODD C. SNELGROVE: Why did that happen?

BO-INGE STENSSON: Two events occurred simultaneously. First, our CEO saw how we were quantifying and measuring true value and total cost of ownership on our sales side and wanted a structured process within procurement, because in the past we weren't measuring all the possible costs and benefits of different supplier offerings. Second, the executive board implemented a centralized procurement operating model to make sure SKF could reach its long-term strategic targets in terms of operating profit margin, return on capital employed, and growth. By leveraging SKF's total sourcing volume across all SKF businesses and by developing a capable strategic supplier base, we've built a strong foundation to give SKF competitive advantages in the markets where we operate. By this we also fully make use of our strategic supplier base capacities and capabilities to drive performance.

TODD C. SNELGROVE: Give an example of when SKF paid a higher price because of a better value.

BO-INGE STENSSON: I can give many examples across both direct and indirect material sourcing. A rigid strategic sourcing process across all categories we buy includes evaluating cost drivers and value drivers across the entire supply/value chain. This process enables us to evaluate, in a transparent way, total cost including price, reduced material usage, shorter setup times, better cash flow, lower energy consumption, faster time to market, and reduced capital tied up in inventories. We can look at hundreds of different drivers of cost and value. Value of shorter lead times, risk management, and better supply chain agility/resilience is also considered.

TODD C. SNELGROVE: How important is it that suppliers quantify the value they create?

BO-INGE STENSSON: It's very important. In general, suppliers have trouble selling us on their value if they can't quantify it. It's very important that suppliers are able to present a convincing business case that substantiates how their offer will improve our own key metrics.

DOI: 10.4324/9781003177937-18

It's critical to profitably grow in today's competitive business landscape. Suppliers need to understand their customer's value proposition and what drives value in the supply chain.

TODD C. SNELGROVE: What's in it for the suppliers who can quantify value for SKF?

BO-INGE STENSSON: More profitable growth, access to leading business practices when dealing with a world-class and leading company. Trust me – they'll have a better chance of getting a price increase if they can demonstrate the value they have and will deliver for us.

TODD C. SNELGROVE: How was the procurement function within SKF perceived in the past, and how is it perceived today?

BO-INGE STENSSON: In the past, I would say, we were generally seen as a non-strategic function, and many times the business units only brought us in to finalize agreements they'd already made. Procurement today, however, is seen as a true strategic business partner delivering value to the bottom line. Through a smart procurement/sourcing business model that forges business requirements with a global category and supplier strategy, we ensure that we focus on the right business priorities and deliver results quickly.

TODD C. SNELGROVE: How did suppliers respond when you said they had to start proving value?

BO-INGE STENSSON: We've been ruthless for many years when it comes to supplier performance. Supplier performance is measured in terms of QCDIM (quality, cost, delivery, innovation, and management capabilities) focused on driving total cost and value thinking. For almost 10 years we have stayed the course, and this also now pays off in a better understanding of value and total-cost thinking.

TODD C. SNELGROVE: I've noticed your new email signature and the – we can call it – branding of the SKF Procurement Team. Can you touch on that briefly?

BO-INGE STENSSON: "Turning costs into value." We've also incorporated the 3Ps – performance/profit/progress – in our procurement brand. It really states the DNA of a high-performing global procurement organization. It sets the direction for what we want to achieve in our daily business.

TODD C. SNELGROVE: How do you get the businesses to engage procurement early on so that a discussion based on real needs, benefits, value can be determined?

BO-INGE STENSSON: First of all, now business units come to us, because they see us as a valuable resource. Now all people in the businesses that work with purchasing/supply-related operations either report or belong to the global purchasing operation. This gives us huge leverage to use our global resource base in an agile, adaptive, aligned manner. Every year we agree, with our business partners, on the top priorities via a signed SLA (service-level agreement). Through monthly follow-ups we can then ensure progress and performance and that targeted profit levels are achieved.

TODD C. SNELGROVE: How is your procurement team measured?

BO-INGE STENSSON: Before, it was very much about price reductions and annual negotiation results. Today it's all about how we can reduce the total cost impacting the company's bottom line, looking much more on a holistic basis of what's good for SKF (see Figure 14.1). Second, we are also measured on how well we've developed and how well we run our supplier base in terms of QCDIM. Third, we're also measured based on how well we continually move our procurement operation toward high performance, by developing people and talent and through continuous capability-building via training programs.

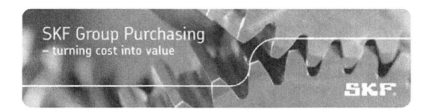

Figure 14.1

TODD C. SNELGROVE: Does SKF enter into pay-for-performance agreements, where suppliers are paid based on the value delivered?

BO-INGE STENSSON: We're entering into more and more performance-based contracts including fulfilment of our Responsible Sourcing Program. This program outlines how suppliers can contribute to reduce Green House Gas – emissions in our supply chain – reduce waste, and drive circular economy activities.

TODD C. SNELGROVE: Is this a culture change for the procurement team at SKF?

BO-INGE STENSSON: In the last four years we've undergone a procurement transformation at SKF. I'm very proud of what we've achieved: business- and demand-driven, innovative procurement. The journey is the target. To constantly change and drive continuous improvements will ensure that we maintain SKF's global competitiveness, generating value for shareholders, customers/suppliers, society, and our employees.

TODD C. SNELGROVE: Any final comments?

BO-INGE STENSSON: For the future it is so important that our business partners understand their customers' value propositions and that we understand our suppliers' value propositions. Understanding the end-to-end value chain and what creates value will create differentiation and competitiveness.

Reducing total cost of ownership and creating sustained value for the final customer are a key priority. To do so, our partners need to be able to measure their impact, not just offer vague promises.

Update 2021 Perspectives – as an expert in supply chain and procurement, working globally and in numerous industries, what new insights do you have now that should resonate with sales?

TODD C. SNELGROVE: What are some things that Procurement Organizations do that unintentionally leads to loosing value?

BO-INGE STENSSON: Not taking your time to build a TCO and Value Sourcing strategy. It is also a leadership issue. Top Management needs to walk the talk and set the right culture and performance indicators to drive the right behavior in the organization.

TODD C. SNELGROVE: What are the things that sales people do that unintentionally hurt their sales performance?

BO-INGE STENSSON: Too short term focused, to save the quarterly results. Salespeople should understand that it is not companies that compete, it is the supply chains. Salespeople should invest more in understanding their customers' value proposition, what are the burning platforms, what problems can my product and service offering solve, and what opportunities can they create. How can my company make my customers successful by delivering profitable growth, competitiveness, and differentiation?

TODD C. SNELGROVE: What reactions have you seen the procurement profession doing during the recent crisis, and what will be the impact for them in the future and how do salespeople address?

BO-INGE STENSSON: The last 5 years or so, the business risks in global business have increased, underpinned by the trade wars, the pandemic, and political uncertainty among other things. The sustainability and environmental agenda have got a much higher and important focus both from investors, customers, and shareholders. Also, the inflow of new disruptive technologies and business models creates both challenges and opportunities.

The reactions? Driving risk mitigation strategies, building resilient supply chains, and developing a sustainability business models based on total cost and value have never bene more important.

15 Using best value to get the best bottom line

Vitasek, Kate

Many buyers and suppliers are easily frustrated when it comes time to negotiate a fair price for value. In fact, the situation is somewhat paradoxical. On the one hand, the parties are discussing value; on the other hand, they're bickering about what is fair with conventional tug-of-war negotiation tactics. Bertini and Gourville (2012), in the *Harvard Business Review*, issued a plea for action, challenging companies to rethink how they price for their services. They asserted: "The way most companies make money is not just broken; it is destructive" (p. 96).

Traditionally, the best suppliers demand a price "premium" for their product or service as a way to justify what they perceive to be a higher-value offering. In other cases, they charge very high consulting fees to justify the "brainpower" in value-added services, regardless of whether the solution provided creates the desired results.

No other subject gets as much attention when two companies are entering, or extending, their business relationship as the effort to establish a fair pricing structure. Architecting a fair price and pricing framework dominates the procurement field, and rightly so.

But for progressive procurement and sourcing professionals, price is not just about "the price" or about pitting buyers and sellers against one another as they sit across the negotiation table. The key to sustainable profits is to unlock the hidden value in buyer – supplier business relationships – and then buy on *best value*. This means shifting focus from "the price" and beginning to adopt more sophisticated approaches such as total cost of ownership (TCO) and "best value" supplier selection techniques (Vitasek, Snelgrove et al., 2012).

While TCO and best value have become industry buzzwords in the last decade, the use of both concepts is far from widespread. The good news is that there's a growing and welcome realization in the sourcing and procurement world that lowest price is not the same as lowest cost, nor does it necessarily create long-term value.

Price versus best value: Why a best value approach is needed

As mentioned, the value mantra is this: *it's not how little you pay, it's how much you get.* That's the basic difference and tension between price and value. And today's procurement professionals not only need to understand this difference; they should use their procurement toolkit to help them put the concept into practice.

When used, best-value approaches become the bridge that spans that tension, because determining the true cost and value equation assures companies they are getting the best "deal."

DOI: 10.4324/9781003177937-19

Unfortunately, the usual modus operandi for many businesses is to seek price reductions that provide immediate gratification rather than buying on best value, which for many managers is too long term, involves too many departments, and is too complicated and abstract. Picking a supplier on price is so prevalent that many corporations and even government agencies have had policies that enforce the "lowest price" practice for decades. For example, beginning in 1954, the Minnesota Supreme Court ruled that state agencies were required by law to award contracts to the supplier with the lowest price using an open-bid process. The rationale? To divest public officials of discretion in order to avoid even the appearance of "fraud, favoritism, and undue influence" (State of Minnesota, 1954).

Low-bid approaches are paved with the good intentions of "watching out for taxpayer dollars." But this approach also has fundamental flaws. Insisting solely on low-bid contracts does not necessarily generate savings (Vitasek, Snelgrove et al., 2012). Indeed, cost and time overruns are often run-of-the-mill, and there is little motivation for the contractor to innovate or bring expenses down because doing so may reduce profits.

While many organizations do not have to follow "low-bid" policies, too often they fail to do their due diligence in digging below the purchase "price" to determine overall total costs of ownership and conduct a proper best-value analysis.

A good example of a company not doing its homework is an original equipment manufacturer that chose to move from an onshore supplier to an offshore supplier in China. Original estimates showed a price savings of almost 75% compared with work performed by the supplier in the region. What the company did not factor in were the increased costs to manage the relationship with the Chinese supplier. The company's travel budget increased by 400% as engineers and quality teams flew business class to visit with the supplier for new product launches and quarterly reviews. This example shows how 100% of the promised savings did not hit the bottom line because the company failed to factor in the total cost of doing business with an offshore supplier before making the final decision (Vitasek, 2013).

Here's the good news: Best-value approaches, tools, and methods such as TCO are gaining traction. Even government agencies that traditionally relied on competitively bid "lowest price" policies have begun to deploy best-value concepts. In 2001, the state of Minnesota enacted Statute §161.3410, which infused discretion back into the process. The Minnesota Department of Transportation used the new law for selecting the contractor to build the I-35 bridge replacement after the bridge's sudden collapse in 2009. Why? It would enable them to balance cost, quality, and timeliness as key factors in how they chose the contractors that would ultimately be charged with rebuilding the bridge. The result? They selected a contractor that had the highest price – yet offered the overall best value – resulting in one of the most successful bridge construction projects in history, winning over a dozen awards, and being erected in a staggeringly short time frame of less than 18 months (Vitasek, Manrodt et al., 2012).

Suppliers are also seeing the value of applying best value and TCO concepts. Some companies such as SKF – a market leader in bearings and related industrial products – have embraced the concepts of best value and TCO. SKF is so serious about it that the company appointed a full-time Global Manager of Value to study, improve, and institutionalize the concepts within SKF. For SKF, seeking to better understand TCO and best value has advantages (SKF, 2014). By knowing their costs and the value their products provide, they can help their customers conduct business cases that help support SKF's premium price (Vitasek, Snelgrove et al., 2012).

Total cost of ownership – the foundation for determining value

The concept of TCO first emerged in the 1950s when experts such as Michigan State's Bowersox (2007) challenged conventional approaches to understanding the costs associated with logistics. He and a few colleagues believed that warehousing professionals needed to understand the total cost of a shipment – not just warehousing and transportation costs. Bowersox and other thought leaders established the National Council of Physical Distribution Management, now known as the Council of Supply Chain Management Professionals, to promote what they called total landed costs. The concept of total landed costs has evolved and expanded outside of the logistics profession. Today most industries refer to the concept as TCO.

TCO began to gain widespread traction in the information technology field in the late 1980s with the Gartner consulting group, where TCO was used to calculate all the costs of owning a desktop device, including capital, technical support, administrative, and end-user costs (West and Daigle, 2004). The TCO concept has evolved considerably over the years to embrace a more holistic approach to understanding the entire economic investment associated with any product – including costs of acquisition, operation, and disposal. In fact, this cradle-to-grave mentality is the basis for how most people define TCO. The existing literature and market consensus is that TCO is the "sum of purchase price plus all expenses incurred during the productive life cycle of a product, minus its salvage or resale price" (Anderson et al., 2004: 98). However, this definition assumes that total costs – once calculated – are static. Contemporaries are pushing the concept of TCO further back in the supply chain and encouraging suppliers to capture their total costs, challenging a more dynamic approach and encouraging companies to consider risks as well.

The TCO concept can best be described through a simple example of buying a car.

Each person considers different criteria to be important when purchasing a car. Intuitively, once the specifications are chosen, such as a four-door family sedan with automatic transmission, air conditioning, and a certain size engine, then one could assume that the choice is made based on a unit-price comparison of the options that meet those criteria. However, the costs of owning a car do not end with the initial purchase. The operating costs such as fuel consumption, average cost to repair or service, financing, insurance, depreciation rates, and numerous other costs live well beyond the acquisition of the car. Using these data, one might find that the car that initially appears to be expensive will actually provide the *lowest total cost* and therefore is a "better deal."

Practical approaches for applying TCO to comparing cars are gaining traction. There are even free TCO calculators available on the Internet to help people determine the costs of owning different types of cars; they include such costs as depreciation, interest on the loan, taxes and fees, insurance premiums, fuel costs, maintenance, and repairs. Edmunds, a website for car buyers, has created its own TCO acronym, "true cost to own," which allows customers to calculate the cost differences between cars (Edmunds, 2014).

Determining total cost of ownership

The only way to get to the real total costs is to document total costs from an end-to-end perspective – capturing the costs from *both* buyer and supplier. This includes all cross-departmental costs within the buyer's organization as well. The earlier example of the procurement group that moved to a Chinese supplier is a good example of how costs "popped up" in other areas – such as travel – that were not obvious to the procurement team when they first did their price comparison.

The following definitions and calculations help clarify the concept of understanding a buyer's total cost (Vitasek, Snelgrove et al., 2012: 6):

Supplier's Costs = Supplier's Direct Costs + Supplier's Indirect Costs
Supplier's Cost ≠ Supplier's Total Costs
Supplier's Total Costs = Supplier's Cost + Supplier's "Hidden" Soft and Hard Costs + Costs Associated with Supplier's Risk
Purchase Price = Supplier's Total Costs + Supplier's Profit
Buyer's Total Costs = Purchase Price + Buyer's "Hidden" Soft and Hard Costs + Costs Associated with Buyer's Risk

A baseline TCO analysis includes the costs under the current scenario as well as what is projected based on the set assumptions. As mentioned, the preferred approach is always transparency, where the total costs to own a product or use a service over time are factored into the price. Some of the most common items to include in a TCO analysis include these:

- Design and development costs
- Hard costs (e.g., labor and assets)
- Operating costs (e.g., energy and maintenance costs)
- Soft costs (e.g., overhead, "corporate allocations," training)
- Installation and commissioning costs
- Governance costs (e.g., cost to manage the relationship)
- Software costs
- Supply chain support costs
- Retirement, disposal costs, or residual value
- Opportunity costs, including reduced downtime, increased production yield, or sales value or increased sales or margin for developing a better product
- Transaction costs, including cost of switching suppliers and costs associated with a competitive bid and contracting process
- Environmental or sustainability costs or savings

While this list provides guidelines, the physical act of identifying true total costs is not entirely straightforward and often not easy. Borrowing from a tried-but-true concept, the "Priceberg" graphic depicts the "below the surface" costs, which ironically are estimated to contain roughly 80% of total costs. The Priceberg (Figure 15.1) illustrates the importance of looking at the hidden costs (Vitasek, Snelgrove et al., 2012).

Understanding only the price (above the waterline) is analogous to seeing only the tip of the iceberg. Often what is out of sight can and will cause the greatest damage. For example, many companies do not consider disposal costs, which can be significant. Numerous studies confirm that initial purchase price can often be the smallest component of an organization's costs. For example, an Accenture Consulting report shows that the purchase price of industrial equipment (such as pumps, fans, or gearboxes) represents only 12% of its total cost (Snelgrove, 2012).

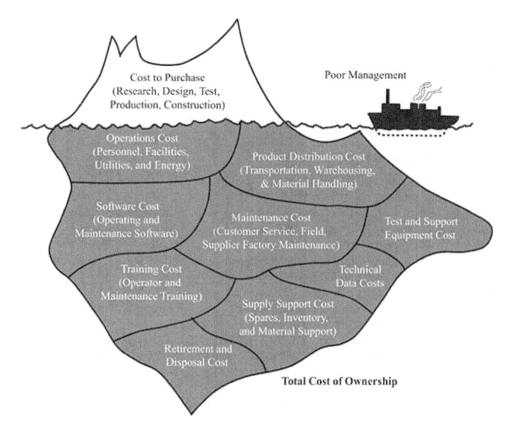

Figure 15.1 The Priceberg

Although cost models are the foundation for TCO, leading authorities of TCO are further pushing the boundaries of what should be included in a TCO analysis, arguing that cost of risk should be also be considered. Over the last decade, supply chains have grown increasingly vulnerable to supply chain disruption (Murphy, 2006). The costs associated with these risks – if realized – are real and should be factored into any TCO decision.

Examples of risk include natural events (blizzards, earthquakes, floods, hurricanes, tornados, tsunamis, wildfires); external man-made events (labor strikes, riots, terrorist attacks, trade embargoes, and wars); and internal man-made events (industrial accidents, business failures, product recalls, machine breakdowns) (Murphy, 2006).

To illustrate the cost of risk, consider Mattel in 2009; it was fined $2.3 million for importing toys from Chinese suppliers that violated lead-paint safety standards. In addition to the fine, Mattel incurred the hard cost associated with the recall of approximately 20 million toys (Kavilanz, 2009) as well as the soft cost of consumer reaction.

A good approach to determining the impact of risk on the potential costs is to do a risk assessment and sensitivity analysis. Companies can develop a model to determine the impact of various assumptions and risk factors. When developing a sensitivity analysis, companies should rank the probabilities of specific outcomes. Some companies even invest in risk simulation software using the Monte Carlo method to help boost awareness of the various risk probabilities and their impacts. Monte Carlo simulation methods were originally used for space exploration, but they are more routinely used by regular businesses to help predict the probability and impact of risk events. (Monte Carlo simulation is a problem-solving technique that uses computers to approximate the probability of certain outcomes by running multiple trial runs, called simulations, using random variables.) Once companies understand risk probabilities, they can create approaches in their pricing model that help offset the risk in the smartest manner. Offset approaches could include insurance, training, and detailed protocols.

Open-book approach as an enabler

The best way to capture the true boundary-spanning TCO components is with a high degree of transparency that exposes the hidden costs across all parties – the functional silos within an organization and the supplier. Although it might be hard to capture internal costs, it will be impossible to capture costs without transparency with a supplier.

A transparent approach to sharing an organization's and supplier's costs often starts with what is called an open-book approach. Using an open-book approach with suppliers allows the parties to build a fact-based discussion around actual costs. By understanding true costs, the companies can shift their focus from sitting across the table negotiating price to probing how both parties can collaborate to eliminate non-value-added activities, duplicative efforts, and risks that drive up costs.

Buyers and suppliers often have differing viewpoints about transparently sharing costs and profit data. Unfortunately, they may tend to avoid transparency. Concerns and criticisms about openly sharing costs, profits, and other key data are real, so buyers and suppliers should openly address concerns about transparency early on in their discussions.

Suppliers can feel especially exposed when sharing costs. If a supplier reveals its true costs, it is easy for the buyer to determine the supplier's profit – which makes many suppliers uncomfortable. A major fear is that the organization will use the information to attack the supplier's margins, which in turn reduces profitability. Buyers that do attack a supplier's margins often find that suppliers are good at hiding real costs, which results in a shell game as the supplier shifts costs around to maintain their target margins. Smart buyers will work collaboratively with their suppliers to drive efficiencies and reduce non-value-added work rather than focus on margin reduction as a quick win for a price concession.

Another criticism of transparency involves the buying organization. Often when it comes time to share, the buyer will look at transparency as a one-way street – the supplier is supposed to share information, but the buying organization is exempt. This situation occurs often, but there are ways to address it.

One way is to have a clear understanding of the business at hand and mutual agreement on a statement of intent that specifies margin targets and what the organization will do with the TCO assessment. For example, a statement of intent might indicate that the goal of transparency is to allow the buyer to identify cost drivers and develop improvement initiatives that can help reduce costs. Or a major retailer and supplier might work together on packaging to decrease shipping costs. If margin targets are properly set early in the discussions, the transparent sharing of costs, and of margins, is easier and more comfortable.

Another approach is to jointly create an end-to-end process map: using this approach enables the parties to discuss and allocate costs to the various buckets of activities as a way to highlight where value is added (or where there is duplication of effort).

Choosing transparency will enable a much higher shared understanding of the true TCO. Although transparency is strongly favored in establishing accurate total costs, it may not be feasible for some companies. Therefore, the only way to get close to a true TCO is for both buyers and suppliers to share as much information as possible. Over time, companies become more trusting, and they can revisit and refine the pricing model as they learn more.

Best value

The conventional definition of TCO is exclusively concerned with the cost side of customer value. However, the real power is that TCO provides a foundation for making best-value sourcing decisions. TCO is defined as the foundation for making best-value decisions (Vitasek, 2010). The advantage of using a TCO model is that by quantifying expected outcomes, organizations can make clear and informed decisions when it comes to price/value decisions.

To be successful, procurement professionals need to examine and weigh what the best net value is for the whole organization. Unfortunately, sometimes outdated thoughts such as "That's not what I am measured on" or "That's someone else's problem" creep in. It is imperative that management insist and consistently reaffirm that shareholders care about the best net long-term decision and not focus on one function saving a little while costing another function a lot more.

How to "buy" best value

But how do you determine the value side of the equation? An easy way to explain the concept of best value is through a basic example, such as picking a restaurant for lunch. There are many reasons why someone might pick one restaurant over another. Criteria might include proximity for reduced travel time, service levels, taste and variety of food, atmosphere, and price. Depending on the situation, different restaurants are chosen. A great choice for a business lunch with a client might not be the same choice someone would make for a quick bite to eat in order to get back to the office to finish working on a report.

Determining best value for a product or service is much the same – it's about picking the best option that fits the current and projected need. The options go well beyond costs. Jaconelli and Sheffield (2000) describe the intent of best value as enabling a balance between cost and quality considerations while ensuring ongoing value for money and promoting continuous improvement to further value for money.

Scotland emerged as a leader in applying best-value thinking (Cooperative Research Centre, 2002). The country is a leader because of a unique political situation whereby the Scottish Parliament was separated from that of Great Britain in 1999. Under the devolution, the Scottish Parliament established 32 local authorities that suddenly gained significant power and budget in procuring public services ranging from education, to street cleaning, to housing, to leisure and cultural services, to welfare services. Local authorities were eager to improve the services received for their money (Wisniewski and Stewart, 2004). Because of Scotland's success in using best-value principles, its parliament established best-value concepts in legislation under the local government in Scotland Act in 2003. The act sets out eight main criteria (Cooperative Research Centre, 2002) to define best value:

- Commitment and leadership
- Competitiveness and trading

- Responsiveness and consultation
- Sustainable development
- Sound governance and management of resources
- Equalities
- Review and option appraisal
- Accountability

It is interesting and instructive that the 2003 Act does not list price as a component. Although the list given earlier is a good one, best-value criteria will vary for every product or service purchased. Again, determining best value is about picking the best option that fits a particular need. Other common criteria include these:

- Environmental sustainability
- Diversity program excellence
- Social responsibility
- Business interface efficiency
- Market penetration
- Brand image
- Speed to market
- Market-dominant supply chain
- Competitive market advantage
- Technological advancement
- Innovation
- Cultural competence
- Growth capability
- Counter trade optimization
- Cash management

Calculating best value

Best value can really be thought of as an equation that balances the decision criteria when choosing from alternatives. The following calculation illustrates how to calculate best value (Vitasek, Snelgrove et al., 2012: 8):

Best Value = Optimum Benefit
(sum of criteria as defined by the buyer)
– Buyer's Total Costs

A good example of a best-value calculation again comes from the Minnesota Department of Transportation (MnDOT) during the process for selecting a contractor to rebuild the collapsed I-35 collapsed bridge (Vitasek, Manrodt et al., 2012). To ensure transparency and objectivity in the selection process, MnDOT was required by law to list selection criteria for every stage of the process and the evaluation weight of each criterion.

MnDOT carefully outlined the performance criteria for selecting a contractor by documenting the formal evaluation criteria and evaluation process. The RFP listed MnDOT's six primary desired outcomes that potential bidders needed to accomplish.

1. Safety

    a. Provide a safe project area for workers, the traveling public, community, environment, and emergency services during the execution of the project.
    b. Provide a solution consistent with MnDOT design and construction standards.
    c. Provide a solution adaptable to the recovery efforts of the collapsed bridge.

2. Quality

    a. Implement a quality management system that ensures the requirements of the project will be met or exceeded and ensure public confidence.
    b. Reduce future maintenance costs by providing a high-quality project.

3. Schedule

    a. Complete construction by December of 2008.

4. Environmental compliance

    a. Provide a quality product with minimal impacts to the environment while using context sensitive solutions.

5. Budget

    a. Implement innovative solutions to maximize the return on taxpayer investment by reducing costs and improving quality of the transportation system.

6. Aesthetics

    a. Utilize visual quality techniques and context-sensitive design to incorporate the bridge into the surrounding environment (quoted in Vitasek, Snelgrove et al., 2012: 9).

MnDOT ultimately created a "best value formula" that would become the litmus test for selecting the winning bidder, with the contract award going to the bidder with the *lowest adjusted bid* representing the best value for MnDOT – not the lowest price. The formula comprised a technical score, the number of days to complete the project, and the contract bid price (Vitasek, Manrodt et al., 2012).

A paradigm shift – from price to pricing models

The trick to "buying" using value-based principles comes from determining the "fair" compensation for the supplier. So how do you establish what's fair? The customary way is to use a competitive process, get bids from suppliers, and compare the various "prices" from suppliers. This transactional approach works well for commodities where there is a great deal of competition, where products and services are relatively standardized, and where the environment is more static than dynamic. But what happens when there is little competition or when the environment is in flux, which can pose risks for either the buyer or the supplier based on changing market conditions? In these cases we suggest making a paradigm shift to using a "pricing model" instead of a "price."

MnDOT best value formula

Three components

- "A" = Contract bid price
- Plus "B" = Number of days to complete project, which is multiplied by $200,000 per day − $200,000 per day based on 50% of road user costs
- Divided by technical proposal average score

Result: Adjusted bid = (A) + (B × $200,000) divided by TPA
    Contract awarded to lowest adjusted bid

It is important to first understand the difference between a "price" and a "pricing model." Simply put, a price is something you pay for each transaction. Say the price for your Starbucks Grande two-pump vanilla latte is $3.25. In the MnDOT example, Flatiron Manson bid a price of $233,763,000 to rebuild the I-35 bridge (Vitasek, Manrodt et al., 2012).

A pricing model is fundamentally different: it is a mechanism that companies use to determine the optimum commercial agreement between the organization and the supplier. In some cases a pricing model consists of nothing more than costs, volume targets, and incentives based on helping an organization achieve value, such as market share, total cost savings, or customer satisfaction levels.

Many pricing models are expressed in a simple spreadsheet; however, some are more like a small, customized software package or macro-based Microsoft Excel spreadsheet. The term "model" is used because a good pricing model enables the parties to manipulate underlying assumptions, allowing them to "model" the outputs relative to the input components to determine a fair way to pay for goods and services. In a dynamic environment, a good pricing model creates a commercial pricing structure that equitably allocates risks and rewards with the purpose of realizing mutual gains for the duration of the agreement.

But how do you establish a pricing model to foster a win–win relationship? Unfortunately, there is no one-size-fits-all approach. There is no generic template or standard spreadsheet to help you get the correct pricing "answer." Establishing the right pricing and incentive mix can be complicated and technical. Yet you do not have to be an accountant, a consultant, or a software engineer to recognize the benefits of a fair pricing model that rewards for value creation.

The good news is that developing a pricing model is not a guessing game. Rather, it is a process that parties go through together with the goal of creating value. The best pricing models are based on transparent relationships that use a fact-based approach that begins with a sound TCO foundation. Buyers and suppliers should develop a pricing model through a best-value lens, striving to understand profitability levers that can add value for the buyer through increased revenue, reduced risk, improved working capital and capital investment productivity, or anything else that positively impacts an organization's profitability. Because value is based on the overall impact on a firm's profitability, the companies should establish the appropriate mechanisms for triggering payments when value is received.

Some of the characteristics of a good pricing model include the following:

- Input assumptions that are changeable. This allows for dynamic business conditions and enables the buyer and supplier to track the real impact of value versus assumed impact.
- Proof points that are supported by references and technical reasoning.
- Ranges of expected outcomes: ranges help focus the discussion based on reference points; in some cases where risk is high, or in extremely large deals, companies conduct sensitivity analysis or even Monte Carlo simulations to clearly show the potential impact.
- Clearly understandable calculations.
- Use of benchmarking data when possible to help set reasonable targets for potential benefits.

Many creative approaches are emerging to help buyers and suppliers establish ways to pay for value received. One of the simplest forms is to compensate suppliers for value through incentive payments. A commonly used approach is known as gainsharing, whereby a supplier receives a portion of any costs savings realized. This in essence becomes a price premium for a supplier. Gainsharing is good when cost reductions are a focus, but different approaches are needed when suppliers help buyers achieve value beyond costs.

More progressive value-based commercial models have emerged where payment to the supplier is tied directly to the supplier's ability to achieve outputs or even business-related outcomes. Two of the more notable approaches are performance-based and vested agreements. The previous chapter highlighted these models. This following section expands on how both performance-based and vested models apply a value-based approach to establish pricing between a buyer and suppliers.

Performance-based agreements

The relationship with suppliers under a performance-based agreement is different than with transactional providers, because some or all of a supplier's compensation is tied to their achieving a predefined output. Performance-based agreements are also called pay-for-performance because they often have an incentive (or penalty) tied to achievement of a predetermined performance target. The supplier's price usually includes guarantees for performance and/or a cost-savings glidepath.

A performance-based agreement typically splits pricing between "base" service fees (e.g., monthly fee to manage the workscope or even a base price per unit/per hour) and incentive/penalty fees tied to the supplier's outputs. For example, an information technology (IT) supplier may charge a monthly fee that typically covers all the basic costs necessary to set up and perform the service, whereas the incentive fee is for achieving the agreed-upon service level agreement (SLA). This method protects suppliers' base cost/ profitability while letting buyers see savings over time from baked-in price reductions and tying suppliers' fees to outputs.

A well-structured performance-based agreement includes an incentive framework, which is a mechanism for measuring performance and triggering incentive awards or payments. Using a clearly defined incentive framework with mutually defined terms is critical for both suppliers and customers. Unfortunately, in far too many performance-based agreements, buyers tend to unilaterally award incentives and assess penalties without input from suppliers or key-user stakeholders. If this determination is not done properly and fairly, a more adversarial buyer-supplier relationship may result.

Vested agreements

A vested agreement is a highly collaborative sourcing business model where both buyer and supplier have an economic (vested) interest in each other's success. Under a vested agreement, buyers and suppliers enter into collaborative arrangements designed to create value for all parties involved earlier and beyond the continuum of conventional buy-sell transaction-based agreement.

A vested pricing model rewards the supplier for delivering desired outcomes in the form of solutions rather than simply using transaction-based approach to pay a supplier for performing activities or supplying goods. The better the supplier is at achieving the buyer's desired outcomes, the greater the supplier's profits. This encourages suppliers to institute innovative and cost-effective methods of performing work to drive down total cost and/or drive up revenue while maintaining or improving service. Properly structured, a vested pricing model creates an economic exchange where the more successful the customer, the more successful the supplier. Likewise, a supplier that is not effective would be paid well below market rates.

Because vested relationships are often longer term and involve supplier investment, it is important that buyer and supplier devise a pricing model that incentivizes the supplier for the effectiveness of its innovations and prevents the supplier from becoming complacent under their longer-term relationship. A vested pricing model usually uses low margins for the base services coupled with incentives that enable suppliers to earn very high margins when they create value by achieving their customers' desired outcomes and solving their business problems.

A general rule of thumb is that "low" means below-market margins if the work would be bid – often as low as 50% of market margin. For example, if the work were to be bid out and the "market" margin was 10%, a vested deal might have a 5% margin for the base services. Using the 10% as "market," the rule of thumb we see in a vested pricing model allows the supplier to earn two to three times the market margin – or up to 20 to 30% profit margins – if they succeed in bringing transformation and innovation to their customer (Vitasek et al., 2013).

Regardless of the approach used to compensate a supplier, it is important for buyers to understand that *suppliers should earn a fair return for their investment.*

Conclusion

As organizations seek (and demand!) more value from their suppliers, they must realize that suppliers must be compensated with a fair return on their investment, ideas, and innovations that are at the heart of creating value.

Organizations are encouraged to take to heart the following lessons:

- Adopt a transparent approach to identifying true TCO and to jointly developing business cases that identify value surplus opportunities.
- Expand the lens with which value is calculated to include a system-wide approach, including developing business cases that look at the profitability factors for both the buyer and the supplier.

- Consider moving away from "prices" and opt for developing "pricing models" that reward suppliers when value is received.
- Learn about and test alternative commercial agreements such as performance-based or vested that shift accountability for delivering value to the supplier yet seek to reward them fairly for their risk.

The bottom line is that those who still use old-school approaches will find themselves in a race to the bottom, bickering over low price rather than seeking ways to establish sustainable supplier relationships that more fairly create value for buyers and suppliers. Moving to a "best-value" mind-set and orientation represents the future of procurement.

References

Anderson, J., Narus, J. and Narayandas, D. (2004) *Business Marketing Management: Understanding, Creating, and Delivering Value* (2nd ed.), Upper Saddle River, NJ: Prentice Hall.

Bertini, M. and Gourville, J. (2012) "Pricing to create shared value," *Harvard Business Review 90*(6), 96–104.

Bowersox, D. (2007) "SCM: The past is prologue," *Supply Chain Quarterly 2*. www.supplychainquarterly. com/topics/Strategy/scq200702future/. Accessed 18 September 2015

Cooperative Research Centre for Construction Innovation. (2002) Best Value Second Interim Report, Project No. 2002-035-C.

Edmunds. (2014) "How to use Edmunds True Cost to Own," www.edmunds.com/car-buying/true-cost-to-own-tco.html. Accessed 18 September 2015

Jaconelli, A. and Sheffield, J. (2000) "Best value: Changing roles and activities for human resource managers in Scottish local government," *International Journal of Public Sector Management 13*(7), 624–644.

Kavilanz, P. (2009) "Mattel fined $2.3 million over lead in toys," *CNNMoney.com.* http://money.cnn.com/2009/06/05/news/companies/cpsc/. Accessed 18 September 2015.

Murphy, J. (2006) *Managing Supply Chain Risk: Building in Resilience and Preparing for Disruption*, Denver, CO: WisdomNet.

SKF. (2014) "Lowest price ≠ lowest cost: Buying on total benefit of ownership boosts profitability by bringing sustainable savings to the bottom line," *SKF White Paper.* http://cdn2.hubspot.net/hubfs/332479/SKF_TCO_TBO_White_Paper.pdf?t=1441284795161. Accessed 18 September 2015.

Snelgrove, T. (2012) "Value pricing when you understand your customers: Total cost of ownership – Past, present and future," *Journal of Revenue and Pricing Management 11*(1), 76–80.

State of Minnesota. (1954) Griswold v. Ramsey County, 65 N.W.2d 647, p. 652.

Vitasek, K., Crawford, J., Nyden, J. and Kawamoto, K. (2010) *The Vested Outsourcing Manual*, New York: Palgrave Macmillan.

Vitasek, K., Ledyard, M. and Manrodt, K. (2013) *Vested Outsourcing: Five Rules That Will Transform Outsourcing* (2nd ed.), New York: Palgrave Macmillan.

Vitasek, K., Manrodt, K. and Kling, J. (2012) *Vested: How P&G, McDonald's, and Microsoft are Redefining Winning in Business Relationships*, New York: Palgrave Macmillan.

Vitasek, K., Snelgrove, T., Evans, D., Tate, W., Keith, B. and Holliman, S. (2012) *Unpacking Best Value: Understanding and Embracing Value Based Approaches for Procurement.* White paper by the University of Tennessee and Sourcing Interests Group. www.theforefrontgroup.com/pdf/unpacking-best-value.pdf. Accessed 15 October 2015

West, R. and Daigle, S. L. (2004) *Total Cost of Ownership: A Strategic Tool for ERP Planning and Implementation*, Philadelphia, PA: Center for Applied Research.

Wisniewski, M. and Stewart, D. (2004) "Performance measurement for stakeholders: The case of Scottish local authorities," *International Journal of Public Sector Management 17*(3), 222–233.

16 Value selling

The crucial importance of access to decision makers from the procurement perspective

Maguire, Rob

It all started so well. I had recently left my position as European Head of Materials and Indirect Procurement for Reckitt & Colman following a year-long stint as Head of Procurement Transformation. As the leader of a new and aspiring procurement consultancy, I was delighted to be asked to be the keynote speaker at a sales conference of a major global telecoms company. My theme was "Understanding the buyer's mind-set – co-creation in a commercial environment."

When I arrived on site in Barcelona, I was greeted by the organizing team and introduced to the conference leader. "We've got 500 of our best salespeople here, and we are expecting a lot of them," she said. "They are very interested to hear from a procurement expert and to try to get under the skin of the professional buyer."

She introduced me to my host for the event and moved on. It's at this point that it started to go downhill. His greeting "Pleased to meet you at last" seemed a bit abrupt, but I thought "That's salespeople for you." "I tried for two years to get 60 minutes in your diary and you wouldn't even return my calls," he added.

Clearly, as a senior leader in a global business with purchasing authority for nearly €10 million of spend across Europe on telecoms, I was an important person to the Head of Corporate Sales at EMEA. But, and it's a crucial but, just because I was important to him didn't mean he was important to me. I understand my importance as a customer from the fact that I have €10 million to spend. Why, though, does the fact that I spend €10 million in a marketplace make any particular salesperson more important to me than any other salesperson or even important enough for me to want to spend time with them?

To understand how we ended up here, we need to examine how a buyer thinks and acts:

- How they analyze expenditure.
- How the buying cycle works.
- How they approach strategy.
- Where they focus their time.

We can then look at the scope to build better relationships and examine how to get that crucial 60 minutes with a key decision maker or influencer.

First of all, consider my role as Head of Procurement. I have upward of 60 categories of spend, responsibility for almost €1 billion of contracts, and 30 factories across 12 countries all clamoring for my attention. To every factory, brand manager, department head, or budget holder their crisis, new product, or innovation is my highest priority.

Helping a salesperson meet their customer relationship management (CRM) target for meetings or their sales target for corporate sales is not high on my agenda.

DOI: 10.4324/9781003177937-20

Most corporate buyers would use as a start point some variant of the Kraljic (1983) portfolio purchasing model to prioritize their time and the focus of their attention.

Kraljic's portfolio model first came to prominence more than 30 years ago and proposed that suppliers and the goods and services they supply can be segmented according to the profit impact on the business and the risk or criticality of the supplies to the business.

The resulting four-box matrix (Figure 16.1; after Kraljic, 1983) presents a clear statement of intent for each of the portfolio segments.

High

Bottleneck	**Strategic**
Reduce risk	Partnership
Continuity	Value engineer
Conformance	Negotiate

Supply Risk/ Criticality

Routine	**Leverage**
Ignore	Leverage
Automate	Exploit
Bundle	Switch

Low   High

Profit Impact

Figure 16.1 Purchasing portfolio matrix

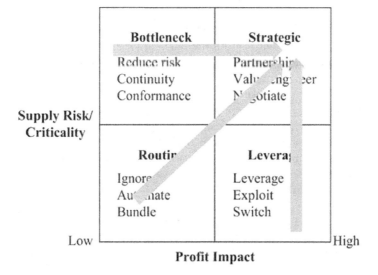

Figure 16.1a The Kralijc framework – supplier view

This is the first problem for the aspiring value seller – making sure the buyer sees you in a segment that gives you the opportunity to sell value.

Whenever I ask strategic account or key account managers (KAMs) where they see themselves, the answer is almost always in the Strategic quadrant.

The problem is that this is based on the seller's view of the seller's importance to the buyer. Frequently, this view can be supported by the customer's budget holders or users. It doesn't, however, take account of the buyer's views with reference to other areas of expenditure.

Bottleneck. If you find yourself in this quadrant, the good news is that there is unlikely to be much competitive pressure. The spend is of low value and is difficult. The key focus of the buyer is to avoid problems and to ensure security of supply and appropriate levels of service and quality. The bad news is that you are unlikely to feature high on the list of people that the buyers consider to be worth spending a lot of time with.

Routine. I think of these purchases as nuisance expenditures, which is a departure from Kraljic's original framework – he used the term "Routine." This is a bit of a blunt description of purchases that are seen as routine and of little commercial interest. I believe, however, that "nuisance" better describes how buyers see spend in this area – high-volume, low-value transactions that clog up the business. The goal is to have as little as possible to do with them.

The focus for the buyer is to reduce the cost of the transaction. Recent advances in digital marketplaces have made this a particular focus for web-based purchasing and ordering strategies. The objective is to spend as little energy as possible in this arena. Many buyers have completely distanced themselves from this quadrant by outsourcing this expenditure to services companies or aggregators who offer to take all the pain away by supplying everything in this quadrant as a one-stop shop.

Leverage. This is where the buyer is most at ease. The value of the expenditure is high enough to be worth spending time on, and the purchases are not so critical that they will expose the business to undue risk if something goes wrong. The buyer has power in the marketplace due to the potential size of the account and a number of suppliers to choose from. If you find yourself in this quadrant, then competition is everything. This isn't about the value you bring but about how you compare with other potential suppliers of similar products or services in the marketplace. You probably will get time in the buyer's diary – to discuss your prices and your response to their latest tender request or even reverse auction.

Strategic. This is the holy grail for the strategic account manager. The value of the spend is high enough to be important to both the seller and the buyer. Importantly, the buyer sees the goods or services as making a major contribution to his or her business performance. This is the quadrant for partnership and joint initiatives. Accounts that operate in this quadrant will have regular planning and strategy sessions, and access to the key decision makers is assured.

Let's return to our telecoms sales executive. He clearly sees himself and the products and services he supplies as strategic to his customer. After all, a company can't function without the ability to communicate with its customers, staff, and suppliers. Add email, online ordering, and remote working to the mix, and there is a clear case to be made for the Strategic quadrant.

Look at it, however, from the buyer's perspective:

- Sure, €10 million is a lot of money, but is it that much in the grand scheme of things?
- There are lots of telcos in the marketplace, and their products are all the same and interchangeable.
- Telecoms is really a utility. It's hard to see how any supplier could add value over another one.

So where would you put it? Certainly not high risk or critical. It is either, then, routine or leverage.

Neither of these options is very attractive for the strategic account manager trying to sell value. The result is a battle for control of the account and the agenda.

As a buyer, my primary objectives are to reduce risk to my business and deliver cost reductions and commercial success.

At one level, this is best achieved by driving as much spend as I can into the Leverage quadrant.

The rise of corporate procurement teams, consultants specializing in procurement, and e-auction technology have all helped fuel growth in this area.

The buyer has three primary tools to help them create Leverage spend:

Aggregation. Centralizing spend control has become much easier with the growth in enterprise computer systems like SAP and Oracle (other alternatives are available). Purchasing authority for everything from stationery through maintenance to travel and training has been taken away from the individual manager or maintenance technician and centralized in a corporate procurement organization. This has driven a focus on large, one-off tenders. In some marketplaces, buyers have gone beyond aggregating similar purchases and created entirely new marketplaces. Industrial distributors who once supplied bearings and fastenings now supply bottled water, cleaning supplies, and safety clothing – anything where they can add more top-line turnover to the account.

Standardizing. From the buyer's perspective, reducing the number of different items I buy concentrates my expenditure on a smaller number of higher-expenditure items. Experience tells me that the greater the expenditure on each item, the easier it is for me to get a better price. Once I have aggregated my spend and reduced my number of suppliers, the next thing is to reduce the range of products or services I take. In addition to greater price leverage in the marketplace, fewer items means reduced complexity and

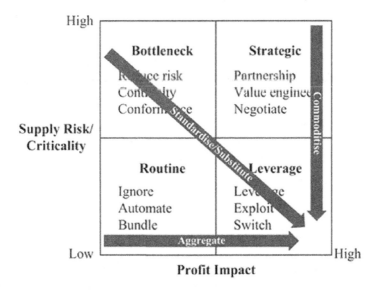

Figure 16.1b The Kralijc framework – customer view

a reduction in Stock keeping units (SKUs), stockholding, and cost of warehousing or servicing.

Commoditizing. To leverage my spend and drive prices down, I need competition. This means I have to remove differentiation and specialization. This drives a culture of "good enough." One supplier's product might be better than another's, but if they are all good enough, then the better aspects of one supplier's product over another's have no value. "Fit for purpose" is the cry: I don't need your extended life, value-added services, or technical support.

Whatever you think about the benefits of your product to the customer and whatever sales methodology you choose to adopt, you can't sell value anywhere other than the Strategic quadrant. Okay, you might have some successes in the Security quadrant, and these shouldn't be ignored. The big money, though, is in the Strategic quadrant.

The mistake many sales teams make is to try to sell value to a buyer who has them positioned in the Routine or Leverage quadrants. If you are positioned in either of the bottom quadrants, the focus is on efficiency of the procurement process or comparison of your price with prices from suppliers of similar products or services. The value sale is not a product or a service sale – it is a positional sale. You need to sell your strategic importance to the buyer before you can start to sell your value.

Back to our telecoms salesman. When he tried to get his 60 minutes, what I heard was someone wanting to talk about phones or the price of cellular minutes or megabytes of data. If I see him in the Routine box it's not worth my time. More likely, I see it as a Leverage spend because of the value, and I don't need a series of meetings to get a pricing sheet filled in. If I did, then I've got a junior buyer or category manager to deal with it.

What I learned in Barcelona was that the KAM didn't want to talk to me about cell minutes or megabytes of data.

"You completely missed the point," he said.

You had no idea how frustrated your sales team were about the poor connections they had or how many orders they lost because they couldn't get access to stock information or process an order in real time. What we wanted to talk about was salesforce effectiveness and productivity, not the price of the calls. We were confident we could improve the efficiency of your front-line salesforce by about 1 hour a day – what would that have been worth?

And the honest answer is that I had no idea, and I'm still not sure I could answer that question now. With hindsight, he was probably right, and it would have been one hour of my time very well spent.

So what went wrong?

Fundamentally, the sales approach was out of synchronization with my focus and expectation as a buyer. To understand this misalignment, it helps to understand the corporate purchasing cycle. This is explained by Figure 16.2.

- *Need identified.* The cycle begins with the identification of a requirement by the business – a need for a component, good, or service. This need, or more accurately the problem needing to be fixed, is the ultimate determinant of value. Fix the problem, and the economic impact of the solution or realization of the opportunity is the real value delivered.
- *Specification established.* The next stage in the process is to turn this need into a specification – a description of what we want or are trying to achieve – that the buyer can take to market. Immediately, the value seller is under pressure. If the need excludes

Figure 16.2 Typical purchasing cycle and value opportunity

or fails to recognize attributes or benefits of your products or services or, worse still, skews the specification toward a competitor, the opportunity for you to demonstrate value and get paid for it begins to disappear.

- *Potential suppliers identified.* The buyer then defines the pool of potential suppliers that will be asked to provide prices. If the buyer doesn't see you as a potential supplier, you won't even be given the chance to pitch. Consider the case where a manufacturer of high-performance industrial components has a range of extended-life products that would reduce long-term maintenance costs and downtime and increase productivity and profitability. If the buyer sees the procurement as a wide-ranging MRO exercise where they want a one-stop shop for the whole range of MRO materials and consumables, the value player won't even be considered a suitable supplier.

- *RFQ.* The buyer puts the requirement into the market as a request for proposal or invitation to tender. Often, this uses the previous step to develop a pre-qualified list of SQEP suppliers: suitably qualified experienced providers. Each potential supplier is considered capable and fit for purpose.
- *Proposals received.* The buyer compares the bids against one another and chooses a short list of the most favorable to negotiate with. This is finally where the buyer fully engages with the marketplace and the potential suppliers. But look what has happened. In the buyer's mind they have already established the need, locked down the specification, decided who might be suitable and asked for proposals against a standard pricing grid, and, probably, ranked them against one another.
- *Negotiate.* The buyer enters into detailed negotiations with short-listed suppliers and agrees on prices and terms. This is not a strategic negotiation about what value can be generated and delivered but a tactical negotiation using competition and leverage (the threat of losing the business) to drive prices down. There is very little value left by this point. What remains is a price reduction or some kind of improved service. Neither of these is likely to be enough to make a step change in the buyer's business or to generate enough measurable value to deliver enough money to pay for a significant price difference. We are in a commoditized marketplace.
- *Contract agreed on and awarded.* The process is now turned over to the lawyers and the agreement converted into a formal contract.
- *Performance.* The buying team and the sales team disengage and turn the operation of the contract over to their respective operational colleagues. They, in turn, operate the contract and the relationship to deliver the goods and/or services to satisfy the need.

When you ask buyers where they focus and put most of their energy, the answer shows a high emphasis on the stages from RFQ to Negotiate. What this means is that they are focused on getting prices from the market.

What the buyer is asking for is a price to meet an established need – whether it is for a bearing, a computer, or a cell phone.

I often describe the organizational buying process as "getting the least worst answer to the wrong question from a bunch of people you've met online."

Often, what the strategic account seller is trying to do is talk about fulfilling the real business need – which is where the value sits. Buyers don't always realize that the opportunity to reduce costs, improve productivity, and potentially increase profitability diminishes as they progress through the cycle. When they invite their chosen supplier(s) to submit tenders for a specification they have decided on, they have probably already limited the seller's opportunity to add value.

The greatest opportunities for innovation and performance improvement happen at the stage where both buyer and seller are jointly defining the need. By the time the customer has created a specification they will already have excluded some options, possibly without even knowing they've done so. Alternatively, the buyer may have specified the requirement in such a way that she or he has built in complexities, manufacturing, or service elements that make it hard to deliver or more expensive to deliver the product or service. In essence they have built in inefficiency and waste.

It seems obvious now that the telecoms salesman and many other salespeople over the years have known as much or even more about my business and my needs than I have and that I should have given them the opportunity to contribute this knowledge to my business. This would have allowed them to add genuine value to my business, deliver productivity improvements, and reduce costs.

In the 30 years since Kraljic proposed his purchasing portfolio matrix, the corporate world has transformed beyond recognition. The dual creeds of core competence and out-sourcing mean that businesses no longer buy simple components and services to combine these into end products. Increasingly, businesses are buying complex assemblies, services, and even finished products through complex, multi-tier supply chains.

As outsourcing has increased and procurement has centralized, buyers have become more remote from the technical and performance aspects of their purchases, and the technical voice of the buying company has become smaller.

The business criticality is often hidden or misunderstood until something goes wrong. The value of expenditure is too blunt an instrument to look to differentiate between sup-pliers and marketplaces.

Buyers need to look differently at how they segment suppliers to take account of this knowledge.

For value to be created and rewarded, the value seller has to persuade procurement to look differently at how they see the seller's role in the purchasing cycle.

The Market Knowledge Continuum (see Figure 16.3) segments purchases into three areas – price, benefit, and solution – based on who knows more about what the purchaser is buying: the buyer or the seller (the market). The segment the purchase is in determines the nature and style of the relationship and the technical purchasing skills required.

In the Market Knowledge Continuum, knowledge represents value, knowledge about

- how costs behave in the customer business (cost drivers and cost reductions);
- how performance can be improved;

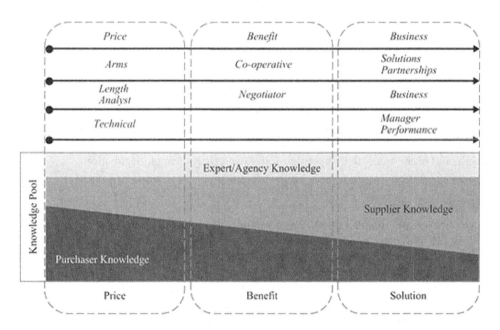

Figure 16.3 Market Knowledge Continuum

- unnecessary complexities driven by buyer behavior;
- how the specification can be reengineered;
- other ways to deliver the outcomes required;
- market innovations; and
- competitive advantage to be gained.

This knowledge needs to be converted into hard economic value, with monetary statements of the investment required represented by the higher price charged by the value supplier and the return on this investment delivered through the quantified and monetized expression of the additional benefits delivered.

The value isn't in the products or services being sold; it is in what those product and services can *do* for the customer – knowing about the customer's problems and opportunities and how to deliver solutions and, most crucially, how much they are worth to that customer when implemented.

In the Market Knowledge Continuum the decision about how to buy the products or service is made through an analysis of the balance between the knowledge and expertise of the buying company (supported if necessary by experts, agencies, or consultants) and the selling company.

Price

On the left of the Market Knowledge Continuum we have areas where the need is simple and the buyer knows everything they need to know to specify their requirements and meet their business objectives.

Typically, these are commodity purchases or goods specified in a way which reduces them to commodity. The buyer may have produced a technical (input) specification that details how the goods should be made and wants to achieve the specification at lowest price.

Price markets and purchases can be handled through competitive tenders, auctions, or agents regardless of their value.

There is very little that suppliers can bring to add to the knowledge of the buyer. Each supplier will, more or less, provide the same goods and/or services, and what remains is price, reliability, and residual aspects of service. They really are all the same.

The buyer's focus will be on developing a clear specification and an efficient RFQ and contracting process. Procurement analysts will compare bids, keep suppliers at arm's length, and focus on using competition to reduce prices through negotiation.

Benefit

As we move to the middle of the Market Knowledge Continuum, the buyer doesn't have as strong or complete knowledge about what is being bought as they had in the price segment. The buyer may have strong knowledge about what they need to achieve, but not necessarily the best way to go about it. There's a danger that if buyers assume they know the best way to go about achieving a desired result, they may develop an inappropriate technical specification and get what they asked for, not what they need. Buyers in the benefits segment need a more co-operative approach with the market; they need to negotiate with suppliers to jointly work out the best way forward. The buyer recognizes that different suppliers can bring different proposals and that it is not just a simple matter of comparing prices. For example:

- Life span will be different.
- Running costs could change.
- Consumables will be more (or less) expensive.
- Reliability and maintenance profiles need assessing.
- Productivity will drive benefits.

This is the arena of total cost of ownership (TCO) procurement: comparing the costs to procure, use, and operate the goods and services rather than the price to buy. TCO has been used by major organizations in the automotive and fast-moving consumer goods sectors for component and direct material expenditure since the late 1970s and in other sectors such as IT and construction since the mid-1980s. It has never really gained much of a foothold (despite the best efforts of many buyers and sellers) in services and indirect expenditure.

Business solution

As we progress through the continuum, the knowledge needed from the marketplace increases to the point where, ultimately, the buyer can only really say what they want to achieve and need to leave it to the supplier to specify the best way to achieve it. This is the business solutions market. It requires in-depth, collaborative working with the most capable suppliers to engineer the right solution for the business.

Buyers need to concentrate on finding the right supplier(s) and to work with them to deliver solutions to business problems: delivering real, hard-cash improvements to the performance and profitability of the business and sharing the prize. It is here that real value can be created and sold. This is the arena for genuine business partnerships.

The job of the value seller is to move the buyer into the business solution segment BEFORE they try to sell to them. As the buyer moves from price to business solutions, they need to get suppliers more involved earlier in the purchasing cycle – arguably as early as need identification – and certainly before specification.

This is tough for buyers. They have to give up their competitive power and take what they perceive as a significant commercial and personal risk. It's much easier to say, "I got four quotations and took the second cheapest" than it is to take responsibility and accountability for a business recommendation that the company should invest in a more expensive solution that will deliver additional economic benefits over and above the price increase.

What this all means is that if you want to sell value, then you have to reduce the perceived risk involved in paying a higher price with the possibility that the additional benefits won't materialize – convince me that you know something that I don't and that you can make something happen that is of real value to me. If you are going to improve my salesforce efficiency by 1% or extend the maintenance interval of my machines by six months, you need to be explicit about what that means for me in economic terms and convince me you know how to do it.

But, and it is a big BUT, if I don't see you as someone with knowledge to bring to the table, only products, you won't get the audience. You won't get out of the price bucket. Don't expect me to do the work for you. I probably don't have the knowledge anyway.

The importance of this was brought home at a recent meeting of Cranfield University's Key Account Management Club. I asked the 100 or so sales executives in the room to imagine that the room itself was the *Knowledge Continuum* and to stand where they thought represented the knowledge split between them as experts in their customers' businesses and their key account customers. If the knowledge was equally shared, they would be in the middle of the room. Of the 100 people, none were left of center (Price segment). There was a very significant belief that they as sellers had more knowledge about how their products and services could benefit their customers' businesses than the customers had.

So far, so good. I then asked them to move to where they believed the customer would position them. Everybody moved left. There were still a few Benefit and Business Solution players, but the vast majority of people were now tending toward Price.

Think about it. Your customer doesn't recognize you as having something to say or value to add. They see you as someone to be bought on price or at best compared with other offers. Value never makes it to the table other than as a marginal differentiator between you and your competitors.

Remember, too, that once you have told me something, I know it, and that knowledge is no longer unique to you. Think of it as a giant bungee cord pulling everything to the left. You need to keep creating new ways to improve my business and turning them into real hard (dollars and cents) statements of value to me, not impressive presentations about your products or services.

And, to be really successful, you need to drip-feed them to me one by one to maintain my interest and get your reward. Showering me with all of your solutions in one great wave is fine. But what are you going to do next?

My telecoms salesman never got the chance to sell me salesforce effectiveness because I had him pegged as a Price player in a market where I know enough about what I want to buy on price. He was right and I was wrong, and we both lost. I never gave him the chance to generate the value, and he never got the chance to sell it. Neither of us got any value.

So what can we do about it? For me the lessons seem clear.

Before we can sell value, we have to sell the concept that we have value to share. Then we can sell it and, ultimately, negotiate our share of the prize.

To sell value you need to drive the customer backward (anticlockwise) around the purchasing cycle to open up the potential markets you are in, create flexibility in the specification and, ultimately, redefine the need if you can.

Investigate

Be curious. Find out all you can about your customer's problems and what they mean for their business.

Go in the back door sometimes instead of through the shiny reception area. Sometimes, walking through the factory or the warehouse or even past the reject bins will give you information about the problems in the customer's business. What is wasted? What could be done better? What could you do for the customer over and above what they think to ask you for?

Elsewhere in this book, Todd C. Snelgrove writes about SKF's decades-long investment in their Documented Solutions Program (DSP). This is a database of delivered solutions that totals in excess of $5 billion worth of savings and productivity improvement. The job for the SKF value seller is to exploit this knowledge and match delivered solutions in one environment to a problem in another.

Quantify

As a value seller you need to do the work to quantify the value you will bring:

*   How much will it be?
*   How will I (the buyer) get it?
*   What do I as a customer need to do to make it happen?

Sales teams need to become much better at speaking the language of business commerce and investment – net present value payback and return on investment. Treat your sales pitch as a business-case presentation. The competitor's price or the available budgets become irrelevant if you are proposing a self-funding business improvement that delivers a payback or return several times greater than the cost of your proposal.

Engage

Next, you need to engage at the right level with the right message. I was never going to meet someone to talk about cell phones – I couldn't see the need. You need to find the right channel to get to the right person and be willing to talk about business issues, not products or services.

Having found the right channel, you will need to engage with procurement. However, the initial engagement is about moving into the solution part of the Knowledge Continuum – convincing the buyer that you have knowledge to bring that is special to you and of real importance to them. Don't sell too soon. Do not give away your knowledge for free and then hope to get rewarded for it in product or service sales.

Sell

Now you can start selling – selling your ability to deliver agreed-upon quantified value to the customer's business. New money! Why talk about the price of your products or services when what you are selling me is the change in profit of my business? Your products or services are just a means of facilitating the value. Other people have similar products or services, and they are probably cheaper. Lose control of this component, and the bungee cord will drag you back to price every time.

Selling in the context of value is about agreeing on what you are going to do – not on how much you are going to charge. Selling is about agreeing on the changes that are going to happen in the customer's business, what the effect will be, and what your role is in delivering the prize. This is where you leverage the outputs of your investigative work and the quantification of the benefits to sell your company as a value player.

Negotiate

Selling is about agreeing on what you are going to do. Negotiation is about agreeing on how much you will get paid. This is about how much of the share of the value created and delivered you are going to get as your reward for the cost reduction, productivity improvement, or additional profit you have delivered. Price is irrelevant. It's probably going to be a fraction of the value created.

Don't look toward the cost of your product or service or the price of the competitor's offer. Your focus needs to be on the unique knowledge and abilities you bring and how you share in your customer's success.

Contract

Marco Bertini (Associate Professor of Marketing at Esade) expresses the problem very well:

> Companies spend too much time thinking about how much they are going to charge and not enough time thinking about what they are going to charge for.

We need innovative contract mechanisms that link payment and rewards to outcomes, not to inputs.

We continue to work with procurement teams to get them to be willing to recognize the need to create the space for sellers to create value and to get paid for it. The burden, though, will always rest fundamentally with the seller.

Companies who provide products frequently find it difficult to know how to charge for benefits when they are used to charging for pills or bearings or disks.

To get paid for value, sellers need to rethink the way they get remunerated. Companies in industries as diverse as pharmaceuticals (Pfizer), aviation (Rolls Royce), and software (Microsoft) are changing the way they charge customers for the goods and services they supply.

Healthcare payers are now asking pharmaceutical companies to contract for outcomes – substantial elements of the payments made will be linked to successful healthcare outcomes. If the patient requires more drugs, therapy, or care the supplier will provide these at no additional cost. These no-win, no-fee arrangements have existed in some markets such as litigation and real estate for a long time and are now becoming more normal as sellers seek higher returns on their knowledge. Microsoft now requires you to lease its Office suite of products on a yearly basis and, in a dramatic turnaround, will give you its latest operating system for free.

Back to SKF. A simple review of their DSP library suggested that there was over a billion dollars' worth of replicable cost savings that could be rolled out across existing clients. How does SKF get paid for that? There probably isn't enough additional product sales available to constitute a fair reward for the benefits they deliver. A value-based contract mechanism will need a major rethink of what they charge for: services? savings? reduced downtime? This will require a new way of thinking about how contracts are constructed and potentially a major change to sales pipeline management.

The contract will no longer be for the supply of a component or service but for the outcome achieved. The ability of the value seller to quantify value and link outcomes to their knowledge and activities and to be willing to share risk for a higher reward will be a core part of new contract structures.

Conclusion

Selling value is no easy thing, especially when the prevailing culture for many buyers is price and negotiation. To sell value you need an intelligent buyer, someone who understands the concept and values the concept of business solutions.

You cannot rely on the buyer to have the knowledge or the willingness to translate your proposals into an explicit statement of value. In the absence of a hard number, the buyer will perceive any higher price to be paid as a risk. The Price bungee will always drag the buyer back to a lower price option if value is expressed as "improved service," "longer life," "better performance," "reduced costs," or some other general statement.

Slowly, aspects of the procurement world are changing. Buyers that understand that strategic suppliers are a key part of their competitive team are beginning to engage in a more open dialogue with their suppliers and adopt a more outward-looking approach to procurement. The chief procurement officer at a major utility business has challenged his procurement team to deliver "Relentless Insight" to their business stakeholders – a constant stream of knowledge, ideas, and innovations about how to make the business better.

This is a big and challenging change of mind-set, but this is the kind of buyer the value seller needs. It is the buyer who is willing to look beyond comparing fixed prices for a given specification that allows the seller to identify and create value.

That's the fundamental rub with many value-selling methodologies – you can't sell value to someone who doesn't get it. If you can't find an intelligent buyer, be prepared for the long haul of educating him or her.

Reference

Kraljic, P. (1983) "Purchasing must become supply chain management," *Harvard Business Review* 61(5), 109–117.

17 The sourcing continuum to achieve collaboration and value[1]

Vitasek, Kate

Adam Smith's *Wealth of Nations* showed the way for modern markets – and societies – to thrive through competition with an "invisible hand" among trading partners. What emerged is, for the most part, what continues to the present day – competitively driven transaction-based business models.

But that was then. What's needed today is what we might term a post-modern approach that embraces the need for strategic collaboration and value-building among business partners. The nature of business today is shifting. Handfield and Chick point to supplier collaboration as "the new way . . . the old adversarial posture of procurement is as outmoded as it is inappropriate." They call for a clear and definitive break between old-school procurement practices and those of today. In short, they argue that everything that has been done and learned in the past is of little use in the dawn of procurement's new value proposition.

Academic research on collaboration and sourcing methods has exploded over the last 20 years. Research at the University of Tennessee shows that innovation and collaboration are not mutually exclusive; rather, they feed and build upon each other. Innovation happens most effectively *through* collaboration. And the best organizations not only *say* they want innovation and collaboration, they also go all-in and *contract* for it (Lafley and Charan, 2008).

Why is a new sourcing approach necessary? Although statistics vary, most experts in the procurement field agree that typical organizations spend between 40% and 80% of revenue with suppliers that help them develop, manufacture, sell, and service their goods/services. Indeed, the automobile industry spends 70% of its revenue with suppliers (Henke et al., 2014). This means that roughly half an organization's procurement spending is on services that require a more sophisticated approach to sourcing. Today's procurement professionals must maneuver in a complicated, evolving environment that is more dynamic than ever. They must embrace and change as business needs change, and this means balancing what seems to be insurmountable, conflicting goals of reducing cost structures and driving innovation and mitigating risks.

But the message is clear: succeeding now depends on harnessing the power of an organization's suppliers. Simply put, they should be embraced as resources, as strategic partners, not as necessary cost centers. The playing field is based no longer on lowest cost but on highly collaborative relationships with suppliers that can help drive transformation and innovation in the organization. If firms are going to compete "supply chain to supply chain," shouldn't all the links in the supply chain work together?

DOI: 10.4324/9781003177937-21

Sourcing is a continuum, not a destination

Organizations typically think of procurement as a "make versus buy" decision. This is especially true as organizations begin to explore outsourcing. Many assume that if they "buy," they should use competitive "market" forces to ensure that they are getting the best deal. This is the essence of a transaction-based sourcing model. It works well for simple transactions with abundant supply and low complexity where the "market" can correct itself. After all, if a supplier does not perform, one can just rebid the work.

But as organizations outsource to procure more complex goods and services, that logic no longer works. All too often buyers become co-dependent on suppliers, switching costs are high, and suppliers have a "locked-in" position. Oliver E. Williamson – professor of economics at the University of California, Berkeley – has challenged the "make versus buy" concept through his work in Transaction Cost Economics (TCE). Williamson received the Nobel Prize in Economic Sciences in 2009. One of his key lessons is that organizations should view sourcing as a *continuum* rather than as a simple market-based make-versus-buy decision (Williamson, 2008).

A good way to approach Williamson's work is to consider sourcing as a continuum, with free-market forces on one side and what Williamson refers to as "corporate hierarchies" on the other (see Figure 17.1). In the middle ground, Williamson advocated that organizations use a "hybrid" approach for complex contracts.

The Industrial Revolution enabled corporations to capitalize on large business ventures, and the result was vertically integrated companies designed to build upon and leverage their power. The default was for organizations to "make" rather than "buy" the goods and services they needed to sustain themselves, whether in the private or public sector. The result? Large, powerful – and bureaucratic – organizations.

Peters and Waterman delved into this idea in their best-selling book *In Search of Excellence* (1982). The make-versus-buy decision began to shift with Drucker's "sell the mailroom" article (1989). Prahalad and Hamel took the debate to a new level in their pioneering *Harvard Business Review* article, "The Core Competence of the Corporation" (1990), which encouraged organizations to evaluate their "core competencies." Their finding? Most organizations cannot focus on more than five or six core competencies.

CEOs and government officials around the world began to shed internal assets. Goods and services that were customarily controlled in-house (e.g., information technology,

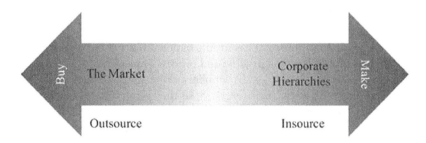

Figure 17.1 The sourcing continuum.

call center/customer care, supply chain services, back-office finance functions) were outsourced.

Williamson's work with TCE supports Drucker's common-sense approach with math. TCE theory posits that there are many hidden transaction costs associated with performing work that is non-core to the organization. One of the downfalls is that when work is performed by an organization's internal resources, there is no competition; this provides little incentive to drive inherent improvements in cost and quality. There is also high administrative control and a legal system that is "deferential to management." As a consequence, innovations that might come from the market or from third parties are not shared or developed as rapidly as management typically likes – if at all.

Because these are additional bureaucratic costs, Williamson (2008: 12) noted, "the internal organization is usually thought of as the organization of last resort." Thus, if at all possible, organizations should not invest in developing goods and services that are non-core.

Buy relationships

Organizations that procure goods or services, rather than produce them in-house, will typically use what Williamson (2008) calls the "market mode" to do so. The market mode employs the free-market economy to determine how organizations will do business, including establishing a price. It assumes that free-market forces incentivize suppliers to compete on low price and high service. This approach also features an absence of dependency; buyers or suppliers who are unhappy can switch at any time with relative ease. Governance of the supply base is accomplished by switching suppliers or customers if a better opportunity comes along. As a result, the market approach can rely purely on classical contract law and requires little administrative control.

The big advantage to using the market is simplicity. The market mode enables a competitive process to determine whether an organization is getting a good transaction price. Its foundation is a transactional business model. Competitive bidding processes establish market prices for everything from a per unit price for a spare part, to a price per call for technical support, to a price per pallet stored in a warehouse, to a price per hour for a janitor to clean a building.

The disadvantage to the market mode is that it often assumes that the purchase is somewhat standardized and therefore available from a variety of suppliers. Consequently, suppliers often "compete" into contracts that pose unnecessary risks. For example, Williamson (2008) points out that service providers might have "specialized investments" that can easily expose the business to significant loss if the contract fails and there are no safeguards in place.

One form of specialized investment is in innovations that create value for the buying organizations, such as asset-specific product and process improvements designed to create competitive advantages for the buyer. As suppliers make specialized investments to support innovation, they look at risk versus reward, so they often raise prices to reflect their increased risk level. However, buyers naturally want lower prices as well as the benefits of the innovation. Buyers and suppliers often find themselves in a "give and take" as a normal part of market-based negotiations and suppliers seek to develop contractual safeguards.

Williamson (2008) showed that using the market for more complex contracts drives up transaction costs. He argued that such contracts should use what he calls a "hybrid" approach, based on a conscious decision to build more trusting and secure supplier relationships with the goal of driving out opportunism and injecting efficiencies in the buyer – supplier relationship.

Hybrid relationships

Although the market and hierarchical approaches offer advantages, they also have clear disadvantages. Williamson (2008) points out that the market doesn't always work as efficiently as theory would lead one to believe. And buyers may find that they lack the necessary skills or funds to invest in certain competencies. Game theory teaches us to view a problem through a different lens: one designed to optimize for the problem under review. Every day, more and more research is proving that collaborative – not competitive – games yield consistently better results (Axelrod, 1984).

Unfortunately, procurement tools today are designed to promote commoditization and competition. This can put buyers and suppliers in a catch-22 situation. (A catch-22, based on the title of Joseph Heller's novel, is a no-win situation that uses contradictory or circular logic.) Why a catch-22? Organizations say they want a "strategic," collaborative supplier, but the nature of how they buy and contract tells a different story – one of low-price commoditization and competition.

More catch-22: it is not uncommon for procurement professionals to be measured on (and often incentivized on!) driving cost (price) reductions through a purchase price variance (PPV) metric (PPV is a procurement metric that measures a procurement organization's – or an individual procurement professional's – effectiveness at meeting cost-savings targets). This drives short-term emphasis on "price" paid versus overall value or a focus on reducing total ownership costs. To top it off, far too many lawyers hunker down with the single-minded goal of shifting risk and emphasizing shorter-term contracts to limit supplier dependency.

These practices are magnified when combined with a conventional transactional business model where a supplier is paid for each activity. The transactional model pits buyer against supplier with conflicting goals. The more hours, the more units, the more calls, or the more lines of code written – the more revenue and profit for a supplier. Buyers find that their suppliers meet contractual obligations and service levels, but they do not drive innovations and efficiencies at the pace the organization wishes. Suppliers argue that investing in their customer's business is risky because buyers will simply take their ideas and competitively bid the work.

On one hand, organizations want suppliers to close gaps when they lack core competency, wanting suppliers to be innovative and provide solutions. On the other hand, they drive competition and commoditization, which curbs supplier incentive to invest in innovation. The result is an industry at a crossroads, with buyers and suppliers wanting innovation – but neither willing to make the necessary investments.

Seven sourcing business models

Research by the International Association for Contract and Commercial Management (IACCM, 2010) shows that most organizations operate under conventional transaction-based models that are constrained by a formal, legally oriented, risk-averse, and liability-based environment. And there is growing awareness that transaction-based approaches do not always give each party the intended results (Williamson, 2008).

University of Tennessee research and industry-specific experience in applying alternative output- and outcome-based approaches for complex contracts demonstrate that alternative sourcing business models are viable approaches to conventional transactional methods. Both output- and outcome-based approaches are gaining momentum as senior leaders see positive results from carefully crafted collaborative agreements.

There are seven sourcing business models that fall into the three categories along Williamson's (2008) sourcing continuum.

- Transactional (Williamson's "Market" category)

  - Basic provider model
  - Approved provider model

- Relational (Williamson's "Hybrid" category)

  - Preferred provider model
  - Performance-based/managed services model
  - Vested business model

- Investment (Williamson's "Hierarchy" category)

  - Shared service model
  - Equity partnerships (e.g., joint ventures)

A brief overview of each model follows; each model differs from a risk/reward perspective and should be evaluated in the context of what is being procured. Figure 17.2 shows how the sourcing business models fall along the sourcing continuum.

Basic provider model

A basic provider model uses a transaction-based model, meaning that it typically has a set price for individual products and services for which there are a wide range of standard market options. Typically, these products or services are readily available, with little differentiation in what is offered. Examples can include janitorial services or procurement of office supplies.

A basic provider model is used to buy low-cost, standardized goods and services in a market where there are many suppliers and where switching suppliers have little or no impact on the business. Buyers typically use frequent competitive bidding (often with pre-established electronic auction calendar events). Often a purchase requisition triggers transactions that signal that the buying company agrees to buy preset quantities of goods or tasks (e.g., widgets or hours). Some organizations even use purchase cards for these types of simple purchases.

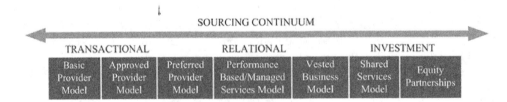

Figure 17.2 Sourcing business models along the sourcing continuum

The buyer–supplier relationship is based largely on a review of performance against basic criteria. For example, did the supplier work the hours claimed? Did the goods received meet the agreed-to quantity, cost, and delivery times?

Approved provider transaction model

An approved provider model uses a transaction-based model where goods and services are purchased from pre-qualified suppliers that meet certain performance or other selection criteria. Frequently an organization has a limited number of pre-approved suppliers for various spend categories from which buyers or business units can choose. The use of multiple suppliers means that costs are competitive, and one firm can easily be replaced with another if a supplier fails to meet performance standards.

An approved provider is identified as a pre-qualified option in the pool of basic providers. Approved providers fulfil preconditions for specified service through a set of criteria or through previous experience with performance reliability. To reach approved status, suppliers frequently offer some level of differentiation from other transactional suppliers and provide a cost or efficiency advantage for the buyer. The differentiation could come in the form of geographical location advantage, a cost or quality advantage, or a minority-owned business and is ultimately "approved" to assist with meeting an organization's social responsibility goals.

Procurement professionals often turn to approved providers as regularly solicited sources of supply when bidding is conducted. An approved provider may or may not operate under a master agreement, which is an overarching service contract with the buying organization. Approved providers may or may not also have to meet volume thresholds to be in an "approved" status. In addition, approved providers may or may not participate in supplier management reviews.

In order to create a seamless and readily accessible supply chain, many organizations develop lists of approved providers. The advantages are many. For example, a pre-approved list saves time when seeking particular goods and services. The approval process ensures parity between bidding qualified suppliers. As an organization selects its approved provider list, it molds the required qualifications to its unique business objectives and strategy.

Intel uses approved providers as part of its Supplier Development Program (SDP), which identifies and confirms that all bidding suppliers are at parity. For that reason, Intel feels confidence in its field of competitors. When it is time for the bid process, Intel can select the lowest-cost (price) supplier without concern about the supplier's capabilities. Intel knows the supplier can meet its needs. In essence, Intel works to commoditize what it is buying to drive pricing competition in the market (Vitasek and Kling, 2015).

Preferred provider model

Like the basic and approved provider models, a preferred provider model uses a transaction-based economic model. A key difference between a preferred provider and the other transaction-based models is that the buyer has chosen to move to a supplier relationship that offers the supplier the opportunity to add differentiated incremental value to the buyer's business in order to meet strategic objectives. This insertion of the supplier's contribution into the buyer's business processes creates the need for a relational model. Thus, contracts with specifically chosen supplier(s) assume a more collaborative relationship. Repeat business and longer-term and/or renewable contracts are the norm.

Similar to an approved provider model, buyers seek to do business with preferred providers to streamline the buying process. Buying organizations typically enter into multiyear contracts using master agreements that allow them to conduct repeat business efficiently. Preferred providers are still using transaction-based economic models. However, the nature and efficiencies of how the organizations work together go beyond a simple purchase order and begin to consider how a supplier can provide value-added services.

A preferred provider is a pre-qualified supplier. Often they offer unique differentiators such as value-added benefits and services and/or demonstrated acceptable and predictable levels of performance. For example, a preferred provider may have a superior software that interfaces with an organization's own system. Sometimes a preferred provider is chosen because of its high-quality workforce and difficult-to-duplicate expertise. Typical conditions for supplier down-selection of a preferred provider are the following:

- previous experience
- supplier performance rating (if the buying organization has a rating system)
- previous contract compliance performance
- evidence of an external certification (e.g., such as ISO certification)
- additional contributions to control costs such as inventory management, training resources, and aligned geographical positioning.

Under Microsoft's Preferred Supplier Program (MPSP), suppliers are divided into two distinct levels – Premier and Preferred. Preferred and Premier suppliers are a small subset of Microsoft's overall list of approved suppliers referred to as the Approved Supplier List (ASL). Premier suppliers are the featured supplier by category in Microsoft's e-procurement system, meaning that when an employee seeks to buy goods or services, the Premier suppliers are the source *recommended* by Microsoft's procurement organization. This leads to substantial revenue increases when business units or employees "buy" products or services using the procurement group's recommendation.

Microsoft's Preferred and Premier suppliers also enjoy added benefits. Microsoft issues invitations to special events during which its executives share insights and strategies. Premier suppliers also have access to Microsoft Executive briefings. It is not easy to become a Preferred or Premier supplier with Microsoft (the company shares its procurement program details at www.microsoft.com/en-us/procurement/msp-overview.aspx).

Performance-based/managed services model

A performance-based model is generally a formal, longer-term supplier agreement that combines a relational contracting model with an output-based economic model. A performance-based model seeks to drive supplier accountability for output-based service-level agreements (SLAs) and/or cost-reduction targets. A performance-based agreement typically creates incentives (or penalties) for hitting (or missing) performance targets.

Sourcing decisions are based not only on a supplier's ability to provide a good or service at a competitive cost but also on its ability to drive improvements based on its core competencies. Performance-based agreements shift thinking away from activities to pre-defined *outputs* or events. Some organizations call the results outcomes. However, note that a performance-based agreement should hold a supplier accountable only for what is under its control. For that reason, in performance-based models, the word "outcome" typically refers to a supplier's "output." An output is a well-defined and easily measured event or a deliverable that is typically finite. Performance-based agreements require a higher level of collaboration than preferred provider contracts because there usually is a higher degree of integration between a supplier and a buying organization. In addition, buyers need to apply more formalized supplier relationship management efforts to review performance against objectives and specify the incentive or service credit (also referred to as a malice payment or penalty) payments that are embedded in the contracts.

Some service industries are seeing an evolution in managed services agreements where a supplier guarantees a fixed fee with a pre-agreed price-reduction target (e.g., a 3% year-over-year price or cost decrease). The assumption is that the supplier will deliver on productivity targets. These guaranteed savings are often referred to as a glidepath because there is an annual price reduction over time. Managed services agreements are a form of a performance-based sourcing business model.

The U.S. Navy set out to improve the performance of the H-60 FLIR system, which enables the Navy's H-60 helicopter to detect, track, classify, identify, and attack targets such as fast-moving patrol boats or mine-laying craft. When first developed, the FLIR was expected to have at least 500 hours of operation before failure but was averaging less than 100 hours. The Navy and Raytheon implemented a 10-year, fixed-price agreement that was priced per flight hour and valued at $123 million. This fixed price by flight hour contract gave Raytheon incentive to improve reliability and helped reduce the need to remove these units from the aircraft. Raytheon also implemented an online Maintenance Management Information System that allowed for real-time data collection by NADEP Jacksonville; an online manual has eliminated the need to have printed copies made and distributed.

In the first 3 years of the contract, the H-60 FLIR components experienced a 100% availability rate and achieved a 40% growth in system reliability improvement as well as a 65% improvement in repair response time. Originally cost savings were projected to be around $31 million but exceeded $42 million after just 3 years. The Navy was recognized by the U.S. Secretary of Defense for its "Performance-Based Logistics" contract with Raytheon for its H-60 FLIR program (Department of Defense, 2006).

Vested model

The vested model is a highly collaborative sourcing business model where the organization and the supplier have an economic interest in each other's success. The vested model is a hybrid relationship that combines an outcome-based economic model with a relational contracting model that incorporates the Nobel Prize – winning concepts of behavioral economics and the principle of shared value. Using these concepts, companies enter into highly collaborative arrangements designed to create and share value for buyers and suppliers above and beyond conventional buy – sell economics of a transaction-based agreement. In short, the parties are equally committed to (vested in) each other's success.

The vested business model was popularized when University of Tennessee researchers coined the term after studying highly successful buyer – supplier relationships. A good example is Microsoft and Accenture's multiyear agreement, in which Microsoft challenged Accenture to transform Microsoft's back-office finance operation processes. The agreement is structured so that the more successful Accenture is at achieving Microsoft's goals, the more successful Accenture itself becomes.

A vested model is best used when an organization has transformational and/or innovation objectives that it cannot achieve by itself or by using conventional transactional sourcing business models (basic provider, approved provider, preferred provider) or a performance-based agreement.

These transformational or innovation objectives are referred to as desired outcomes. A desired outcome is a measurable strategic business objective that focuses on what will be accomplished as a result of the work performed. Desired outcomes are not a task-oriented SLA such as those typically outlined in preferred provider or performance-based agreements. Rather, desired outcomes are strategic and often can only be achieved with a high degree of collaboration between the buyer and provider and/or with investment by the supplier.

Desired outcomes form the basis of a vested relationship because the provider is rewarded for helping the buyer achieve mutually defined desired outcomes – even when some of the accountability is shared with the buying organization. Desired outcomes are generally categorized as an improvement to cost, schedule, market share, revenue, customer service levels, or overall business performance.

Shared services model

Organizations that struggle to meet complex business requirements with a supplier can always invest to develop capabilities themselves (or in-source). One approach is to develop an internal shared service organization (SSO) with the goal of centralizing and standardizing operations that improve operational efficiencies. A shared services model is typically an internal organization based on an arm's-length outsourcing arrangement. Using this approach, processes are often centralized into an SSO that charges business units or users for the services they use. In some instances, SSOs are formed externally to the company (such as a subsidiary).

SSOs act like outsourced suppliers, performing services, and then "charging" their internal customers on a per-transaction or actual cost basis. SSOs generally mirror conventional preferred provider models. The main difference is that the SSO is an internal rather than an external supplier.

Organizations can use a shared services model for a variety of functional services such as human resources (HR), finance operations, or administrative services (such as claims processing in health care). For example, large organizations may centralize HR administration into an SSO to provide benefits management to their own employees and even external clients. Small enterprises can benefit from a shared services model by joining forces to create specialized service centers that economically provide a functional service to each of the smaller firms.

In 1995 Bell Canada's distribution operations were operating at service levels 10% to 15% below industry average and at a cost base of $100 million. Bell Canada (the largest telecom services organization in Canada) decided to spin off the assets and the staff of the distribution business into a stand-alone, wholly owned subsidiary known as Progistix Solutions Inc. (PSI). The idea was that by creating a separate shared services entity with its own P&L, PSI would be driven to operate more efficiently. PSI was chartered to provide a full range of order-management and inventory-management business processes for all of Bell's operating businesses, and a new CEO was brought in to turn the business around. The management team was driven through profit-sharing incentives to dramatically reduce costs in all parts of the organization. As a result, PSI reduced costs by $45 million, yielding a breakeven position in 1998. In addition, systematic improvements raised service levels to industry standards, with over 95% of the orders processed during the day being picked, packed, shipped, and delivered to customers by the end of the next day. During the next two years, PSI was able to generate industry-standard profits and grew revenues by 15%.

Equity partnerships

An equity partnership creates a legally binding entity. These take different legal forms, from buying a supplier (an acquisition), to creating a subsidiary, to equity-sharing joint ventures, to entering into co-operative (co-op) arrangements. Equity partnerships are best used when an organization does not have adequate internal capabilities and does not want to outsource.

Some organizations decide they do not have internal capabilities and do not want to invest in an SSO. In these cases, organizations may opt to develop an equity partnership such as a joint venture or other legal form in an effort to acquire mission-critical goods and services.

Equity partnerships, by definition, bring costs "in house" and create a fixed cost burden. As a result, equity partnerships often conflict with the desires of many organizations to create more variable and flexible cost structures on their balance sheet.

Different models – different systems

While business needs have evolved, the fundamental nature of how goods and services are procured has not. The vast majority of organizations (public and private) still use the same transaction-based approach to procure complex goods and services that they use to buy simpler commodities and supplies.

Unfortunately, many business professionals wrongly assume that a transaction-based business model is the only way to architect a supplier contract. *For simple transactions with abundant supply and low complexity, a transaction-based business model is the most efficient model.*

The real weakness of a transaction-based approach emerges when any level of complexity, variability, mutual dependency, or customized assets or processes is part of the equation. This is because the transactional approach cannot produce perfect market-based price equilibrium in variable or multidimensional business agreements. In many instances, hybrid sourcing business models built with relational contracts and output- or outcome-based economic models are more appropriate.

Think of a sourcing business model as a "system," because each is purpose-built to optimize the business needs given critical operating factors. Each situation is different: there is no one-size-fits-all sourcing business model.

It is thus vital that organizations work together to choose the most appropriate sourcing business model for their situation.

Note

1 Content for this chapter is primarily based on ideas and research by the University of Tennessee in the book *Strategic Sourcing in the New Economy*, by B. Keith, K. Vitasek, K. Manrodt, and J. Kling, New York: Palgrave Macmillan, 2015. Reproduced with permission of Palgrave Macmillan. Additional content is based on the White Paper "Unpacking Sourcing Business Models: 21st Century Solutions for Sourcing Services," available at www.vestedway.com/vested-library/

References

Axelrod, R. (1984) *The Evolution of Cooperation*, New York: Basic Books.

Drucker, P. (1989, July 25) "Sell the mailroom," *Wall Street Journal*. www.wsj.com/articles/ SB113202230063197204. Accessed 15 September 2015

Henke, J. W., Jr., Stallkamp, T., and Sengun Yeniyurt, S. (2014, May/June) "Lost supplier trust, . . . how Chrysler missed out on $24 billion in profits over the past twelve years," *Supply Chain Management Review*. www.ppi1.com/uploads/wri-profit/scmr-lost-trust.pdf. Accessed 15 September 2015

International Association of Contracting and Commercial Management. (2010, April) "Contract negotiations continue to undermine value," IACCM Ninth Annual Top Ten Terms Report, Ridgefield, CT.

Lafley, A. G. and Charan, R. (2008) *The Game-Changer: How You Can Drive Revenue and Profit Growth with Innovation*, New York: Random House.

Peters, T. and Waterman, R. (1982) *In Search of Excellence*, New York: Harper & Row.

Prahalad, C. K. and Hamel, G. (1990) "The core competence of the corporation," *Harvard Business Review 68*(3), 79–91.

Secretary of Defense Performance-Based Logistics Awards Program for Excellence in Performance-Based Logistics. (2006) www.aia-aerospace.org/assets/PBL_Winners.pdf. Accessed 17 September 2015

Vitasek, K. and Kling, J. (2015) *The Innovator's Dilemma: How Intel and DHL Drove a Paradigm Shift in Procurement, Vested for Success Case Study* (Teaching ed.), Knoxville, TN: University of Tennessee, Office of Business Administration.

Williamson, O. (2008) "Outsourcing: Transaction cost management and supply chain management," *Journal of Supply Chain Management 44*(2), 5–16.

Part V

Value quantification and organizational change management

18 Interview

Implementing value quantification in B2B

Hinterhuber, Andreas and Heutger, Matthias

ANDREAS HINTERHUBER: Value quantification is arguably a critically important capability for many companies. Based on your experience, for what type of contract or customer is value quantification especially important?

MATTHIAS HEUTGER: In the world of logistics, value creation and subsequent value demonstration are important for most customers and most contracts. Value quantification is especially important if products are standardized – that is, if customers view them as commodities – and we're in a competitive situation where we need to justify premium prices. It's also essential when we require the customer to make changes or investments; in this case, a solid business case is essential so that customers can quantify the value and justify a solution to the business.

ANDREAS HINTERHUBER: Let's illustrate this with an example. Let's assume that I'm a major customer of DHL and that I tell your account manager, "Your price is 10% to 15% higher than the offer from your main competitor." How do you think your account manager will respond? Are there any best practices you wish to share?

MATTHIAS HEUTGER: All of our account management and sales teams are briefed and trained to make sure they are able to articulate the potential value of our products to each different customer. How we do this varies. For a product in our DHL Express service line – let's say a straightforward shipping product which could be seen as a commodity, at least relative to many other products we offer – we articulate the characteristics of our offer and demonstrate the product's advantages compared with competitive products. For more complex products, this will change substantially. These types of products include our warehousing, managed transport, and other complex outsourcing solutions. With this complexity, a simple price comparison between competitive offerings is insufficient. So I'm convinced it's essential to analyze what our solution does for the customer's end-to-end costs and value creation. The most direct benefit we can offer with any solution is cost savings within the supply chain – we achieve this by doing things more efficiently, using our scale and experience. For example, we can help customers by better consolidating and managing their logistics flows, using fewer trucks and reducing warehouse space, so it's very direct. For our more complex solutions, we tend to create additional direct benefits like reducing the cycle time, improving time-to-market, increasing product availability, and enhancing security so that fewer goods are lost – which is not a direct cost saving per se, but it improves total landed cost and can help to drive revenue growth and raise satisfaction levels among our customers' customers. So in everything we do for the customer, we are always looking for the customer benefits and value across their whole supply chain. Does this answer your question?

DOI: 10.4324/9781003177937-23

ANDREAS HINTERHUBER: Yes. What I took away is: For some types of products – I'm not sure I would call them commodities, because, in my view, there are no commodities – you provide customers a kind of scorecard, not unlike the one you get at school, highlighting reliability, on-time performance, etc., without necessarily translating your own competitive advantage into quantified customer value. The customer, in the end, quantifies the value and . . .

MATTHIAS HEUTGER: . . . in most cases you don't have to do this quantification. You describe the service quality, on-time performance, etc., to the customer, but the value is so obvious that you don't have to make the value calculation for them. They already know the importance of on-time delivery and reliability; it's common sense, so to speak. Let's look at another set of products, such as Air & Ocean Freight. If you're smarter, you can offer better consolidation through better routing than competitors. With this you create an advantage for the customer that leads to direct or indirect cost savings. You could recommend using rail instead of ocean services, which might save a couple of days and which may help reduce customer inventory – all of this relates to end-to-end process optimization. If you're in a competitive bid but you haven't yet established a level of trust with a specific customer, you will need to quantify and articulate the value you deliver. And even if you're not obliged to quantify the value to get the business, I would still advocate doing it. You can always go to the customer at a later date and say, "Hey! Look, this is what we did for you." This certainly helps to keep customers loyal and increase renewal rates.

ANDREAS HINTERHUBER: You say that value quantification is beneficial also after contract signature in order to facilitate contract renewal and maintain customer loyalty. This relates to the idea of scorecards which we touched upon earlier.

MATTHIAS HEUTGER: It's important to get the customer to recognize and agree with the value quantification. This means that you must have the data to share with the customer; that's the best way to ensure customers appreciate the value you deliver to them.

ANDREAS HINTERHUBER: Value quantification requires collaborating with customers. Now, some customers may be very reluctant to share with you what your product or solution does for their profitability because they fear this knowledge could be turned against them. Put differently, once the account manager knows – thanks to their customers! – that their products produce benefits that are sometimes greater than the ones the account manager has anticipated, the supplier factually has an incentive to increase the price. Is this a concern in your environment, or do you say, "I'm happy to have the customer take a larger share because this will help us in long-term collaborative relationships anyway"?

MATTHIAS HEUTGER: That's a tricky question. If you really want to achieve a true partnership, both the organization and the logistics provider need to recognize sufficient value to make continued investment worthwhile. And then of course the question is, how should you share a 100% gain? Should it be 50/50 if one party invests more or has taken on higher risk? This is a case-by-case decision and also depends on the maturity of the relationship with the customer. We do enter into gainsharing agreements. These require a certain level of openness: you need the facts and information visible so that gainsharing works for both parties. If we deal with a new opportunity, we tend to use benchmarks from previous comparable case studies and discuss these with customers. In many instances, these benchmarks help us to get to the center of the conversation with the customer.

ANDREAS HINTERHUBER: Are these gainsharing agreements something you do frequently, or do you do them for a quite narrow scope of contracts which you know very well?

MATTHIAS HEUTGER: We do gainsharing agreements frequently but not for the majority of contracts. Typically, they are a viable option in our contract logistics business when, for example, you enter a multiyear contract that aims at continuous optimization and improvement. We need a certain project period to make gainsharing work; we would rarely enter a gainsharing agreement in a one-year contract; there needs to be a longer-term agreement such as a fourth-party logistics (4PL) solution or a complex outsourcing agreement. It's also possible to start with an open-book contract for the first one or two years, so that we establish transparency and both parties can gain some experience, and so that we establish a baseline. After this, we can move into a gainsharing agreement. For a new customer, new solution, or new product, I would not recommend gainsharing right away; otherwise one party or both might lose.

ANDREAS HINTERHUBER: I would reckon that the advantage of gainsharing also depends on risk perceptions. For contracts that you perceive as low risk – you know you can do the job – you probably prefer gainsharing. Conversely, if you perceive outcomes to be risky, you probably will prefer a fixed-price agreement over a gainsharing contract.

MATTHIAS HEUTGER: Yes, in some instances gainsharing doesn't make sense. In my view, you enter into a gainsharing contract because the objective is to improve and change. You will only create more value if there's a mutual agreement that both parties will continue to improve and change things. For something standard – a "this is how we do it" solution – where neither party can bring in new ideas, then gainsharing doesn't work. You need a certain level of innovativeness and an ability to bring in new ideas to jointly create new value.

ANDREAS HINTERHUBER: So you suggest that these gainsharing agreements work for longer-term collaborative agreements where both parties are willing to experiment and to innovate?

MATTHIAS HEUTGER: Experimentation is probably not the word I would choose, but both parties need to commit to a certain level of change and continuous improvement to make it worthwhile, yes.

ANDREAS HINTERHUBER: Do you have any rules of thumb for how you share value with your customers? Let's assume that a complex logistics contract creates €1 million in incremental value for your customer. Are there guidelines for how you split this value with your customer, or is it left to the individual sales managers to negotiate this when it comes to pricing?

MATTHIAS HEUTGER: There are no rigid guidelines. But how value is shared is not left to sales managers; we deal with it case by case, taking into account risk factors, the contribution of each party, and the overall pricing model. There are many different ways you can share gains, and so I can't give you an answer that's valid across the board.

ANDREAS HINTERHUBER: Let's get down to the individual sales manager. What are in your view characteristics – that is, personality traits – of sales managers who excel at value quantification? What are, by contrast, personality traits or behavioral characteristics that make the individual sales manager less effective at value quantification?

MATTHIAS HEUTGER: I can't tell you all our secrets! On top of having a good product and a good solution, the other key to success is having the right salespeople. We have invested significantly to identify the ideal profiles of an account manager and a relationship manager. Besides the usual list of requirements, we look for people who can strategize. They must be able to see how a product or service fits into the customer's setup and how that solution adds value for the customer. And they must know how to articulate this value creation to the customer. This approach demands a strong customer focus, some strategizing, and a lot of listening.

ANDREAS HINTERHUBER: You talk about "strategizing": Is value quantification also a matter of entrepreneurial orientation? Do you feel that the sales managers who are more dynamic, more risk-taking, are better at value quantification than other sales managers who are maybe less entrepreneurial or less risk-oriented?

MATTHIAS HEUTGER: I'm not sure I'd call our people "risk-oriented." In the end, the operation owners need to sign off on contracts, so risk must be properly managed. But our managers need to be dynamic, proactive, think about different ways of doing things, and be interested in exploring new ideas.

ANDREAS HINTERHUBER: One obstacle which your sales managers may come across day to day is the purchasing organization. In some cases purchasing managers are rotated precisely in order to avoid the development of long-term relationships with suppliers that you advocate. Furthermore, some companies may be contractually required to purchase based on LPTA (lowest price technically acceptable) criteria, meaning that criteria are defined first and the selection – on price – occurs thereafter. Can you share some insights on how to change these purchasing criteria of hard-nosed B2B purchasing executives?

MATTHIAS HEUTGER: We tend to encourage our sales managers to seek access to decision makers, that is, to the business, but we need to make sure that we don't lose purchasing people along the way. We also encourage our people to get access to purchasing managers who have a little bit of a strategic view. Value-based discussions require you to access people who appreciate the issues: business owners and purchasing managers who understand supply chain and value creation more holistically.

ANDREAS HINTERHUBER: Once you have access to the business owner, then you can also work on changing purchasing criteria.

MATTHIAS HEUTGER: Yes, at least, that's the first step.

ANDREAS HINTERHUBER: Where does value quantification not work? Are there some types of contracts or some types of customers where value quantification will not work? You could also answer this question from the viewpoint of individual sales managers: Do you encounter instances where individual sales managers say, "Value quantification is a nice idea that works in theory, but I find it not helpful and basically I go on in my old way of selling, whatever that is."

MATTHIAS HEUTGER: I think it does always work. It always helps if you know the value for the customer, regardless of whether the organization is procurement-driven. But – as we discussed earlier – in some cases it takes a lot of effort and a lot of work to get value quantification right. So the questions are: In what situations does value quantification help turn the decision in our favor? And when should we make the effort and investment to quantify value? Of course in B2C it's different, but in B2B it's all about that value creation. And a simple value creation is cost reduction. Although we pride ourselves on knowing the markets very well, sometimes you are working in the dark – you know your own rate and you bid but you may not know your competitors' current rates, so quantifying the cost difference is difficult. So it is especially important to look at the value creation end to end. But I believe the customer will always do the value quantification for themselves – maybe sometimes in a too narrow scope.

ANDREAS HINTERHUBER: Current research we conducted on value quantification suggests that, broadly speaking, there are four categories of quantitative customer benefits: revenue/gross margin improvements, cost reductions, risk reductions, and capital expense savings. These four types of quantitative customer benefits are undisputable – since they represent hard "green" money, that is, monetary benefits the customer can touch and see. Now the question: Which type of value is easiest to sell? What type of value messages does your salesforce focus on most in value-based selling?

MATTHIAS HEUTGER: This varies a lot between products. For us the easiest sell is direct cost reductions, by which I mean direct saving of logistic costs. The next easiest sell is service quality improvement – like faster delivery times – which for customers can mean lower inventory and an improved ability to provide better services to their own customers, and this can lead to revenue and gross margin improvements. Risk reduction and security are also important, particularly in warehousing and transportation. It's important that we help customers to reduce stock-outs, improve customer service, boost customer loyalty, and increase revenue growth. Risk mitigation is very important: think of the life sciences sector and its requirement to keep pharmaceutical products in a certain condition (e.g., an end-to-end cold chain); by achieving this, we help customers reduce costs and protect their brand. On balance, I think the most important value drivers are cost savings – in all forms: logistic costs, inventory costs, etc. – and service improvements for our customers' customers. Revenue increases are also important: if we give customers a better solution, it may enable them to enjoy an advantage vis-à-vis their own competitors.

ANDREAS HINTERHUBER: Great answer. Are there any issues which you would like to add to the topic of value quantification, value-based selling, and pricing?

MATTHIAS HEUTGER: As you know, we practice value-based selling and we quantify the value to customers. Value quantification is important, especially for complex B2B contracts. For us, quantifying value in a credible way is very important. It shows that we actually deliver value.

ANDREAS HINTERHUBER: How can you make value quantification credible and plausible to customers?

MATTHIAS HEUTGER: You have to deliver – that's the basic requirement. So we invite our customers to do a test drive – that's an important thing. And we make sure we are talking to the right people on the customer side, the people who can really appreciate the value. To facilitate this type of interaction in support of sustainable value management, we regularly invite customers to our DHL Innovation Centers (located in Germany, Singapore, and the Americas). Here we showcase our latest and future logistics solutions. We also publish trend reports to keep customers informed of the technologies and innovations that are likely to impact their business. And we conduct customized Innovation Workshops to trigger the co-development of solutions and subsequent proof-of-concept pilots with our customers.

ANDREAS HINTERHUBER: You mention "test drive." You thus suggest that starting small, testing, and scaling up are key elements of value quantification.

MATTHIAS HEUTGER: That depends on how a customer wants to do it. If you say, "Hey, we have an idea here" – and let's assume this idea requires a lot of customer change and implementation effort – in order to manage risk, the customer may say, "Yes, let's test it on a small scale. If we can see the value, then we will expand." This is one option. Another option is that, if the value of a solution is clear, if we've done it before, then we could start right away – without a test. It's always helpful to bring in case studies or best practices from other customers or other industries to demonstrate that you've done this before and substantiate the value that you've created.

ANDREAS HINTERHUBER: Talking about the organizational transformation toward value-based selling: How did the change toward value quantification and value-based selling come about? Was it driven by top management? Did it start at middle-management levels?

MATTHIAS HEUTGER: Some years ago, we decided to change the way we engage with our customers and the way we sell. That's when we started our consultative selling approach and value-based selling. Once we'd begun this journey, it changed our way of doing business and the way we sell. This decision to change wasn't taken lightly. It required considerable training, new processes, and for senior management to "live it." To do this right required a true change management effort. And then of course we had to define the profiles of key personnel in order to implement this change to value-based selling. When we began this journey we made a conscious decision – a management decision – to change our selling approach. This profoundly altered our organization, our processes, and the type of people we now hire.

ANDREAS HINTERHUBER: What kind of advice do you have for those companies who have, like DHL, a competitive advantage but do not have, unlike DHL, processes and capabilities to quantify their competitive advantages into monetary benefits for the customer?

MATTHIAS HEUTGER: My advice is work with the customer. The closer you are to the customer and the more customer knowledge you have, the easier it becomes to do the calculations required for value quantification. If you can't do this because you don't have that access to the data or don't have a relationship with the customer, then I suggest that you obtain a case study of a similar customer or a similar solution and use this as the basis for value estimation. Going in with that estimation will, in many instances, prompt the customer to validate that value with you.

ANDREAS HINTERHUBER: So it really comes down to changing the way you interact with your customers.

MATTHIAS HEUTGER: Absolutely. We truly changed how we interact with customers. We have some really great customer relationships now in which we jointly innovate and co-develop solutions. And that's ultimately what you want to do. The discussion is no longer about price; it's now about trust, mutual benefit, and the willingness to grow together over time.

ANDREAS HINTERHUBER: Mr. Heutger, perfect. I thank you for this insightful conversation and the privilege of this first-hand intellectual exchange.

19 Interview

The ring of truth – value quantification in B2B services

Hinterhuber, Andreas and Kemps, Pascal

ANDREAS HINTERHUBER: Let's explore the topic of value quantification in the context of strategic account management. For what types of contracts or customers do you think value quantification is especially important?

PASCAL KEMPS: It really depends on the nature of your relationship with your customers. It's not just black and white, but if I look at certain tele sales and field sales customers, then you're talking about relatively small customers. Our service is often not part of their customer value proposition, so typically they just want convenience. In such a case, it's hard to quantify the value in the convenience of doing business or in the reliability of the service. Certainly you've got to have good tools, the right salespeople, friendly couriers, a smooth and friendly experience, but it's difficult to put a number on it. It's not impossible, but you don't typically have discussions where you actually physically quantify the value. Of course, if you move up the chain of customers to the key accounts and the strategic accounts, then value quantification is something you need to consider for pretty much every customer. If all is well due to the nature of the strategic relationship, you're playing a significant role in their business. You're delivering part of their service; you're delivering part of their promise to their customers, which essentially means you're part of their value chain; and then of course in every pursuit you've got to come up with your value; otherwise, it turns into a very simple price negotiation. That's the last thing you want in a strategic account setting, although it does happen. And yes, some customers have become pretty clever at setting things up; there are RFQs (requests for quotations) and there's very little room for value quantification. I must admit, though, that more and more you start to see these big customers realizing that this type of behavior [the focus on price] comes at a relatively high cost of change, with difficulties in implementation and with an inability to achieve the targeted savings. I'll give you one very concrete example. Particularly with Express we've got some big customers, and they actually tell us,

Okay, well, I'm going to split up my business. I'm going to give every possible Express provider a chance to bid for our business. And then, basically, we'll just force the user to always use the cheapest one for each individual shipment.

That approach has two fundamental problems. One, you've got a theoretical savings, which procurement can come up with, but obviously the user is going to sit there and is going to use, for example, different systems from different providers, which potentially causes extra workload and cost. Two, the service levels will not always be comparable, like how late a collection can be made, how long the lead time is, and so on. So, potentially, inventory levels need to be adjusted. Those are all things that with this type of procurement approach simply get lost, and that's not

DOI: 10.4324/9781003177937-24

even talking about how a supplier would position their pricing in this bid, because that type of cherry-picking allows cherry-picking in the other direction as well. Why would you lower rates in areas where there is no real alternative? Or bid low on lanes where your network is full? And what you then see is that although you've got nice savings on paper, they never really get implemented: the actual savings never achieve what's expected.

ANDREAS HINTERHUBER: How do you deal with this type of purchasing organization that tries to create an unhealthy level of competition, that is, a competition that ends up being counterproductive for the customer?

PASCAL KEMPS: Well, it is what it is – there's nothing we can really do about it. And it's a perfectly valid choice – we do think that it's probably not the best choice, but it is a fair choice and it is their prerogative to do this, so we adapt to it. You may have heard that we've got our own in-house quality program where we look at process optimization, and this can easily be applied in bid responses. There's value for us in customers who behave in an extremely predictable way in the sense that they can help us streamline our own processes. I personally, years ago, led a project where we knew exactly what the customer's RFQs were going to look like. So we worked out a process that allowed us to respond much more quickly, and each time we met the pricing and the quality benchmarks they set, and we spent 80% less time on it. We could reuse part of that time to quantify whether there is some extra value – like, for example, is the warehouse we're proposing inside or outside a toll parameter, and what does it do to the total cost of ownership? In short, we simply adapted to the customer. Figure 19.1 shows the process improvements we were able to realize on our end after changing the way we respond to this customer's RFQs. It's the natural flow of things, and it's not the case that just because the customer takes a very trans-actional approach you shouldn't be taking a strategic approach to it, because that level of predictability is something we can work with quite well and derive value from, in the sense that we know we'll be able to respond within a specified time with limited effort and with a price and a quality that meets the customer's benchmark. I think it's a natural part of being in sales. There is a second aspect to this type of customer behavior: if you gain a critical mass with the customer – whether due to the number of similar operations or simply due to the nature or size of any individual business you have – you can start to identify opportunities for optimizing costs and services. Part of these you keep in-house to improve your own bottom line, and part you give back to the customer. Even if the customer then takes these achievements into their next RFQ, there will still be knowledge and expertise in your business that allows you to be more competitive than the competition and retain healthy margins. To make it concrete, for one customer, we operate a network of warehouses, spread all over the world. They all have the same function, so we've created an internal community that actively shares best practices, tips, and tricks . . . and meets face to face once a year at one of the sites (each time a different one to maximize the learning experience). During our last community call, we had 22 participants from 14 countries all over the world. This is an inexpensive and easy-to-implement way of working, but the results are spectacular: our hit rate on new business is more than two times higher than our average, and retention is de facto 100% (the only exception occurred when a ware-house was closed down due to structurally slow sales in that region). It's hard to beat a competitor that is always on the mark in terms of price, consistently makes cost-savings commitments in the contracts, and consistently wins quality awards – even if

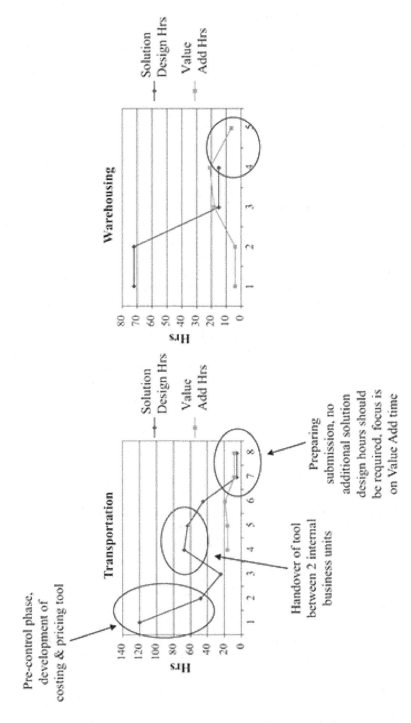

Figure 19.1 Responding to RFQs – process optimization

the customer has a very RFQ–driven culture. And for us, this is really good business – it's financially healthy – but also because it will earn a good strategic account manager (SAM) access to different customer levels and departments.

Fair enough; it's easier to create value with a customer that has a more balanced approach. But to write off transactional customers is to cut off a very interesting source of revenue and business.

ANDREAS HINTERHUBER: Let's get down to a specific example. Your customer sees your price for a complex service contract, and he says that this price is too high because he can get a substantially similar offer for 10% or 20% less. Could you give an example where you were able to overcome these objections with a quantification or documentation of value? In other words, a case where you show your customer that your higher prices are actually less if considered over the life cycle of a contract or if the customer considers further factors, which actually end up saving him money?

PASCAL KEMPS: Yes, there are plenty of examples. I'll give you a very traditional one which you find in logistics. We deal with logistics departments. We get called in for an RFQ. And, when we do our site visits – *gemba* walks, as we call them – we notice, for example, that the packing is not optimal. We have teams of packaging experts who then help design a significantly optimized supply chain. So far competition can follow, but because very few companies in the world buy more packaging than we do, we can actually say, "Why don't we look not only at this project, but also at your overall usage of packaging in their supply chain? And help you procure it or work out a rental scheme?" That's one example. Another example relates to material handling equipment. We buy a lot of material handling equipment. We're also very good at designing warehouses. We're designing not only warehouses but also their continuous improvement. So we can throw these types of elements into the mix and say,

If you're after this, that's fine; here's the price – however, have you thought about this? Because right now you're looking for the cheapest rates on an ocean container, for example, but we can tell you that the ocean container is half-full.

We can do a lot more than that; here's a real customer example where we did both: we suggested a different way of working as well as optimizing packaging. This relates to an otherwise quite commoditized transport service, Ocean Freight. So when you're doing traditional purchasing, you can save a few percent. But we've actually reduced the total cost of operating these Ocean Freight lanes by 50%, and the trigger in that was not only buying; it was redesigning the entire supply chain as well as the packaging, because that particular company was simply not filling their containers as they should (see Figure 19.2). That case was a learning experience for us as well. It's one of those situations where value begins when somebody has an idea, somebody who's walking through a place spotting a latent demand who then links that thought to the latent resources within our organization. From the packaging example, we've developed lots of packaging now for our automotive sector that's enabling us to go in and say,

We're not talking about the €4.5 million that your transport is going to cost; we can tell that you're only going to need 70 runs instead of 100, so it's not going to be €4.5 million, it's going to be €3.8 million.

That's the type of discussion we can then have.

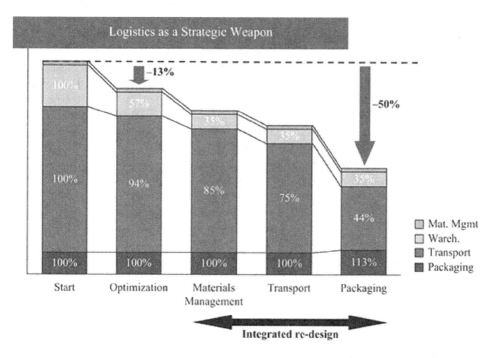

Figure 19.2 Customer value creation in B2B through process redesign

ANDREAS HINTERHUBER: So this process optimization can then mean that you end up making a lower turnover? This means that you sell less?

PASCAL KEMPS: Yes, true, because that's a sacrifice you have to make, and of course it's not always an easy discussion. Really, I call it a sacrifice, because even if we're in a luxury position where we as DHL can offer (almost) any logistics service, these are not pleasant internal discussions. On the other hand, neither are pure pricing discussions or poor attrition rates, and that's often the only alternative: if you're just going to offer what the pack is offering, then somebody else will do it cheaper tomorrow. However, if you're the one who comes up with the ideas and you are seen as authentic – that is, genuinely walking the partnership talk – then when the customer has a problem, challenge, or a question, they come to you, and you have good strategic discussions up front. Your discussion no longer starts with an RFQ; it actually starts with an up-front value discussion: "How on earth are we going to fix this? How can we do this better?" Then you're building something. That's the "strategic" in strategic account management.

ANDREAS HINTERHUBER: Very well. What you're saying is that you care less about short-term revenue losses and more about building consultative or collaborative relationships with your customers.

PASCAL KEMPS: Exactly. I don't know if the expression even exists in English, but in Dutch we say, "Trust comes on foot, but leaves by horse." It means that it takes time to build trust, so either you can invest in always becoming cheaper and cheaper, or you can invest in building up a meaningful business relationship. Now, I believe both models work, but generally speaking the latter one is more satisfying for the employees and also more sustainable. It's also the more difficult part, because it's a lot harder to create a strong relationship, a value-added relationship through commercial operations, than it is to lay people off or invest in cost-bound technology automation.

ANDREAS HINTERHUBER: Fantastic example! Let me lead to the next question, which is, I think, tricky for many companies. And before I ask the question, I will make a small premise: some companies do value-based selling, and they do value-based pricing very well. One obvious example is a company such as BMW or Audi or Volvo. And, of course, these companies quantify the value of safety, prestige, or luxury for you. But this does not mean that you pay for your Audi or your Volvo based on the amount of luxury, safety, or prestige you enjoy. You pay up front, and that's a fixed price. So the question I would like to explore is that value-based pricing for some companies means they quantify the value and then they charge a price, which reflects that value, but this price is fixed. On the other hand, there are other companies that practice value-based pricing, and these companies interpret value-based pricing as performance-based pricing. They define relevant performance indicators together with their customers, and then price will vary depending on how the company performs against some of these performance indicators. What's your take on this? Do you think value-based pricing requires performance-based pricing, or do you think value-based pricing is also possible by setting a fixed price like, for example, how Volvo does?

PASCAL KEMPS: I think performance-based pricing – that is, the performance-based contracting like you find in the public sector – has its strengths and its weaknesses. In my humble opinion, you too often fall into a scenario whereby you manage by statistics, but it doesn't necessarily mean that you're managing what matters. On-time delivery, for example, can mean absolutely nothing, and I'll give you one example. Let's assume, for the sake of argument, that with a large car dealer we've got an 80% on-time delivery service (which is very, very bad; it's just to make the example easy). If he ordered five boxes of parts, that means that one box out of five didn't get delivered. Now, the way order and pick-and-pack processes work in big warehouses, you don't necessarily have all the parts for one car in the same box – they may be spread out over several boxes depending on, for example, the location of the parts in the warehouse. That means that in that one box that didn't get delivered, there may be parts for every single car that that dealer wanted to repair on that specific day. Our performance actually looks like it's 80%, but in reality there was no service because the dealer simply couldn't finish any of the cars that he had.

ANDREAS HINTERHUBER: Great example!

PASCAL KEMPS: So there you've got to be cautious. There is one customer whose name I must keep confidential for whom we don't measure the statistics; he measures the logistics service by the number of customers who didn't receive service, which then creates a totally different discussion because then the 80% would show as zero service basically. And thus you have a more holistic view of things. I'll give you another simple example of how KPIs can be misleading. Say we try to ship something, but the pickup is too late because the material in the warehouse isn't ready for whatever reason when our driver shows up. The driver does what he can, but he gets to our terminal late, and so the shipment doesn't get loaded in the right container; it misses a sort and is delivered late. It looks as if it's us, the transport provider, who's at fault.

But in this case it's the warehouse's fault. As the transport provider we could easily pump up our KPIs by refusing late collections, but that can't be the spirit, surely. Now, we could have been the warehouse and somebody else could have done the transport, but this is just for the sake of the argument. In such a case, when you just measure by KPIs and performance, it just doesn't mean much, to be honest. I'm not saying it doesn't mean anything – it does have value, but it certainly doesn't help anybody in this example. So I think the performance-based contract only works if it's properly set up and thought through. And if I'm perfectly honest, I don't know many examples where that's done in such a way that it truly serves the best interests of the customer and their customers, because it's difficult to do. It's not something you can pull out of a hat any time you need it. And that goes back to the fixed price. There are two aspects to it. In some cases we can get away with it. If I look at our service into emerging markets, then we know we are there much faster than anybody else. So, yes, there is a premium, there is a fixed price to it, and it will be more expensive than the competition's. The irony of it all is that often competition even outsources the business to us. So, in that case, you can simply say, "Here is the price," and that's it. You can't go crazy on it either – it always has to be reasonable – but we do know that there's a very significant service advantage. If you look at other markets and other areas, it's virtually impossible to use a fixed price, because what you can physically do as a service is too similar to what others can do. Then you've really got to start looking at other options, like the example of packaging I gave. There's no clear-cut answer to this one, at least not in logistics.

ANDREAS HINTERHUBER: You clearly caution against the folly of managing by statistics. Some companies, you find, are excellent at collecting data. But unfortunately, you suggest, you will frequently find that these data don't mean anything to the customer.

PASCAL KEMPS: Well, yes, I mean, the statistic becomes the goal, and that's simply wrong. I'll give you another example I think most people will be able to relate to easily, even if they're not in logistics. Let's imagine that you ship something. Then there could be all kinds of reasons for a delay: it could be totally uncontrollable – like customs being difficult – or totally controllable – like a missort in one of our facilities – or even customer controllable – like a customer's decision to accept shipments only on specific days of the week. Imagine that somebody decides to send a shipment down to, for the sake of argument, Argentina, and that the receiver in Argentina says, "I don't want you to deliver it today, but deliver it to me every Thursday," so we're going to have the shipment there, we're going to fly it out there like it's urgent, and then it's simply going to sit there for X days. And the statistics guy would show this item as an uncontrollable factor, so it's deducted from our gross performance and therefore doesn't show in the net performance. We can say, "Okay, our net performance is 95% to 96%." But the real question is, "Why on earth are we shipping this urgently?" Obviously, the receiver doesn't need it urgently; there are better ways – this isn't giving better customer service to ship it quicker. You can start to think, "Let's consolidate several shipments and airfreight it down to that customer; it will be cheaper for everybody." In summary, because they look at net performance, which is 95% to 96%, that statistic doesn't really tell you that actually we're probably spending money on something we shouldn't be spending money on. Or the example of the late box that I gave you, the 80% – well, that can be very well 0%; the 80% isn't going to tell you anything.

ANDREAS HINTERHUBER: The key in your experience is thus to move from meaningless KPIs to a few business indicators that truly matter to your customers in the sense of being specific to each customer's unique circumstances.

PASCAL KEMPS: You've hit the nail on the head. I think we should start calling it key business indicators and actually measure the impact of the value chain on the customer. The last thing I personally, as a customer, want is the message "service delivered" when I don't have the stuff on my doorstep. So how did the value chain perform? I'm sitting at the end. I receive goods from whoever, it doesn't matter. Did I get it, or not? Did I get it on time? Did I get it undamaged? Simple question: yes or no. Did we achieve it or not? That's the only thing that matters. And behind that, there can be a million key performance indicators. But the only thing that matters is those business indicators, because that's going to determine my satisfaction, my repeat purchase, my loyalty. As a service provider it's crucial to think about these things, because therein lies your potential to create value. If you don't think about it, not only are you missing opportunities, but the customer will get challenged by the market sooner or later and you're just a domino stone in the chain.

ANDREAS HINTERHUBER: There is only one key question: By how much did the profitability of your customer improve thanks to your performance?

PASCAL KEMPS: Yes, exactly – the performance of the value chain – because if you look at just how complex many products and goods have become and how complex the delivery of those products and goods has become, you've got to look at the value chain and work your way backward: "Okay, this didn't work; this customer did not get what he asked for – why?" How many customers did not get what they ordered and what they asked for? And then, work your way backward. And then, based on that, determine for the whole value-chain key business indicators. Going back to the earlier example – we get our material one hour after the normal departure time of the courier, so we're going to try to push it through, because if it misses the sort window and it's left behind, it's going to show in our performance because we accepted it and yet we are late. But did the problem happen within our area? No, it's further up the value chain. This is typically an easy one to address, but there are far less easy ones to tackle. And yet I see examples every day where even the easy ones are not being addressed, because the KPIs drive different behaviors – or no behavior at all ("I'm hitting my numbers – what's the problem?").

ANDREAS HINTERHUBER: Value quantification of course is easier if you can link your own performance to financial outcomes. The classic example is this: If you can say, "I saved you one million in inventory costs" you can then say, "Let's find a way to share this." Easy. But what about some intangible benefits that you provide to your customers? You could be seen as the most innovative logistics company. You could be seen as the company – turning back to our example earlier – that collaborates and co-creates value in consultative relationships with customers better than anyone else. The key challenge thus is: Is there a way you can put a reliable price premium or value premium on all these capabilities? Or do you attach a value premium intuitively? In the latter case you would probably say:

Okay, I know there's a competitor, I have a feeling for the price levels they practice with my key accounts, and I estimate that whatever we do on top of this competitor has intangible benefits that must be worth around 5% to 10% or so.

PASCAL KEMPS: In order to determine this, you need to understand the buying process within your customers. Some customers have a rule that the buying occurs in the business, which means you're going to be dealing with a guy who's going to run the operation. He's not only buying it; he's also taking the responsibility for making sure that it works. So clearly there you can have a much more qualitative discussion with less quantification. There you can have these discussions saying, "We're working on this. Why don't we look at that?" And you just can't quantify it, because in the course of the project, you don't have the time, the knowledge, the data, the expertise available to make it happen. But you can simply say, "Fine, as part of our response, here's the financial picture, here are some quantified benefits, here are a bunch of things that we will commit to looking at together with you, and here are the time frames." You can say, "Fine, this is what we are going to do." That, then, is a very concrete application. Now, if you're dealing with organizations where the buying and the operations are split, it's a completely different situation (although things are never 100% black or white). There, basically procurement will have been given a mandate to buy something, and often they will be shielding potential providers as much as possible from the users because they want to keep full control over the RFQ over the life of the project. It's much more difficult because these folks have to meet a set of user-specified criteria, and obviously they don't contain these non-tangible benefits necessarily. If you know the criteria up front – and this is again where the customer intimacy comes from and what I mentioned about building up a sustainable value relationship with a customer – then you can insert them and you can influence the RFQ. But it's certainly more difficult, especially in the earlier stages of development of the customer, to do this. It's still, then, valuable to do it because those types of intangible benefits open good discussions, they create customer intimacy, and they create a positive atmosphere. The customer will start to think,

Maybe we're not doing much business with them. But let's go talk to them because I remember they have some good stuff when it comes to supply chain risk management, they have some really good stuff when it comes to packaging. They've been doing some work with augmented reality/vision picking in warehouses.

Then you come to the table and have a discussion. For example, we have an innovation center in Germany, Troisdorf – you are very welcome to visit it one day – where we have a team of researchers who research relevant topics such as crowd logistics. Have a look at www.delivering-tomorrow.com. We've looked at augmented reality, unmanned aerial vehicles, self-driving vehicles. These are big hypes today, but we have really mapped out "What can it mean for logistics?" "How could this work?" and then tested them in real-life operations. Very few companies have done this, but along with the "paper" insights, we allow customers to experience different options in person in the innovation center and talk to subject-matter experts. That makes things tangible, and as a result we're soon going to open another innovation center in Singapore. We have lots and lots of customers who go there and who really enjoy going there because they actually see what's going to happen in their area going forward. And the beauty of it all is that it's an environment where we have very open, friendly discussions with them about what will be the future of logistics, what projects are running up there, what's on their minds, etc. It helps you build a potential value proposition going forward.

ANDREAS HINTERHUBER: Fantastic example! The point is that you show them softly who is the thought leader in the logistics industry and you softly sell them the idea that they could partner with a thought leader, that you could take them in a direction they themselves don't have a full idea about, and that you are the most reliable partner to take them into an undefined future.

PASCAL KEMPS: Exactly. And if these are people from the business and they are the ones who sell you on a project, then they are actually very suitable for these discussions because they will take these considerations into their business decision. If you talk about very procurement-driven types of organizations, then it's a way to create a positive, open atmosphere, to get out from behind the brick wall that's often in place; you get a friendly discussion and you get an early visibility on project needs and requirements. It's your starting point for a value approach; that's it. So there are two angles to it. With regard to your point on thought leadership, it indeed helps them feel reassured about you as a company. In our case the scale is large because we can offer a broad range of logistics solutions, but for smaller companies there's no reason why this can't be done within a narrower focus. A lot is possible in today's world.

ANDREAS HINTERHUBER: Let's explore the individual characteristics of the SAM. We could argue that selling in the old days was different, and we don't talk about the golf course or the whiskey or the martini at two o'clock in the afternoon, but selling in the old days was all about selling features or benefits. And if we take our conversation through the natural consequence, then we say selling today and in the future means that at least for some of your strategic accounts, selling is all about co-creating value, quantifying value, and selling business impact. This then leads to the question: At the level of individual characteristics or even personality traits, what are some of the characteristics that are required at the level of the SAM today? What, by contrast, are some of the behavioral characteristics where you see that they simply don't fit, that these people don't make the cut, and you maybe have to reassign them to a different role because they may find it difficult operating in this new environment?

PASCAL KEMPS: Crucial – and this is rule number one – is being aligned with the customer. You've got very transactional customers for whom you need somebody who's really good at project managing and sales pursuits in order to be able to standardize and industrialize these responses and work for the procurement – see the earlier example. Then you've got the ones – customers from Asia, for example – who really work around a trust-based, snowball type of development and whose trust you have to earn by taking on smaller projects and then gradually building them up. They will be very loyal to their providers, and you can really only get in if you come up with new ways of doing things. Both customer profiles require different account manager profiles. I'm giving you two extremes on the spectrum, but that's number one: There's got to be a good fit between the customer and the salesperson. The second point, then, is that when you build such a team, you need to look at the different characteristics within that team. At a minimum, there needs to be somebody who can think very much outside the box. The guy who, when you send him to a customer, comes out and says: "These are the five things the customer wants, but here are ten other things we can think about, because I think they need this or I seem to understand they've got this challenge" – really outside-the-box thinking. Now, the trouble with those profiles is that you sometimes need to get them back on track. So, in my mind, then, you need to always have a healthy counterbalance with somebody who is more of a day-to-day-like person. The one who says: "Let's roll up our sleeves and get down to business." The variation depends on each customer again, but in my humble opinion, you need a balance between those two. And that then links to the culture of the customer. If you look at certain Asian customers, some people will have a big problem working with them. Why? Because of the snowball development required. These are the guys who run from one big project to the next, the so-called hunters. They're the ones who essentially score the touchdown after the team has brought them forward. They are, I'm generalizing, not necessarily always a good match with Asian customers – I'm putting it in very black-and-white terms now. So you need to have somebody with those traits on a team, but for Asian customers you need outside-the-box thinkers. It's a very simplified view, to be honest, because there are so many dimensions you need to look at and so many character traits that you need to look at. Another profile example is that you need to have, on each and every team, a data miner, because in logistics everything we do is data, so you need to have somebody who can really read within the operations and pull out where the inefficiencies are, where the service issues lie, how things can be improved. So you need to have somebody with that type of brain as well – not necessarily in the sales function, but very closely supporting them. When you talk strategic accounts, it's a team pursuit. It's not that you need a dozen dedicated people on each strategic account; you can make a mix. In fact, these differences between customers are a great way to help your people learn/develop new skills by diversifying their portfolio. So, to summarize, the number one point is that you need to align the right team with the customer's culture. Then you will be successful internally and externally.

ANDREAS HINTERHUBER: Yes. And the second point, which you stressed, is this snowball effect, which means that you have to find people who are comfortable developing or investing in long-term collaborative relationships without seeing an immediate benefit.

PASCAL KEMPS: Yes, exactly; that's crucial in the development of any customer, even if you have those customers who put out big RFQs where you can win or lose multimillion euro deals every two or three years, like you see with a number of customers. Then, even there, you need to have such people who can get to a value-based discussion with customers. Let's put it like this: by using the elements you mentioned – like innovation, like pointing out to users and procurement, "Yes, you're optimizing the container, but you're not optimizing what's inside the container; you can actually be using a lot fewer containers." So these types of discussions you still need to have. Even with customers who have a transactional mentality, the long-term vision of the strategic account managers is necessary because ultimately they are also there to provide a customer service and to manage their business. At some point, somewhere in the organization, there will be people listening.

ANDREAS HINTERHUBER: We touched upon one constituency, the purchasing function, which may or may not be aligned with the business function. And you mentioned how the relationship between purchasing and the business function on the customer side might evolve. But maybe you could provide one example of how to change the purchasing criteria of the purchasing function. To put it a bit more bluntly, some companies say value quantification is all nice and fine, but you deal with purchasing, and purchasing tells you there is one purchasing criteria, which is price, and the second one is price, and the third one is price as well. Put differently, a bit more technically again: A number of companies are more or less required to put out RFQs based on LPTA (lowest price technically acceptable), which basically means that they first define the criteria and that once you pass them, then of course they select on price and price alone. What are your thoughts on how to change the decision criteria of the purchasing function?

PASCAL KEMPS: There are a couple of points. First of all, what people sometimes forget about procurement is that it also has a benefit for the likes of us, and that is that we tend to get information and data in a structured, easy-to-work-with way. If you work directly with business owners, they're typically not used to running a lot of RFQs, so what you get is sometimes very difficult to work with. So I think procurement, which most companies are very good at, guarantees a certain level of quality standardization and clarity that is difficult for business owners to produce. But, as you mentioned, many organizations – arguably all of them – officially go for the LPTA. This means that at some point procurement will go into the business – they will be starting to gather information from the business – and that's where you actually need to be. At that point, you will need to have proved your point and exposed them to the potential value so that the RFQ, the technical specifications, is written in such a way that it factors in these value elements. That's it. And that can take a very long time; it's not always easy to do. It also depends on the state the company is in – needless to say, companies in a financially difficult situation will simply be going much more for the lowest price and won't be bothered too much about changing the technical specifications. I work mostly with the automotive industry, and we know what kind of crisis they've been through. That was a time when (almost) everybody was saying,

Listen, you're absolutely right; we know we can do things better, but right now we just can't afford the time to work on that. Even if your idea brings value, right now we just need to come down with costs and with rates short term. So, we apologize, but it has to go like this.

The beauty of it all is that if you then make the investment to show the customer how they could improve – never waste a good crisis – eventually the times turn. Yesterday I was with a customer I'd spoken to two or three years ago about something, and he said, "Well, actually you mentioned that back then, and we couldn't do it, but I would like to talk to you about it now because we are ready for it, and I remembered that this was something really useful." In Japan, there's a beautiful expression, "You have to be prepared to sit on a rock for three years," which means that sometimes you have to be in a difficult, painful situation before you get results. I know that's difficult for many of my colleagues, but fortunately I'm in an organization where it's understood that things may take time, and it's accepted that sometimes you need to make an investment to service a customer in order to achieve a longer-term sustainable success. I'm well aware that that's not the case in all organizations, which means the SAM organization needs to be more careful balancing the short-, mid-, and long-term development activities.

ANDREAS HINTERHUBER: You talk about the cultural or strategic fit with customers. Are there some types of customers who are your preferred customers, whom you would target preferentially? And then, by contrast, what would be some of the cultural traits or strategic traits – whatever we could call them – where you see that there is less of a fit between what you have to offer and how they would like to purchase? What is your take on that?

PASCAL KEMPS: I personally don't have a real preference. Like I said, things are what they are. I understand that individuals, particularly on the sales team, will have certain preferences. The hunter will be totally frustrated with certain types of customers who will only give him small pieces to test and build up trust. The hunter wants to feel the rush of the big RFQs, sail the waves of adrenaline, and celebrate the big win. That's a great fit for a transactional customer – as long as the hunter is counterbalanced by somebody who's good at project-managing and bid-structuring. Coming back to what I said earlier, if you've got a very procurement-driven transactional customer, then you have to adapt yourself to it. Certain people will do well with that, certain others won't, but those who do well are probably going to struggle big time with the more relationship-driven customers.

ANDREAS HINTERHUBER: It's a great answer, because you suggest your company is big enough to deal with all types of customers; that's the point.

PASCAL KEMPS: You can look at things negatively, or you can look at positives. For a small company with a transactional customer, for example, it can mean that they can cherry-pick the business they want. It means they can work in a very structured process, which they can align with. If you're small, it allows for very efficient responses on the pieces of business you can/want to do. I'm playing the devil's advocate certainly, but I mean it. Like the example I gave earlier: We've had a customer like this, and we've streamlined our internal response process to it, and we were able to respond in time with the right quality and the right prices every time in the first round already with an 80% reduction in the time spent, so we can free up those resources for somebody else.

ANDREAS HINTERHUBER: Great! Let's talk about your own lessons learned. Some companies will look at DHL and say that DHL is really an excellent example of a company that develops collaborative relationships with customers and that can quantify its own contribution to the customer's bottom line. Some companies, however, are truly at the beginning of this process, either because they sell only based on features or because they have to sell heavily on price, simply because they don't know how to quantify value. So what are some of the lessons you learned during this journey? What advice would you give to companies that have a well-defined competitive advantage but in some ways struggle to convert this advantage into quantified and documented customer benefits?

PASCAL KEMPS: One is the Japanese example of sitting three years on a rock. It's going to hurt, you're going to hit a wall, you're going to misjudge customers at times, you're going to misjudge projects, you're going to misjudge your own capabilities, your own competitive strength. It's all part of it. We've had this, too: Even if we've always had growth – it's pure fantasy that you can get away without growth – in the last couple years in particular we've seen phenomenal growth. It took us years to actually reach this level, simply because we were also in a learning period; that's true for many other customers, for many people out there. And this is not something that an individual can agree to; this has to come from management. There has to be a firm belief that, yes, this is going to work; we're not going to shut the whole SAM organization down after a year. The SAM management and each individual SAM need to make deliberate choices about what short-, mid-, and long-term development they focus on. We – as SAMs – have got to keep growing, learning from our mistakes as we go forward, and we've got to keep investing in the people to keep them on board, to keep them motivated. That's the big learning, having gone through the cycle personally myself and together with this organization. I was here when it started back in 2003, so I've pretty much seen every stage of it and learned. Two is the message I tried to give at the Strategic Account Management Association (SAMA) as well about a very small company, Avonwood. I think it's a beautiful example of a company that's very small on its own, too small to be truly global, to be carrying big investments in innovation. They were in every possible way the complete opposite of our company. Yet they've been able to piggyback on, in this case, the innovation project that we operated with Volvo, the Maintenance-on-Demand project. They've been getting their funding 100% basically from the European Commission, so basically it cost them nothing; they got 100% coverage plus 20% for fixed costs, and now 70% of their sales is coming from the product they developed out of it. Of course, it does take a vision to actually get it, and you have to fall into the right project, but my message there is that there are many resources out there, if you look around, that you can actually leverage. I could give some examples, which are completely outside the box, of low-cost solutions we've put forward that we've developed which would probably be within reach for other companies, too. For example, we've looked at some customers as there was a crunch in the industry; cash was tight; we've worked with banks where we were offering inventory financing. Why? Because we offer certain standards, there's a certain level of trust from the banks, and they said, "Fine, we're willing to buy the inventory and therefore relief cash on the side of the customer as long as DHL, who is working according to these standards, is the custodian of the goods." That's one example – very concrete. The second one is something I call "start-up within our company." It has to do with supply chain resilience, which has built up expertise on scanning hundreds of sources a day on potential supply chain disruptions, and now our customers can subscribe to it as a service for a very low fee. They then get informed, for example, about an accident that happened on the highway: "Stuttgart has been closed off completely, which means the flows are going from A to B, and on that track you might want to divert them." So these are the types of products, this could have been a start-up somewhere in Silicon Valley or what have you, but it's something that we pulled together. I think it's a matter of also looking beyond your scope, and sometimes people say we should just focus on our core, but I think the key question you need to ask yourself is "What is your core?" and you need to be willing to look at it. Those are my two pieces. It's going to take time; that's inevitable. Certain things simply take time. You can't force a tree to grow faster than it can. You can give it the optimal conditions to grow in – but you're going to have to wait until it's big if you want wood to build some furniture. It's as simple as that; there's nothing you can do about it, and it's only up to perfect conditions. And the second point I mentioned is that if you start to look around you'll find that there are more ways to differentiate than you probably imagined. The role of SAM is to foster these thoughts and projects within their people; they don't need to be revolutionary. And, again, it's a great way to motivate and educate people, giving them something different from the day to day.

ANDREAS HINTERHUBER: Two great pieces.

PASCAL KEMPS: The guys from Avonwood are more than happy to show that case. For them, it's also free advertising, but I thought it was a brilliant example. It's a very small company with just a handful of people – it's literally a dad with his son and a handful of other people – and they hooked up with us through this Maintenance-on-Demand project, and now 70% of their sales are from this project – they are active worldwide.

ANDREAS HINTERHUBER: Is there anything we missed in the overall exploration of this topic of quantifying and documenting value to customers? Are there any further questions you yourself would like to raise?

PASCAL KEMPS: Well, there are a couple of points. Basically, I think there's a sensibility that you need to bring when you talk about value. The biggest mistake you often see is that you bring value to the customer, and particularly in a pre-sales, before you sign a contract, and essentially you find out that your competitor can bring the same value. So it won't help you if that value becomes part of the RFQ. If you can apply the law of substitution, you haven't created value, basically. That's something in a pre-RFQ cycle you need to be very cautious with, because clever procurement organizations will simply take it, and you will have made your competitors stronger than they were. The other one is the "ring of truth." I'm sure you get emails in which the claims are just too good to be true. But even if you can't quantify it, can you substantiate how you're going to do it, how you're going to provide it in such a way that the customer will go and you can validate and say, "Yes, this makes sense, I believe what you're saying"? I regularly spend time with our procurement, and it's a great learning for a sales guy. Very often your suppliers come in and state, "We can do this for you," to which the response is,

So could the guy before you. And by the way, where's the proof? Can you demonstrate this? Can you – I understand you can't quantify it – but where did you do this? Facts – hard facts: how are you going to handle this?

And then the sales guy walks away, sends in a presentation a week later, by which time everybody has halfway forgotten the message, and nobody takes the time to read it anyway. That's fundamental: The value mustn't be interchangeable with your competition. So, can you demonstrate clearly that you are able to do this? One example, we can leverage our innovation center because we can show what we do there, but we also offer, for example, virtual tours through certain of our operations. It's a robot that drives around between the staff in a live operation, and the audience – wherever they are in the world – can see, live, what's going on. We can actually show them everything we're doing. That's a simple and effective way to prove that what we say is very real.

ANDREAS HINTERHUBER: You suggest attaching a lot of meat, proof, to your promises is key in this context of value quantification.

PASCAL KEMPS: Yes, but remember it takes time to write something concise. You don't want a 100-page presentation either. You can simply say, "Here's a little movie" or "Here's the process, which we're going to take you through";

We're going to start on this date. These are the people who are there. This is their background. They are going to do this, this and this. They are going to run through your operation. Look at your packaging. They will deliver the report. And by that date, we will be ready to discuss. And by the way, here is some proof of the procurement of packaging in the past with this or that customer.

It's as simple as that. Blaise Pascal once wrote, "Sorry to write such a long letter; I didn't have time to write you a short one." It's about making it and putting it in there, but you don't end up sending a presentation a week later, which nobody is going to read; instead, it's about building it in, in a very concise, easy-to-digest way.

ANDREAS HINTERHUBER: One thing is clear: You don't want to make your competition stronger than necessary. So one dilemma which you face from time to time is: You describe the process, but you probably have to be careful to not describe it in such detail that your customer just takes your description and puts out an RFQ with these requirements.

PASCAL KEMPS: Yes, and sometimes you have to take that risk, and I admit it does happen to us. Sometimes it's the only way to trigger a change, but then at least you were in early and you have access early and understanding early, and your solution will be seen as the benchmark anyway. But you're right, you've got to be very cautious and always ask yourself, "What I'm proposing here – can my competition do the same?" Because if they can, it's not the only proposal you want to go in with; you have to think further and take a conscious decision.

ANDREAS HINTERHUBER: How do you pay SAMs whom you expect to wait on a stone for three years? You probably cannot use only short-term revenue targets. Do you use soft indicators such as customer satisfaction? How do you incentivize them to value-based selling and value quantification?

PASCAL KEMPS: There are two aspects. How do you keep them motivated? You've got to make sure it stays meaningful. You can work around it and give them two types of customers to look after who are at different stages of development, so they can taste success enough – let's put it like this. But the second aspect is exactly like you say: There's a whole host of KPIs – we should say business indicators – that are not only related to revenue. Customer satisfaction – and how that evolves – is a very big one. There's always room for every individual to have some specific strategic targets, which are nonmonetary necessarily. That's all part of the package. Every case will be different, but the only thing that matters is how you keep the individual satisfied. Fortunately, there is so much variety in the world that with a bit of creativity you can achieve a lot for your people, your customers, and your organization.

ANDREAS HINTERHUBER: Great! Pascal, this has been a rich and rewarding conversation. Thank you.

Part VI

Buying and selling on value – value quantification tools

20 A question of value

Customer value mapping versus economic value modeling[1]

Nagle, Thomas T. and Smith, Gerald

To set and justify prices that reflect customer value, one must first be able to measure it. In the early 1980s two very different approaches to measuring customer value emerged in management practice. Both are commonly cited in the marketing literature and used by practitioners and consultants as if the choices between them were merely one of convenience. In fact, the two approaches make substantially different assumptions about customer behavior and have different implications for how to set price for a differentiated product. Since only one can be right, the practical implications of picking the wrong one can be very costly.

Customer value mapping (CVM) emerged from the total quality management movement, in which firms endeavored to measure and deliver superior functional performance more cost-effectively. Authors such as Monroe (2002) and Gale (1994) argue that buyers should and do evaluate competitive products by calculating the ratio of product performance to price (a ratio calculation). For example, Monroe summarizes the ratio view that

> buyers' perceptions of value represent a mental trade-off between the quality or benefits they perceive in the product relative to the sacrifice they perceive by paying the price: Perceived value = perceived benefits (gain) divided by perceived sacrifice (give).
>
> (p. 104)

The alternative, economic value modeling (EVM), stems from the industrial purchasing world in which firms estimated the economic savings they would realize by buying one firm's product compared with the products of competitive suppliers. Here researchers such as Forbis and Mehta (1981), Dodds et al. (1991), Rust and Oliver (1994), and Hinterhuber (2004) argue that value is the utility of quality minus the disutility of price (a difference calculation).

Of the two, CVM has been more broadly applied by marketers, purchasing departments, and even the early developers of the Malcolm Baldridge National Quality Award, because it requires only information about how products in a category are perceived to perform relative to one another, whereas EVM requires understanding how differences in performance affect the customer. Unfortunately, despite its greater simplicity and intuitive appeal, CVM leads sellers and buyers of differentiated products and services to undervalue them systematically, thus undermining the potential for innovative products and services to win sales at prices that reflect their superior worth.

DOI: 10.4324/9781003177937-26

Empirical research, finally, suggests that customer value models that integrate quality and price linearly perform better than models that integrate price and quality as a ratio (DeSarbo et al., 2001).

The flawed logic of customer value mapping

The basic assumption underlying CVM is that customers evaluate products and services relative to each other by comparing their price to performance ratios. A product with a lower price performance ratio, CVM proponents claim, will win market share from competitors as customers discover that it represents a better value. In short, the CVM argument is that customers will prefer a product that offers them the lowest price per unit of performance. So, for example, a new drug that is 50% more effective in treating a disease would be preferred only if its price were no more than 50% higher than the alternative treatment.

The problem with CVM is that it fails to recognize that markets value products and services differently when their related benefits are commoditized – achievable from all brands – than when their benefits are differentiating – achievable from only one brand. "Commodity value" is the worth of the benefits associated with features that resemble those of competitors' products. "Differentiation value" is the value associated with features that are unique and different from those of competitors. The price-per-unit value that buyers should be willing to pay a supplier for features that create unique benefits is greater than the price-per-unit value that they should be willing to pay for features that create only commoditized benefits. That's because refusal to pay a supplier's price for differentiating features means that the buyer must forgo those features and the associated unique benefits. Refusal to pay a supplier's price for commodity features, however, means simply that the customer must buy them from another supplier.

Consider a simple example. You have a product – say a solar panel – that is 40% more efficient than its nearest competitor in generating power per square meter of space. How much higher can you price it? For advocates of CVM, the answer would be simple: You could price it no more than 40% higher if all else were identical. For advocates of EVM, however, the answer would require more information. What is the application, and what are the costs and benefits associated with durability in that application?

Let's say that the answer to that question was that the solar panels are to be placed on the roofs of homes. If good locations for placement were unlimited and free, one could simply purchase 40% panels from the competitor and produce the same result. But if good locations for catching sunlight are limited, then a buyer cannot achieve the same benefits simply by buying more of the competitive panels. In that case, the more efficient panels are truly differentiated.

But what, then, is that differentiation worth, and could you ever charge more for it than the 40% premium that equals its performance advantage? To answer that question, we need to know the economic value of the benefit, which in our example is the value of the electricity generated. Let's say that the next best competitive product will generate electricity with a net present value (NPV) of $10,000 over its life and that your efficient solar panel will generate 40% more with a NPV of $14,000. Due to intense competition among commodity suppliers of solar panels, your competitor's panels sell for only $3,000 each. Although there are additional costs of installation to be covered, at least some of the remaining $7,000 difference between the $3,000 price and the $10,000 benefit value is likely to remain as what economists call consumer surplus and what marketers call the purchase incentive. CVM assumes that purchasers will evaluate competing products by comparing the price divided by the benefits received, selecting the option with the lowest price-to-benefit ratio. If applied in this case, that would create an uncomfortable paradox. The price-to-benefit ratio of your competitor's product is $3,000:$10,000, or 30%. If the same ratio were applied to your product, which according to CVM would be necessary to make it competitive, the maximum price you could expect for your superior product would be $4,200 (0.3 times $14,000). If instead your price were $4,900, your price-to-benefit ratio would be 35%, which CVM advocates claim would make it uncompetitive.

Figure 20.1 illustrates the problem. CVM advocates would claim that the ratio of price to value determined by commodity competitors determines a "fair value line," which in this case has a slope of 0.3. The $4,900 price for your product is clearly out of line, so to speak. CVM suggests that your product will lose share because your position is above what CVM advocates call the fair value line. CVM practitioners would recommend that you reduce your price to $4,200 in order to become price-competitive.

But would a customer who paid $4,900 for your product be making a poor purchase decision? At a price of $4,900 for $14,000 of value, your product would generate $9,100 of surplus value per panel. In comparison, your competitor's product prices at $3,000 for $10,000 of value would generate $7,000 of surplus value for the customer. Assuming the other costs of installation were the same for both products, your more efficient panel would give the customer $2,100 more benefit per panel than the competitive product priced at a lower price-to-benefit ratio. For any economically savvy customers seeking to maximize the value of their sunny locations, this should be a compelling argument for buying your product despite a price higher than what CVM advocates would call its fair value.

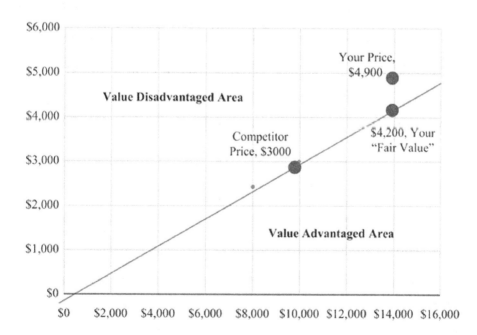

Figure 20.1 Price versus value and "fair value" line

Why do these two approaches to value estimation yield such different results? Because CVM treats all benefits as if they were commodities. If, in the example cited earlier, your differentiated product's added value could be achieved simply by buying 50% more of a commodity brand, then the CVM model would be correct. But if your product produces higher value by offering differentiated benefits that no amount of the commodity product can reproduce, then the CVM model is highly misleading. The correct calculation for value comparison of a differentiated brand is not "dollar worth of benefits divided by price" but "dollar worth of benefits minus price."

Here's an actual B2B example: A semi-conductor manufacturer sold integrated circuit chips to original equipment manufacturers (OEMs) of telecommunications, who sold various products to the consumer marketplace. A key driver of value for these OEMs was "time to market," that is, the time it took to "design in" the new chip into the new product and get the new consumer product to market. This semi-conductor manufacturer excelled at design-in, which enabled its OEM customers to get their consumer products to market usually 2 months faster than it would take to design-in chips from alternative semi-conductor suppliers, out of an industry-average 12-month design-to-launch cycle time. Thus, the improvement in time-to-market "productivity" was about 17% (2 months divided by 12 months).

CVM logic would suggest therefore that the semi-conductor manufacturer could set a price 17% higher than competitors' prices for a comparable semi-conductor. However, the dollar value created per product sold was considerably higher than 17% vis-à-vis other competitive suppliers due to (a) the incremental share of market the OEM company would realize by being first to market, (b) the price premium it would realize before competition effectively entered the market (usually about 4 months of a product's usual 12-month life), and (c) the unit cost savings the OEM would realize by driving volume manufacturing to scale faster than competitors. Figure 20.2 shows an example of a typical semi-conductor offering these advantages with reasonable assumptions: $100 million product market in which competitive reference products cost about $10, 50% contribution margins, 12-month typical product lifetime, first-to-market market share of 30% versus 20% for later entrants, first-to-market price premium of 30% for 4 months, and achieving scale economies 50% faster than competitive products.

The same thing happens in many B2C contexts. BMW promotes its cars, justifiably, as offering greater durability, a more pleasurable driving experience, and more prestige than cars costing half as much. Would buyers of BMWs rate the value of owning one at twice the value of owning a car brand costing half as much? Perhaps not. But owning two of the cheaper alternative, with the potential to deliver twice as much transportation (commodity value), could still not reproduce the unique values associated with owning a BMW. Differentiation values are more costly than commodity values, and not everyone will find them affordable. But a marketer's job is to prove not that differentiating attributes are as bargain-priced as commodity attributes but that differentiating attributes are worth the extra cost relative to the value of the extra benefits they deliver.

The problem with CVM is that it confuses different concepts of value, which need to be clearly understood when communicating price and value to customers.

Use value. The monetary worth of benefits actually received by a customer as a result of using a product or service is what economists call "use value." In *The Strategy and Tactics of Pricing* (Nagle et al., 2011: 18), the authors explain:

> On a hot summer day at the beach, the "use value" of something cold to drink is extremely high for most people – perhaps as high as $10 for 12 ounces of cold

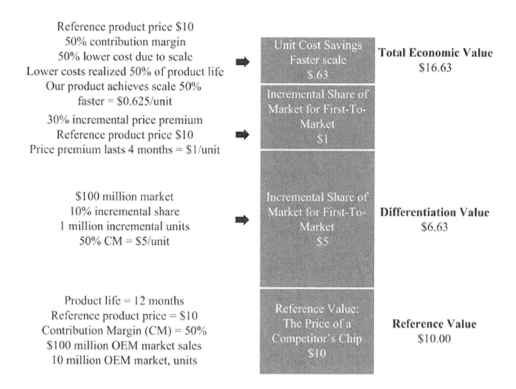

Figure 20.2 Economic value OEM semi-conductor

cola . . . [but] few potential customers would be willing to pay such a price. Why not? Because potential customers know that, except in rare situations, they don't have to pay a seller all that a product is really worth to them. They know that competing sellers will give them a better deal, leaving them with "consumer surplus." . . . [Perhaps] a half mile up the beach is a snack shop where beverages cost just $1.

Richard Thaler's seminal 2008 *Marketing Science* article "Mental Accounting and Consumer Choice" describes this definition of value in use in terms of "acquisition utility" and its value equivalent (i.e., the amount of money that would leave the individual indifferent between receiving the product or its monetary equivalent as a gift). Value in use is realized over the life of the product or service and includes all associated savings and benefits such as installation or maintenance savings or personal or product performance benefits (see Figure 20.3).

Economic value. A product's objective monetary worth to a customer, adjusted for the availability of competitive substitute products, is known as economic value or value in exchange. Even though a product's value in use may be substantial, competitive market forces barter away some of that value through competitive pricing. This value is not lost but simply transferred from sellers to buyers in the form of consumer surplus. Consequently, buyers may be willing to pay sellers in one market less than they pay for similar benefits in another market because the first market offers more competitive alternatives.

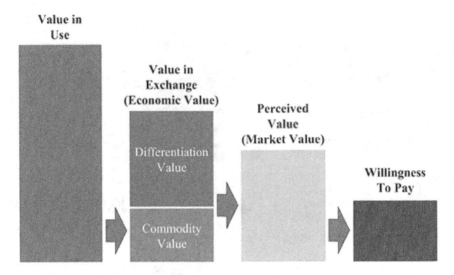

Figure 20.3 Distinguishing between different types of value

To calculate economic value, one must first determine the reference price of competitive substitutes in the marketplace and then determine the incremental use value the product delivers over and above that of competitive substitutes. Shapiro and Jackson (1978) at Harvard Business School advanced this customer-based approach in which the marketer looks at the actual utility or value of the product to the customer and compares that with the utility or value offered by competitors. (See also Nagle et al., 2011 and James C. Anderson, Dipak C. Jain, and Pradeep K. Chintagunta's 1993 *Journal of Business-to-Business Marketing* article, "Customer Value Assessment in Business Markets: A State of Practice Study," which explores the many definitions of value studied by scholars and researchers and settles on this relative conceptualization of value.)

Market value. Market value is the value that buyers perceive a product to be worth. Nagle et al. (2011: 30) comment: "A product's market value is determined not only by the product's economic value (value in exchange), but also by the accuracy with which buyers perceive that value." This means that it's critical not only to understand perceived value (market value) but to understand it separately from actual value so that marketers can compare, diagnose, understand, and recommend strategies to manage the gap between perceived value and real value.

Willingness to pay. This refers to the price that buyers are willing to pay to obtain the value they perceive a product to be worth. Despite their perceptions of value, buyers may be either unable or unwilling to pay for this due to price sensitivity. For instance, heavy-volume purchasers may perceive significant product value but be sensitive to unit price because the total product expenditure is large relative to total income or budget. Thaler's, 2008 description of "transaction utility" and its value equivalent (i.e., the difference between the price an individual pays and some reference price) reflects willingness to pay.

CVM virtually ignores this distinction between use value and economic value. It begins the analysis by asking customers for their subjective ratings of benefits, an indirect way of measuring perceived use value. By measuring only perceived use value, CVM also fails to distinguish between perceived and actual economic value. The consequences of this omission for pricing and marketing are significant since, if a product is selling poorly, an EVM analysis may reveal better alternatives than lowering the price. If a product's perceived value (perhaps as measured by a CVM benefit score) is lower than the actual value estimated by an EVM model, the problem may well be that buyers are uninformed, skeptical, or misinformed by competitors' selling tactics. Rather than lower price to a level that reflects buyers' poor perceptions of value, the firm would be much better off properly educating customers about the product's potential economic value, thus raising its perceived value. Doing so might also reassure risk-averse customers that they will truly realize this actual value, by offering stronger warranties, or perhaps communicate to late-adopter customers that other "opinion-leader" buyers have purchased the product because they know the true value it delivers, and so on.

Finally, the value of the benefits does not tell the full story of why customers may not buy (i.e., why the product is a share loser rather than a share gainer). Willingness to pay merits just as much strategic and analytical rigor as value. Even if customers perceive significant value in a product or service, they may be unable or unwilling to pay because of low budgets or income, because the price represents a large share of their total available budget or for some other reason. In such cases, the answer simply may be to restructure the transaction to facilitate purchase – by offering financing so that buyers can spread payments over time aligned with the timing of the incremental benefits they receive from the purchase.

True measure of value

The process for estimating economic value has been reasonably established by pricing and marketing scholars. Nagle et al. (2011) summarize this process in their textbooks. James C. Anderson and James Narus show a practical application in their 1998 *Harvard Business Review* article "Business Marketing: Understand What Customers Value." John Forbis and Nitin Mehta provide a foundational conceptualization and excellent application in their 1982 *Business Horizons* article "Value-Based Strategies for Industrial Products."

Economic value is the price of the customer's best alternative (the reference value) plus the value of what differentiates the offering from the alternative (differentiation value). Differentiation value identifies all factors that differentiate the firm's product from the competitive reference product; these are sources or drivers of differentiation value. The worth of each of these drivers of differentiation value is estimated by quantifying the savings and gains that customers would realize by using the firm's product rather than the competitor reference product.

To be sure, although rational customers will often pay much more than the price that the CVM model would predict, they are rarely willing to pay as much as the EVM would say a product is worth. Factors such as uncertainty about the promised benefits, switching costs, and perceptions of fairness will all reduce willingness to pay to a level below economic value. Economic value is, however, a useful starting point for communicating value to customers and for building a marketing program that supports capturing a large portion of it in price and increasing the perceived purchase incentive for the customer. CVM's "fair value" is, in contrast, a declaration that innovation and marketing are not true value since, despite building product differentiation and the means to communicate it, "fair prices" are in the end simply commodity prices. We believe that sellers should refuse to accept this flawed proposition, countering it with the logic of EVM.

Note

1 Portions of this chapter were originally published by the authors as "A Question of Value," Marketing Management (July/August 2005).

References

Anderson, J. C., Jain, D. C. and Chintagunta, P. K. (1993) "Customer value assessment in business markets: A state-of-practice study," *Journal of Business-to-Business Marketing 1*(1), 3–29.

Desarbo, W. S., Jedidi, K. and Sinha, I. (2001) "Customer value analysis in a heterogeneous market," *Strategic Management Journal 22*(9), 845–857.

Dodds, W. B., Monroe, K. B. and Grewal, D. (1991) "Effects of price, brand, and store information on buyers' product evaluations," *Journal of Marketing Research 28*(3), 307–319.

Forbis, J. L. and Mehta, N. T. (1981) "Value-based strategies for industrial products," *Business Horizons 24*(*3*), 32–42.

Gale, B. M. (1994) *Managing Customer Value*, New York: The Free Press.

Hinterhuber, A. (2004) "Towards value-based pricing – An integrative framework for decision making," *Industrial Marketing Management 33*(*8*), 765–778.

Monroe, K. B. (2002) *Pricing: Making Profitable Decisions* (3rd ed.), New York: McGraw-Hill.

Nagle, T. T., Hogan, J. E. and Zale, J. (2011) *The Strategy and Tactics of Pricing: A Guide to Profitable Decision Making* (5th ed.), Boston, MA: Prentice Hall.

Rust, R. T. and Oliver, R. L. (1994) "Service quality: Insights and managerial implications from the frontier," in R. T. Rust and R. L. Oliver (eds.), *Service Quality: New Directions in Theory and Practice* (pp. 1–19), Thousand Oaks, CA: Sage.

Shapiro, B. P. and Jackson, B. B. (1978) "Industrial pricing to meet customer needs," *Harvard Business Review 56*(6), 119–127.

Thaler, R. H. (2008) "Mental accounting and consumer choice," *Marketing Science 27*(1), 15–25.

21 Why start-ups should consider using value propositions

Foos, Lennart and Kirchberger, Markus

Why start-ups should consider using value propositions

It is not only large established firms that have to convince potential customers of the value their products deliver; young start-ups do, as well. The commercialization of a product is a complex process, especially when it comes to new technology (Gans and Stern, 2003). Customers need to be convinced to leave behind old and familiar technology and trust a start-up to deliver higher value with their novel product. We researched how, in this setting, value quantification can contribute to successful commercialization.

The start-up setting is especially interesting because a product might still be under development, allowing modifications which increase customer value. Therefore, we see the exchange of information about customer value not as a one-way stream, which serves to convince the customer, but as a means to gain insights. The numerical information gathered on customer value can help shed light on customers' operations and on the application of the product (Wouters and Kirchberger, 2015).

Our case study is set in a start-up from a German technology university; however, our research is not only interesting for other start-ups. In times of open innovation and ever faster disrupting technologies, managers also need to understand how they can work with start-ups or innovate to render their own business models agile, like start-ups do (Chesbrough, 2003).

Callahan and Lasry (2004: 107) found that

> the importance of customer input increases with market newness of a product up to a point and then drops off for very new products, whereas the importance of customer input increases with technological newness of a product without dropping off.

Therefore, start-ups trying to launch a technologically new product need to establish intense contact with potential customers and end users. We propose the customer value proposition (CVP) as an instrument for doing this.

The CVP encourages market and customer orientation and offers a strategic methodical approach to quantifying customer value and eventually marketing a product. Using the structured approach of a CVP can help a start-up find a suitable pilot customer in order to establish a constructive cooperation. According to Lindgreen and Wynstra (2005), customer relationships fulfil two main functions: the direct functions of profit, volume, and safeguarding; and the indirect functions of innovation, marketing, scouting, and access.

However, customer contact can also be used to develop a better understanding of customer needs and the start-up's own competencies and to facilitate organizational learning (Jalkala and Salminen, 2010). The commitment of the start-up and the pilot customer as

DOI: 10.4324/9781003177937-27

well as the bidirectional sharing of information and knowledge is essential and one of the most important keys to success (Ruokolainen and Igel, 2004; Ruokolainen, 2008).

The research described in this chapter was conducted at a public, research-based, high-tech start-up called cubuslab GmbH. Cubuslab has developed an innovative machine-to-machine (M2M) communication solution for laboratory instruments; it was developed during the research assignment of the technical founder at Karlsruhe Institute of Technology (KIT). The first development steps and prototypes were implemented and tested at KIT. Laboratory workers were introduced to the technology, and they gave feedback on its usefulness and how they could imagine using it in their future working environment.

From a practical point of view, we follow the ideas on CVPs formulated in Anderson et al. (2007) and Anderson et al. (2006). We propose that their approach can be enhanced through design thinking (DT) methods. In this work, certain stages of the DT approach and the derived value proposition canvas (VPC) were applied in a supportive manner and extended the existing ideas for crafting a CVP.

We focus on how customer value can be quantified in monetary terms. Additionally, we pay special attention to the determination and access of the target market as well as the establishment of buyer-supplier relationships.

Our perspective on value propositions

We build our research on the current understanding in literature about customer value. This includes the commercialization of new technology based on research and the topic of customer value and its different interpretations.

Challenges for new technology ventures

According to Conceição et al. (2012), academic entrepreneurs possess limited knowledge of the industry and markets they are entering. Aggravating this situation is the fact that inventions that originate from academic research tend to be more fundamental and often need substantial development before commercial application (Thursby et al., 2001). The most challenging part for public research-based start-ups and university spin-offs often is not the development of new technologies but their commercialization. Unlike established companies, new ventures lack market and customer experience. Additionally, they have only a few resources (Gans and Stern, 2003), which limits their flexibility. In order to use their available resources effectively and efficiently, start-up companies should focus on those features and competencies that result in the highest perceived customer value.

Customer value

In the late 1980s, the idea of customer value emerged and had a significant impact on how customers and their needs were treated. That enabled companies to gain deeper insight into the market as a whole, also reflecting their competitors' customers' opinions, and therefore improved their competitive situation. Zeithaml (1988: 14) concludes that customer value is "the consumer's overall assessment of the utility of a product based on perceptions of what is received and what is given." Anderson and Narus (1998) developed the idea of expressing customer value by drawing a comparison between a product and its next best alternative (NBA).

According to Lindgreen and Wynstra (2005: 743), the identification and development of new products, and hence their value, happen through interaction between customers and suppliers, particularly in business-to-business markets. They state, "[O]ne of the most consistent research findings regarding key success factors in new product development is the importance of the degree of market (or customer) orientation adopted by the developing firm." A high market orientation can be achieved through an active relationship with potential customers.

Pilot customers

The requirements of different potential end users and markets vary, so it is best to adopt a market-orientated approach as early as possible. Nonetheless, the decision on a specific target group needs to be carried out conscientiously because it has a significant impact on a company's future. Given that

> the importance of customer input increases with market newness of a product up to a point and then drops off for very new products, whereas the importance of customer input increases with technological newness of a product without dropping off (Callahan and Lasry, 2004: 107)

start-ups that launch a new product strongly rely on customer input and need to establish in-depth contact with potential customers and end users in order to integrate customer input permanently.

Early access to customer data and the support of customers were defined as relevant key factors by Coviello and Joseph (2012). They found that the likelihood of product success positively correlates with the intensity of customer cooperation. The customer and the seller of a product have different perspectives regarding the product's value, and, according to Terho et al. (2012), both play an active role in creating value. Jalkala and Salminen (2010) found that pilot customers provide evidence of a product's functionality as well as insight regarding customer needs and an understanding of the company's internal competencies. This knowledge could be used as a sales tool for promotional activities to win further business. But how can this knowledge be communicated to potential customers?

Communicating value – the customer value proposition

A CVP is a strong and persuasive method for presenting a product's combined value to a customer (Johnson et al., 2008). The main goal is the "monetary quantification of the benefits of a firm's offering" (Wouters, 2010: 2). The process of crafting a CVP is designed to create a good understanding of customer needs and demands. Thus, an offer that fulfils the customers' requirements can be made (Slater, 1997). Through an iterative process, and by implementing small changes in cooperation with suppliers and customers, a firm can increase the value of a product (Anderson and Wouters, 2013).

The literature consists of different streams that focus on how to craft a CVP. On the one hand, Terho et al. (2012) use a value-based selling approach with three dimensions: (a) understanding the customer's business model and identifying key drivers of earnings logic; (b) crafting a CVP, identifying the customer's problems, and customizing the offer; and (c) communicating customer value.

Terho et al. (2012) interviewed 11 managers and directors with a sales focus about an effective implementation of a firm's value orientation. A sales manager stated: "All value selling does is translate back to the customer what your solution does for their business, in terms of dollars and cents, monetary benefits" (Terho et al., 2012: 178). It is important to understand Terho et al.'s first dimension in order to decide how value can be added to an existing business. Regarding the CVP, the authors refer to methods such as "customer specific value calculations, value studies, simulations, return-on-investment studies, life-cycle calculations" (Terho et al., 2012: 180) that allow one to quantify the value of offerings. They highlight the "importance of making the size of the value opportunity visible to the customer" (p. 180) and not the quantification of precise numbers. According to the vice president of a multimillion-euro business, the company's most satisfied customers are those with whom the company has long-term, value-based agreements. These customers even spend more than other customers. This is consistent with Anderson et al. (2010: 76), who reported a study participant as saying that "'value-based pricing is not about squeezing out as much money . . . as you can, but building customer relationships.'" They continued: "Customers that feel good about doing a business with a supplier are more willing to give that supplier a larger share and a more profitable mix of their business." Thus, a value-based selling approach promises to benefit both buyers and suppliers.

How we designed our work and research

We conducted our research in a research-based spin-off, cubuslab GmbH, founded in 2014 by a former KIT student and a KIT research associate. In January 2015 another former KIT student joined the founding team. Cubuslab is a small, new-technology-based company. The technical founder worked for more than four years as an information scientist in the field of life science laboratories at KIT.

During that time, a new database was introduced, as well as a service called Dial-A-Device. The business idea of cubuslab is based on these two projects and the technology behind them. Universities have different goals and approaches to evaluating a new technology than a company in a competitive market. "Value in business markets is the worth in monetary terms of the technical, economic, service and social benefits a customer company receives in exchange for the price it pays for a market offering" (Anderson and Narus, 1998: 54). Universities strive to gain new insights and to expand the limits of what is technically possible.

Thus, technologies developed at universities frequently have a very general purpose and a broader range of application (Conceição et al., 2012). This is also the case for cubuslab's Dial-A-Device technology. It can be used to connect to any kind of machine or instrument that is computer-controlled and that has some kind of data interface. Cubuslab has developed a unique, innovative high-tech solution for M2M communication. After years of development, the potential of flexible instrument control and fully digital laboratory data management was realized and implemented in a business model. This platform-technology can be classified as an Internet of Things technology and could be applied in various scenarios: from smart energy to smart homes to smart factories.

In every kind of laboratory, data must be transferred from different instruments to a database. Until today, most of these data transfers have been performed manually, using a USB stick, printouts, or even handwritten notes. But even if instruments are connected to a computer or network, they frequently use different interfaces, different data formats, different software, and specific databases. Cubuslab offers a solution that provides overall instrument control, automatic documentation, precision, transparency, and full-range compatibility for upgrades and extensions.

We analyzed various internal documents and attended meetings with the founders, in which they explained every detail of their product. Table 21.1 gives an overview of the different data sources used. All regular and additional meetings with members of the cubuslab team as well as meetings with people outside the company were documented in a short summary and coded using keywords in order to process them without losing their intentional content. In addition, external opinions on the value created by this start-up were captured through three mini surveys.

How to craft a monetary customer value proposition

The crafting of a CVP is an iterative process. The first steps focus on understanding the product's possibilities and potential target markets. Subsequently, a deeper knowledge of application scenarios, market segments, important product features, and competencies can be formed through internal and external research. New information gets generated in cooperation with partners and possible users. This information influences the product development and business model and will eventually result in increased customer value. This customer value can then be represented in simple arithmetic value word equations (VWEs) and monetarily quantified.

Laboratory instrument automation market

Understanding potential customers and markets requires a deep understanding of a product's possible forms of application and how the customer's problems are currently being met. The present state of laboratory automation knows two extremes. First is the high-end, high-cost, full laboratory automation solution from a few major suppliers which integrates all instruments into one perfectly working network. The second version is a custom-built automation solution, often found at universities. This version normally results from cooperation between information scientists, laboratory workers, programmers, and industrial engineers. In reality, both solutions are available only for a minority of laboratories: either highly profitable pharmaceutical corporations or highly endowed research institutions.

A vast number of small- to medium-sized laboratories have no access to a solution that offers them the advantages that come with digitalizing and automating their instruments

Table 21.1 Overview of the collected data

Qualitative data collected		
Source	Details	Quantity
Meeting summary	Weekly meetings	24
	with *cubuslab* team	1
	Timeline overview	
Documents	Internal documents	18
	External documents	46
	Excel tool	1
Surveys	Compamed/medica	15
	Laboratory workers KIT	15
	User-interface	12

and processes without the obligation to set up their instrument park from scratch. The lack of suitable products created the business idea for cubuslab.

Determination of target market

Although cubuslab had a very detailed idea about their target market – laboratory instrument manufacturers – it was necessary for them to identify and select specific target groups within the market very carefully. This is one of the most important steps in crafting a CVP; is the basis for subsequent steps; and can help the start-up become more aware of customer needs, problems, alternatives, and competitors as well as market challenges and its own competencies.

To better understand what customers required, cubuslab conducted a mini survey. Regarding the specific features of the cubuslab connector, the following results were obtained. Good handling was seen as a very important feature (80%). Most participants (53.3%) rated the automatic transfer of data as very important. Another feature regarded as very important (66.7%) was the ability to automatically perform tasks. That was also the essence of most interviews the cubuslab founders conducted. A feature seen as a unique selling point so far, remote controllability, was the only feature rated as either very unimportant (6.7%) or unimportant (13.3%).

The second part of the survey assessed the cubuslab technology and pointed toward technically orientated problems and product properties and features. A product characteristic respondents reported as cubuslab's main advantage was the ability to control devices from different manufacturers. Most respondents (64.3%) did not have such a solution at that point but were very interested. An unexpectedly large proportion (21.43%) were not at all interested in such a solution. These numbers are consistent with the proportion of participants who were interested in integrating instruments without an inbuilt network interface into a laboratory network. These insights led to the definition of the key benefits list: (a) remote controllability, (b) multilingual software, (c) saving of time during documentation, and (d) programmability of software.

Developing a value proposition canvas

The VPC uses the DT mind-set to design, test, and evolve value propositions in an iterative search. DT, unlike analytical thinking, is a process that includes the creation of ideas without restrictions. This process helps reduce the fear of failing for all participants and can lead to more innovative outcomes (Plattner et al., 2011). Historically, design was treated as a downstream step in the product development process, and designers had to wrap a technological innovation within something aesthetically attractive. Today, however, companies ask designers to create ideas that fulfil consumer needs and desires – human-centered activities are much more the focus (Brown, 2008). The DT process can be described as a system of spaces rather than a step-by-step approach. The spaces define different kinds of related activities that together form the continuum of innovation.

The VPC is designed to keep a company's value propositions relevant to customers by continuously undergoing an iterative process (Osterwalder et al., 2014). It focuses on two main blocks of the best-selling book *Business Model Generation* by Osterwalder et al. (2010). These are the customer segments and value propositions, and they are designed to help businesses create products and services that customers want and that offer them high value (Osterwalder et al., 2015). The VPC consist of two sides: the customer profile, which clarifies the customer understanding, and the value map, which describes how value for the customer can be created. Eventually a company needs to coordinate how to achieve a fit between these two sides (Osterwalder et al., 2015).

Applying the value proposition canvas

The goal of the VPC was to systematically analyze the problems, needs, and tasks of the target group in order to match cubuslab's products and services accordingly. A number of assumptions about the problems and pains of potential customers were made. Eventually, an end-user requirements scenario was created which resulted in the VPC presented in Table 21.2.

The VPC was based on the experience of the founders and on assumptions about customer needs as well as interviews with laboratory workers and industry experts. These assumptions needed to be verified. This verification was performed through mini surveys and interviews. Some of the assumptions turned out to be right; others were questionable. During the process of crafting the CVP, and especially the VWEs shown later, cubuslab's strategic focus became more and more clear. At the beginning, many features were listed as important. Over time the focus changed to key benefits that customers perceived as high value. In the end, cubuslab defined three very condensed core competencies which they wanted to communicate to their prospective customers (see Figure 21.1). These core competencies were also the basis for the monetary quantification of customer value.

Table 21.2 Value proposition canvas outcome

Pains	*Pain relievers*
• Manual data transfer • Complicated integration of instruments • Incompatibility • Manual documentation • Susceptibility to errors • No standards • Data security, organization, and availability • Handling • Collaboration • Publication • Plausibility • Timeliness	• Comprehensive instrument control • Automatic documentation • Precision • Data loggers • Compatibility for extension and upgrade
Gains • Remote controllability • Time savings • Universality • Multiple languages • Low cost • Little space • Easy to implement • Programmability	*Gain creators* • New use-scenarios • Flexible working models • Fast communication • No lock-in effect

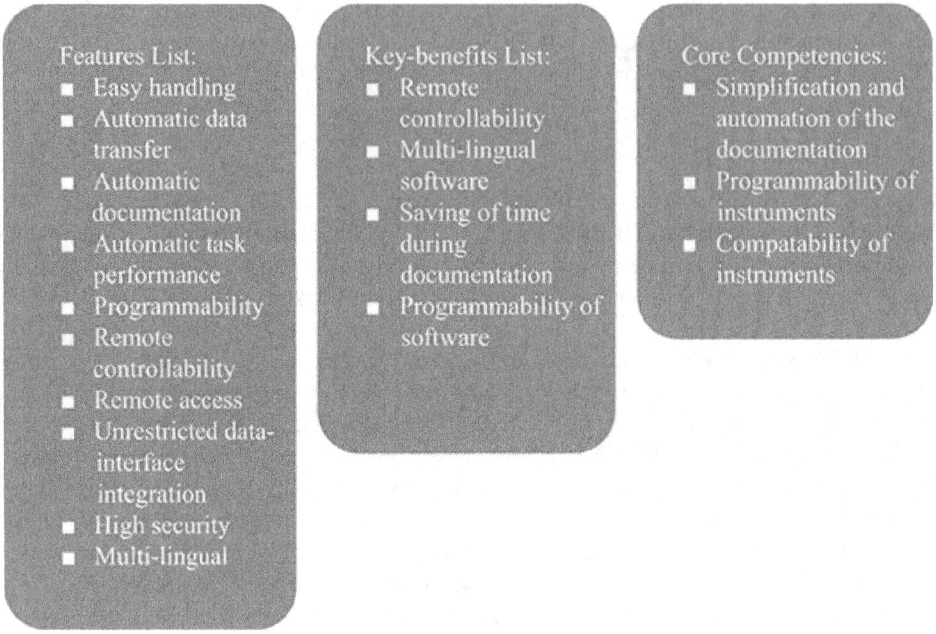

Figure 21.1 The development of cubuslab's strategic focus

Quantification of customer value

The three core competencies and their impact on the customer and end user were ana-lyzed and formed the basis for the monetary value quantification. Through the use of simple words and arithmetic expressions, as proposed by Anderson et al. (2007), the core competencies of the cubuslab solution could be expressed as VWEs.

The improved documentation due to simplification and automation has two positive effects that can be quantified as customer value in monetary terms: time savings and improved quality. The customer value created through time savings can be expressed by the following formula:

$$
\begin{aligned}
Cost_{savings\ reduced\ time\ due\ to\ improved\ documentation} \\
= cost_{laboratory\ worker} * working\_time_{laboratory\ worker,\ daily} \\
- \Big[cost_{laboratory\ worker} \\
* working\_time_{laboratory\ worker,\ daily} \big(share\_work_{Preparation\ of\ experiments} \\
* \big(1 - Improvement_{time\ for\ preparation,\ cubuslab} \big) \\
+ share\_work_{Realization\ of\ experiments} \\
* \big(1 - Improvement_{time\ for\ realization,\ cubuslab} \big) \\
+ share\_work_{Evaluation\ of\ experiments} \\
* \big(1 - Improvement_{time\ for\ evaluation,\ cubuslab} \big) \big) \Big]
\end{aligned}
$$

The monetary customer value created due to better quality as a result of an improved documentation process is captured in the following equation:

$$Cost\_savings_{\text{better quality due to improved documentation}}$$
$$= cost_{\text{—experiments with } Nr\_specimen\_total} * \frac{Nr\_specimen_{badquality}}{Nr\_specimen_{total}}$$
$$* Improvement_{quality, cubuslab}$$

Another core competency is the programmability of instruments, which allows users to optimize the laboratory workflow. This results in time savings, since wait times can be minimized. Additionally, more experiments can be conducted and therefore more profit generated. The third core competency is the full compatibility of the cubuslab solution: There are no limitations with respect to different manufacturers or to the data-interface technology. Full compatibility of instruments allows users to integrate all kinds of instruments into one, platform-based, laboratory network. In this network they can connect old devices with analogue data interfaces to up-to-date instruments that can transfer data over digital interfaces without manufacturer restrictions. Therefore, the number of necessary new acquisitions, as well as installation costs, can be reduced significantly. Due to space limitations, we do not explain in further detail here the formula for the programmability of instruments or the formula for full compatibility.

The monetarily quantified customer value can be calculated for any specific customer scenario with a spreadsheet tool. For a standard scenario, using the introduced equations, precise values could be calculated. Figure 21.2 presents the monetary value of the standard-case scenario regarding the improved documentation. Figure 21.3 displays the accumulated customer value for one year in a laboratory with five employees and 15 existing laboratory instruments.

In order to take into account the concept of resonating focus by Anderson et al. (2006), it was important to specially define a NBA. Instead of using a cubuslab connector, the NBA uses a full-size desktop computer as access point to the laboratory network and bidirectional communication.

Although the previously presented calculations are based partly on assumptions, it was possible to calculate a monetarily quantified customer value. The goal was not to offer a tool for business planning with exact figures and unquestionable numbers but to provide a general range in which the customer value is located, as proposed by Terho et al. (2012), in order to motivate possible customers to upgrade their laboratory infrastructure. These figures represent tangible customer benefits which customers can better relate to than to standard sales arguments. They also provide insight regarding the differential value regarding a status quo or a NBA and therefore can also help set a price range in a value-based selling approach.

The assumed values of the standard use-case scenario can vary greatly from other real-life scenarios, since the quality and cost of laboratory infrastructure also vary greatly. The values are based on the experience of the cubuslab team and on interviews with laboratory workers.

Results/Discussion

Crafting a CVP proved to be a powerful tool and offered a highly structured method while determining the target market and encouraged the start-up to verify their assumptions

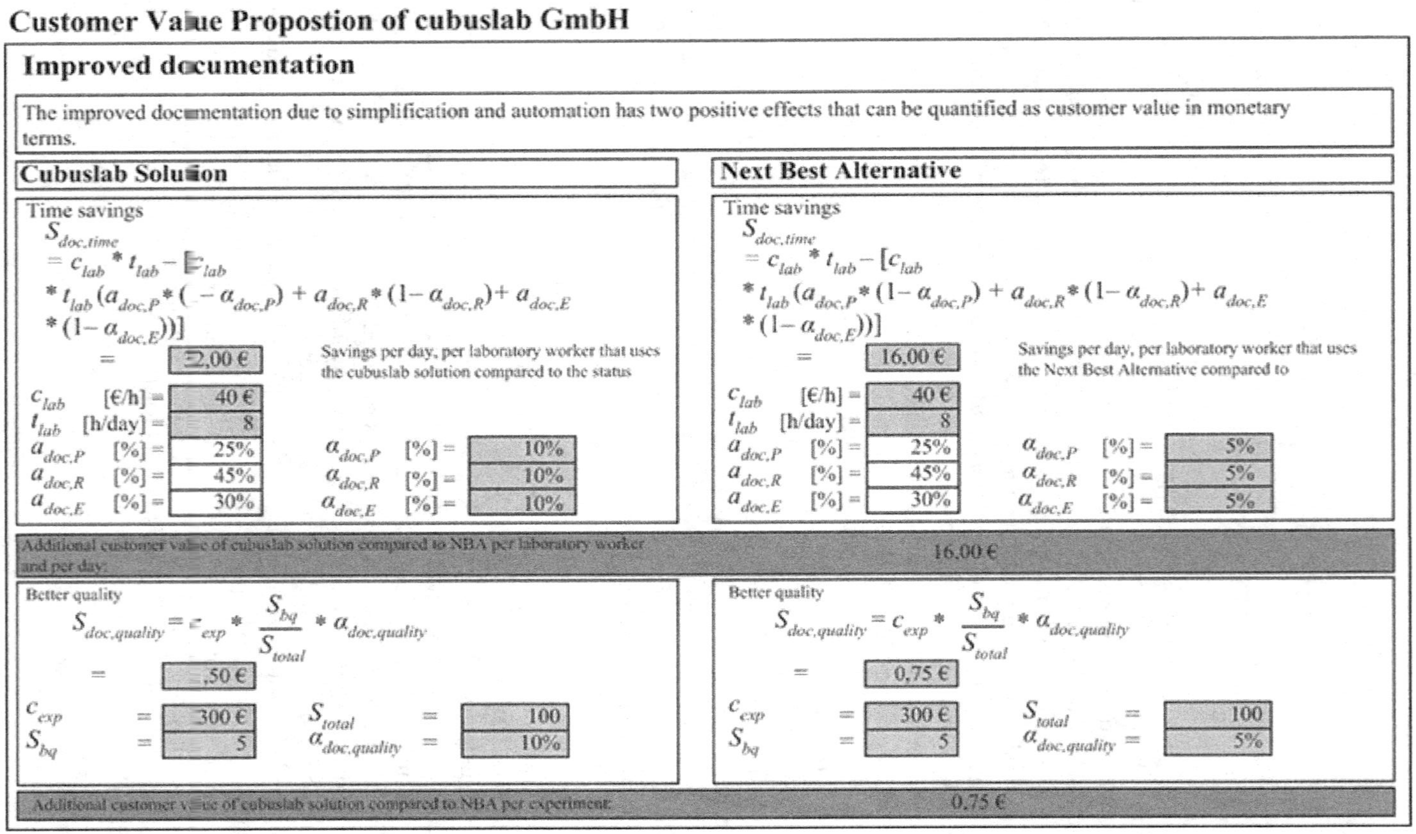

Customer Value Propostion of cubuslab GmbH

Improved documentation

The improved documentation due to simplification and automation has two positive effects that can be quantified as customer value in monetary terms.

Cubuslab Solution

Time savings

$$S_{doc.time}$$
$$= c_{lab} * t_{lab} - [c_{lab}$$
$$* t_{lab}(a_{doc.P} * (-a_{doc.R}) + a_{doc.R} * (1 - a_{doc.R}) + a_{doc.E}$$
$$* (1 - a_{doc.E})]$$
$$=$$

Savings per day, per laboratory worker that uses the cubuslab solution compared to the status

2,00 €

c_{lab}	[€/h] =	40 €
t_{lab}	[h/day] =	8
$a_{doc.P}$	[%] =	25%
$a_{doc.R}$	[%] =	45%
$a_{doc.E}$	[%] =	30%
$a_{doc.P}$	[%] =	10%
$a_{doc.R}$	[%] =	10%
$a_{doc.E}$	[%] =	10%

Next Best Alternative

Time savings

$$S_{doc.time}$$
$$= c_{lab} * t_{lab} - [c_{lab}$$
$$* t_{lab}(a_{doc.P} * (1 - a_{doc.P}) + a_{doc.R} * (1 - a_{doc.R}) + a_{doc.E}$$
$$* (1 - a_{doc.E})]$$
$$=$$

Savings per day, per laboratory worker that uses the Next Best Alternative compared to

16,00 €

c_{lab}	[€/h] =	40 €
t_{lab}	[h/day] =	8
$a_{doc.P}$	[%] =	25%
$a_{doc.R}$	[%] =	45%
$a_{doc.E}$	[%] =	30%
$a_{doc.P}$	[%] =	5%
$a_{doc.R}$	[%] =	5%
$a_{doc.E}$	[%] =	5%

Additional customer value of cubuslab solution compared to NBA per laboratory worker and per day: **16,00 €**

Better quality

$$S_{doc.quality} = c_{exp} * \frac{S_{bq}}{S_{total}} * a_{doc.quality}$$

Cubuslab Solution:
$$= 2,50 €$$

c_{exp}	=	300 €
S_{bq}	=	5
S_{total}	=	100
$a_{doc.quality}$	=	10%

Next Best Alternative:
$$= 0,75 €$$

c_{exp}	=	300 €
S_{bq}	=	5
S_{total}	=	100
$a_{doc.quality}$	=	5%

Additional customer value of cubuslab solution compared to NBA per experiment: **0,75 €**

Figure 21.2 Quantification tool: Monetarily quantified customer value due to improved documentation

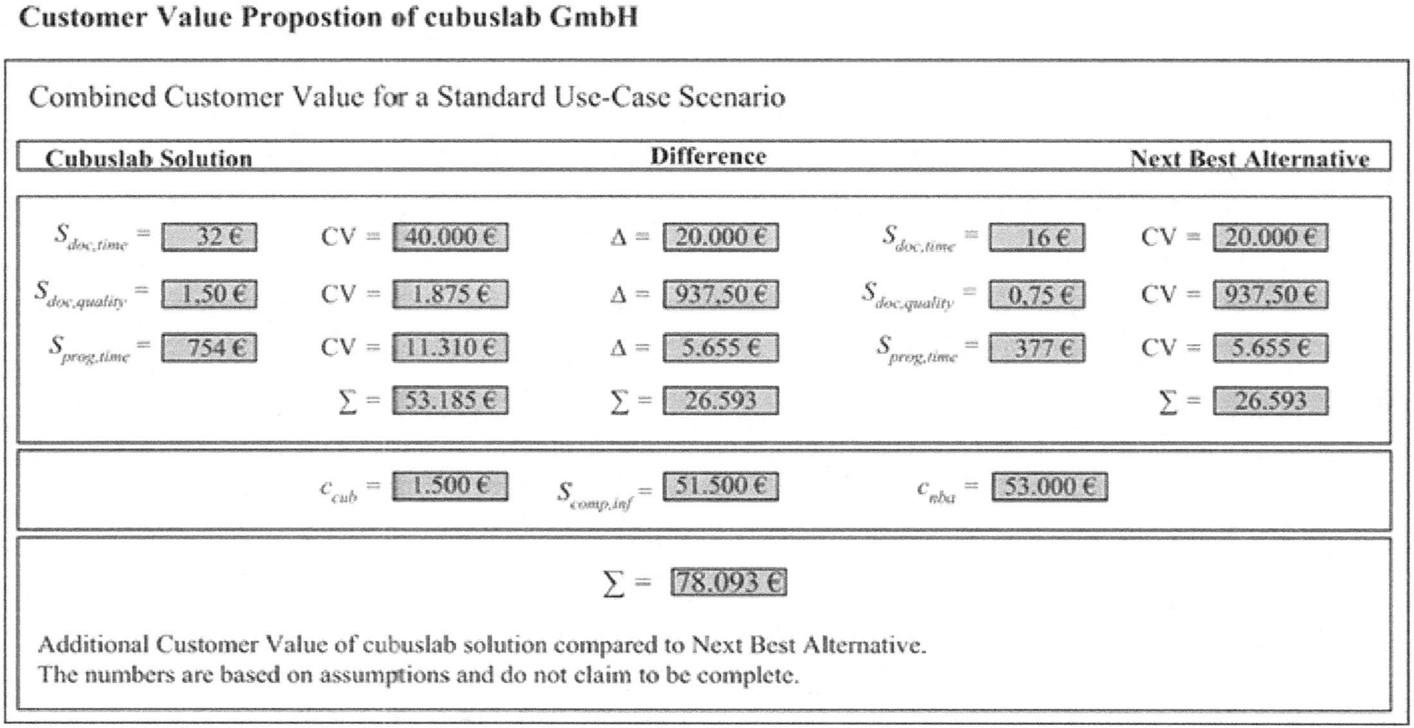

Figure 21.3 Quantification tool: Combined monetarily quantified customer value for standard use-case scenario

about prospective customers and market segments. Although cubuslab had a strong idea about the market they planned on entering, abiding by the CVP framework ensured that this far-reaching decision was based not on a gut-level judgment but on verified assumptions.

Cubuslab's core technology is based on academic research, which often means that the same core knowledge can be used in a variety of applications (Malerba and Orsenigo, 1997). This generality harbors various opportunities due to the versatile application scenarios but can also "have a negative effect on new product development, because it makes it less suitable for specific application" (Conceição et al., 2012: 45).

A critical confrontation with the technology's ability to successfully fulfil the requirements of the laboratory automation market was necessary and took place.

During our 6-month case study, it was not possible to completely establish a value-based selling approach; nonetheless, a subscription model has been created. It was possible to quantify the customer value in monetary terms by basing it on assumptions. It was possible to derive a range, where a future value-based price could be located in order to preserve a positive customer. This range as well as the defined VWEs and the determined monetary customer value were used to define a subscription model. The founders stated that potential customers appreciated the transparency generated through presenting the monetarily quantified value and the relating VWEs.

Due to delays in product development, it was not possible to acquire a pilot customer in the target industry in order to analyze a standard use-case scenario in a business environment so far. Nonetheless, very detailed and compelling equations and calculations could be created that represent the customer value of the cubuslab laboratory automation solution in monetary terms. This shows potential customers that their problems and challenges are understood and can be a great advantage over competitors, since it automatically creates a professional basis for discussion with the customer's technology managers, rather than the usual meaningless phrases employed in sales meetings. For cubuslab, the monetary quantification offered helpful insights into their product and market offering; it also created a starting point for value-based selling approaches. The presented equations and value propositions became main elements of cubuslab's sales strategy. According to the founders, their prospective customers highly value the transparency regarding their value propositions as well as the comparability with other available solutions.

It was possible to combine the process of crafting a CVP with the DT approach. A mutually supportive effect could be demonstrated by merging them into one comprehensive approach (Table 21.3).

The generation of new information, the creation of value-enhancing possibilities, decisions on changes in market offering, and implications for technology development were mostly carried out during the different DT spaces. An increased activity in the CVP main steps "Conduct research with other parties" and "Make decisions based on insight obtained from CVP" could be detected. It is not possible to claim that this would not have happened if the DT approach had not been used. But it appears to be reasonable to consider a beneficial, amplifying effect of the DT mind-set toward the continuous product development and progress in customer value creation.

What you can take away from our case study

We recommend that other start-ups or new product development teams in larger, established firms use one of the available approaches to create a CVP. Crafting a CVP as

Table 21.3 Customer value proposition and design thinking steps performed during the case study

Steps for crafting a CVP	
Main steps	Sub-steps
I Drawing a frame and establishing contacts	
II Select target market	Investigate current understanding
	Identify further feasible applications for the new technology
	Identify your needs for help and suitable partners
	Identify target markets and market segments
	Assess target markets
	Select market segment(s) to first work on
III Conduct internal research on selected target market	Market research
Technology assessment	
	Preparing quantification of customer value
IV Conduct research with other parties	Develop contacts with relevant partners
	Agree on issues that are barriers for cooperation
	Collect existing information
	Generate new information
	Create value-enhancing possibilities
V Make decisions based on insight obtained from CVP	Decide on changes in market offering
	Deduct implications for technology development, to be implemented by the technology venture and by partners
VI Develop technology and market offering with new knowledge	Develop technology and otherwise implement changes regarding the products and services offered
	Use your CVP as a sales tool
VII Administrative topics	Bachelor's thesis
	Preparation of external research
	Theory lessons
VIII Extended concept: Design thinking spaces	Empathize
	Define
	Ideate
	Prototype
	Test

described here forces a company to intensely concentrate on determining its target market and its market offering. Many ideas and assumptions need to be tested during this process. It stimulates discussion about customer challenges and pains that need to be solved as well as product properties and features and their respective importance. The whole business model gets examined, and a company is forced to think about the product from the customer's perspective. An additional effect is that early customer contact is unavoidable if the company has fully committed to implementing the concept. This effect gets amplified when the CVP concept is combined with the DT approach and the VPC, since these concepts require continuous interaction with end users. Figure 21.4 is a graphical guideline to this process.

This work shows how the concept of customer value and its monetary quantification influence the way a new technology venture develops its product and determines its target market. It also provides insights about how contact with potential partners and customers can be made at an early stage. Most important, it shows how early customer contact and

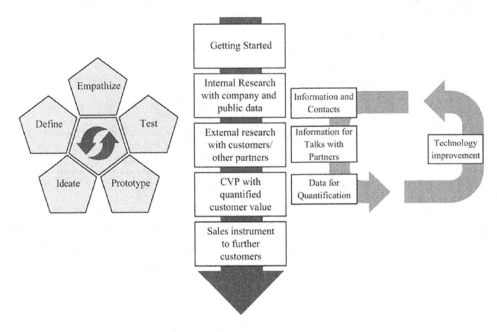

Figure 21.4 Graphical guideline to the applied customer value proposition approach

an ongoing analysis of what customers actually want can lead to continuous innovation. Cubuslab was able to sharpen its profile and create a perfectly fitting industry solution from a general core technology with a wide field of applications.

References

Anderson, J. C., Kumar, N. and Narus, J. A. (2007) *Value Merchants: Demonstrating and Documenting Superior Value in Business Markets*, Boston, MA: Harvard Business School Press.

Anderson, J. C. and Narus, J. A. (1998) "Business marketing: Understand what customers value," *Harvard Business Review 76*(6), 53–55, 58–65.

Anderson, J. C., Narus, J. A. and van Rossum, W. (2006) "Customer value propositions in business markets," *Harvard Business Review 84*(3), 90–99.

Anderson, J. C. and Wouters, M. (2013) "What you can learn from your customer's customer," *MIT Sloan Management Review 54*(2), 75–82.

Anderson, J. C., Wouters, M. and van Rossum, W. (2010) "Why the highest price isn't the best price," *MIT Sloan Management Review 51*(2), 69–76. http://doc.utwente.nl/73918/1/why.pdf

Brown, T. (2008) "Design thinking," *Harvard Business Review 86*(6), 84–92, 141.

Callahan, J. and Lasry, E. (2004) "The importance of customer input in the development of very new products," *R&D Management 34*(2), 107–120.

Chesbrough, H. W. (2003) *Open Innovation: The New Imperative for Creating and Profiting from Technology*, Boston, MA: Harvard Business School Press.

Conceição, O., Fontes, M. and Calapez, T. (2012) "The commercialisation decisions of research-based spin-off: Targeting the market for technologies," *Technovation 32*(1), 43–56.

Coviello, N. E. and Joseph, R. M. (2012) "Creating major innovations with customers: Insights from small and young technology firms," *Journal of Marketing 76*(6), 87–104.

Gans, J. S. and Stern, S. (2003) "The product market and the market for 'ideas': Commercialization strategies for technology entrepreneurs," *Research Policy 32*(2), 333–350.

Jalkala, A. and Salminen, R. T. (2010) "Practices and functions of customer reference marketing – Leveraging customer references as marketing assets," *Industrial Marketing Management 39*(6), 975–985.

Johnson, M. W., Christensen, C. M. and Kagermann, H. (2008) "Reinventing your business model," *Harvard Business Review 86*(12), 50–60.

Lindgreen, A. and Wynstra, F. (2005) "Value in business markets: What do we know? Where are we going?" *Industrial Marketing Management 34*(7), 732–748.

Malerba, F. and Orsenigo, L. (1997) "Technological regimes and sectoral patterns of innovative activities," *Industrial and Corporate Change 6*, 81–117.

Osterwalder, A., Pigneur, Y., Bernarda, G., Smith, A. and Papadakos, T. (2014) *Value Proposition Design: How to Create Products and Services Customers Want*, Hoboken, NJ: Wiley.

Osterwalder, A., Pigneur, Y., Bernarda, G., Smith, A. and Papadakos, T. (2015) *Value Proposition Design: How to Create Products and Services Customers Want*, Hoboken, NJ: Wiley. https://books.google.de/books?id=jgu5BAAAQBAJ

Osterwalder, A., Pigneur, Y. and Clark, T. (2010) *Business Model Generation: A Handbook for Visionaries, Game Changers, and Challengers*, Hoboken, NJ: Wiley.

Plattner, H., Meinerl, C. and Leifer, L. (2011) *Design Thinking – Understand, Improve, Apply*, Heidelberg: Springer.

Ruokolainen, J. (2008) "Constructing the first customer reference to support the growth of a start-up software technology company," *European Journal of Innovation Management 11*(2), 282–305.

Ruokolainen, J. and Igel, B. (2004) "The factors of making the first successful customer reference to leverage the business of start-up software company – Multiple case study in Thai software industry," *Technovation 24*(9), 673–681.

Slater, S. F. (1997) "Developing a customer value-based theory of the firm," *Journal of the Academy of Marketing Science 25*(2), 162–167.

Terho, H., Haas, A., Eggert, A. and Ulaga, W. (2012) "'It's almost like taking the sales out of selling' – Towards a conceptualization of value-based selling in business markets," *Industrial Marketing Management 41*(1), 174–185.

Thursby, J., Jensen, R. and Thursby, M. C. (2001) "Objectives, characteristics and outcomes of university licensing: A survey of major U.S. universities," *The Journal of Technology Transfer 26*(1/2), 59–72.

Wouters, M. (2010) "Customer value propositions in the context of technology commercialization," *International Journal of Innovation Management 14*(6), 1099–1127.

Wouters, M. and Kirchberger, M. A. (2015) "Customer value propositions as interorganizational management accounting to support customer collaboration," *Industrial Marketing Management 46*, 54–67.

Zeithaml, V. A. (1988) "Consumer perceptions of price, quality, and value: A means – end model and synthesis of evidence," *Journal of Marketing 52*(3), 2–22.

22 Creating and sustaining competitive advantage through documented total cost savings

Underhill, Tim

Customers are increasingly looking for the means to improve operating profits, and with an average of 60% of operating costs being spent on goods and services, they are turning to their suppliers to help meet their cost-reduction goals. Price is the obvious savings most customers focus on, because it is easy to prove how much was saved when the price is lowered.

But for those suppliers that add value beyond a lower price, it offers an opportunity to create a true competitive advantage by demonstrating the savings to the customer when the supplier provides value-added products and services. For example, when a supplier provides a product that is a "better fit-to-function" for the application involved, it can often help the customer reduce total operating costs. Or when the supplier performs a service that solves a problem for their customer, it can have a direct impact on the customer's operating profits. While many competitive suppliers offer similar products and services, few can truly demonstrate the savings. And the demonstration of value-added savings can justify why a particular supplier should be the customers' supplier of choice.

As a quick definition of "value added," *suppliers add value when they do something that makes their customer more profitable*. This value can come either from increasing the customer's revenues or from decreasing their costs.

To measure the value added, you must look at how the supplier impacts the customer's operating profits. If you look at a profit and loss statement, there are three categories of profit impact a supplier can affect.

1. *Revenues*. How can the supplier help the customer make and sell additional products/ services? This is often accomplished through minimized downtime, increased production rates, reduced rejected output, or other changes that increase the customer's sales or profit from sales.
2. *Expenditures*. How can the supplier reduce total spend? This can include reductions in the price paid for products/services (both the supplier's products and the impact on purchases from other suppliers), energy costs, utilities, disposal, freight, or other aspects of annual spend.
3. *Processes*. How can the supplier reduce the customer's personnel costs by eliminating or minimizing tasks to be performed? This can include reductions in time to process invoices and cut purchase orders and reduced maintenance, warehouse operations, production time, and many other labor-related costs.

DOI: 10.4324/9781003177937-28

A fourth category can be related back to the profit and loss statement: assets. Assets appear on the balance sheet, but each asset is associated with a possession cost.

4. *Assets.* Reductions in possession costs occur when inventory, equipment, or facility requirements are minimized. Possession costs can include any cost associated with owning the asset such as finance charges/interest payments/working capital, maintenance and repairs, storage, utilities, and other ownership costs.

The possession cost of an asset is the easiest measure of the value from asset reductions. For example, inventory reduction can reduce interest expense, storage, handling, taxes, shrinkage, and other costs. Instead of trying to measure every cost, companies assign a value to the possession of the inventory, often referred to as carrying cost.

Accurately determining which categories are impacted by a value-added solution is critical for measuring the dollar impact provided.

Suppliers should also track both the value they have already added and the value they could add. Determining value already added can help create a "firewall" to assist in retaining a current account. Demonstrating to customers the value of what could be provided can help the supplier obtain additional sales from an existing account or gain sales from a new account.

The value that suppliers add is a function of the type of goods and services they provide. Service companies such as contractors, accounting firms, or engineering companies generally add value through reduced personnel and the expertise they provide around their services. For example, a utility company called for bids on a new project. All the bids came back well over budget. A contractor that worked for the utility company offered to rework the specifications, even though the contractor itself could not bid on the job. The reworked specifications resulted in just under $10 million in savings, cutting the bids in half.

Manufacturers generally add value through their products, but some also add value through services such as failure analysis, reserved production time, custom products, and design support. A manufacturer helped redesign a project that saved a customer over $50 million.

Distributors can improve a customer's operating profits from both the value-added products they offer from numerous manufacturers and the services they provide. A distributor was working with a customer on a flange-failure issue that occurred each year with one of their strategic accounts. After evaluating the process and specifications, the distributor proposed an engineered gasket that protected the total flange face, which when installed saved the customer $300,000 annually through reduced flange spend, reduced downtime, and lowered maintenance costs.

These examples illustrate two points. First, they all show a supplier adding value beyond a low price. In each case the value was added through the supplier's expertise and knowledge. Second, this type of value is not likely to be forgotten by either the customer or the supplier, because the savings are so large. But what about the day-to-day value that many suppliers add that results in smaller savings that are more easily forgotten? It is important to measure and track the value from all the solutions a supplier provides. And the list can be extensive. Some distributors, for example, have identified over 50 value-added opportunities they provide their customers. Here is a partial list of some of these opportunities.

1. *Consignment* is an issue of ownership. When a supplier consigns inventory at a customer's location, they are putting stock, which they own, on the customer's premises and generally do not get paid until the customer uses the stock.

2. *Vendor-managed inventory (VMI)* involves the supplier evaluating the customer's inventory needs on site at the customer's location on a regular basis to ensure that the right products and quantities are always on hand.
3. *Design support* is a service provided by suppliers where they help their customers to design products, production lines, equipment, and a host of other items.
4. *Technical support* covers everything from problem solving and installation guidance to product design or selection.
5. *Product substitutions* can include similar fit-to-function change in the materials used that offers a lower price when the products are true commodities. Better fit-to-function product substitutions that look at the total cost impact often result in an initial higher price paid, but a lower total cost overall.
6. *Kitting* is a service in which the supplier combines a number of products into one bundle, usually with its own part number.
7. *Preassembly* is a service in which the supplier assembles/cuts parts into one larger component so that the customer does not have to assemble it.
8. *Energy audits* are a service performed by the supplier to identify ways in which the customer can reduce their electricity or fuel consumption.
9. *Leak audits* are a service performed by the supplier to identify why leaks in steam lines and/or production lines are occurring and how to stop the leakage longer term.
10. *Failure analysis* is a service where the supplier examines why a failure occurred.

One of the key points to notice in this list is that each of the value-added opportunities requires the customer to change in some way and to have the supplier do something for them. For example, with VMI the supplier takes over managing the customer's inventory; with energy or leak audits the supplier helps find ways to reduce energy costs or leaks in production lines or steam pipes. Suppliers add value when they work with the customer to make a change. If the customer does not change, there is no value added. This is a critical aspect of being able to measure the value that a supplier adds, because it is the change in operating costs and revenue that allows you to measure the value added.

Measuring the financial impact of a change is not new for most companies. There is a whole field of study in accounting called cost accounting that measures the financial impact within a company when a change is proposed or made. Most companies use these cost-accounting principles to make financial decisions around large expenditures or projects, but cost accounting can be used to measure any change. Measuring value added is simply extending cost accounting to include smaller changes provided by the supplier.

For example, in order to measure the impact on the customer's revenues, you need three pieces of information.

Additional units sold: the number of additional units of a product that the customer can make and sell due to the value-added solution. Note that the "and sell" issue is critical in determining whether there is an impact on the customer's revenues. If the customer cannot sell the additional production, there will be no impact on revenues. In such cases there can be a reduction in costs that can be measured.

Unit value or selling price: the customer's average selling price for the units made. This is often a wholesale and not a retail price.

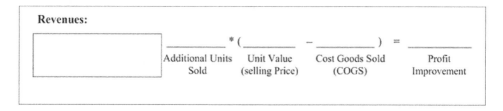

Figure 22.1 Worksheet for measuring revenue impact

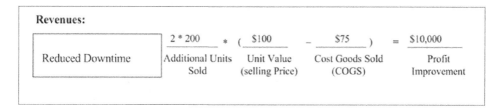

Figure 22.2 Completed revenue worksheet for downtime example

Cost of goods sold: the incremental addition in the raw materials usage due to making each additional unit (the overhead is usually not included since it is not an incremental cost).

To help measure this impact, you can use the simple form shown in Figure 22.1.

If a customer makes widgets and sells them for $100 each, the $100 selling price is not the improvement in profits for each additional widget sold. You have to remove the cost for making each widget. In this case we'll assume that the cost to make each unit is $75. If a supplier recommends a different tool or part that could reduce downtime by 2 hours, and the customer produces 200 units an hour, an additional $10,000 in revenue-based profit is achieved, as outlined in Figure 22.2.

Revenue impact is often overlooked by organizations as a key area for measuring value, but it shouldn't be. Revenues offer huge impact potential. Unfortunately, revenue impact is also hard for the supplier to quantify in many cases, because some customers are reluctant to provide the information needed to measure it.

This brings up a critical point: Information is rarely perfect. Companies need to make reasonable and defendable estimates of the numbers used when measuring the value added, just like the estimates used to make any operating decision. For example, production rates vary, and in the example given earlier, the number of widgets produced could be as low as 195 or as high as 220 widgets per hour. The 200 in this example was used as an estimate that is both reasonable and defendable given production variances. As such, averages, industry standards, and other conservative estimates are often used in cost-accounting and value-added calculations.

As a reminder, not all production-related improvements will impact the customer's revenue streams. If the customer cannot sell the additional units that could be produced, the supplier should look at the impact on operating costs.

Expenditures are the most commonly measured savings because they are the easiest to measure. To measure expenditure savings, you need only three pieces of information, as seen in the worksheet shown in Figure 22.3.

Current price: What was the customer paying for the product before the change?
New price: What is the customer paying for the product now?
Annual usage: How many units will be impacted per year?

If the change is simply a lower price, the worksheet given earlier can be used with no modification. However, if price and quantities vary, it's best to use two lines. For example, let's assume the customer was spending $100 per unit for the ABC Part and purchasing 500 units per year. Then the supplier offered a better fit-to-function substitution. The new XYZ Part costs $110 per unit but reduces the customer's unit usage to 400 per year. The net savings to the customer is $6,000 per year, as shown in Figure 22.4.

There are three important points to be made with this example. First, why did we use two lines instead of one line with two quantity fields? The main reason is ease in presenting the savings. Showing it on two lines makes it easier to see the impact of the change, while still following the standard cost-accounting principles. As such, the "0" on the first line indicates that there are no more expenditures for this product, and the "0" on the second line indicates that in the past there were no purchases of this product for the application under review. However, this formula works just as well if you display all of the savings on one line: (Current price × Current usage) − (New price × New usage).

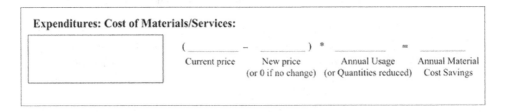

Figure 22.3 Worksheet for measuring material/service savings

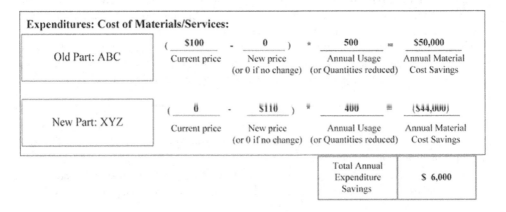

Figure 22.4 Completed expenditure worksheet for the substitution example

The second point is that the savings shown are simply for the price paid and do not reflect any impact in the other cost-savings categories. Because expenditures are the most commonly documented savings, many purchasing organizations start to believe that the real value a supplier brings is a lower price. For suppliers that provide value-added solutions, it is critical to measure savings beyond the price paid for the goods and services provided. To better demonstrate this, an example of another product savings is outlined later showing a higher price paid but where other savings such as energy costs result in a lower total cost.

The third point is the difference between one-time savings and ongoing savings. Some savings, such as the expenditure example mentioned earlier, result in savings year after year, while the revenue example might only impact operating profits once. If you try to combine savings and costs from various solutions with different time frames, it becomes very difficult to determine the actual total cost impact within a given time frame. For this reason, always measure the value for a 1-year period. This way, the forms shown will always reflect the annual impact and can be easily combined with annual spend to determine a total cost for each supplier. Multiyear projections can then be made from these estimates to determine the long-term impact of a solution.

Process savings is the third category to evaluate. Processes deal with the personnel costs that a customer incurs for performing any task: ordering, accounts payable, warehouse activities, engineering, and so on. When a supplier provides a product or service that reduces personnel time, such as time spent on maintenance, there is a value-added benefit to the customer. To document these savings, you need four pieces of information (see Figure 22.5).

Past cost. Before the change, what did it cost the customer to perform the task? (This could be an hourly rate or the actual cost for the task.)

Past frequency. Before the change, how many hours or how many times did the impacted task have to be performed?

New cost. What is the cost to perform the task now? (Keep in mind that if an hourly rate is used, it may show no change.)

New frequency. After the change, how many hours will it take to perform the impacted task, or how many times will it be performed?

Process savings can be measured using hourly wage rates or the cost per occurrence. For example, if you're reducing maintenance costs, you might want to use the hourly rate method. If the customer pays their maintenance personnel $25 per hour and personnel were spending 1,500 hours on maintenance, but after the change they will only need to spend 800 hours on maintenance, the calculations would look like the example in Figure 22.6.

The other method for calculating process savings is cost per occurrence. Summary billing (in which the customer pays once a month for all purchases) is a good example to use.

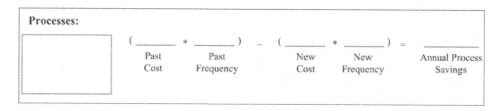

Figure 22.5 Worksheet for measuring process savings

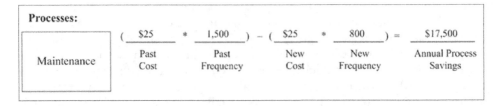

Figure 22.6 Completed process worksheet for reduced time in maintenance example

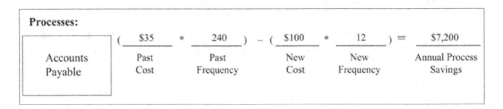

Figure 22.7 Completed process worksheet for process acceleration (example)

If the customer has determined that it costs them $35 to process an invoice and there are 20 invoices a month, the cost to the customer will be $8,400 a year to process invoices from this supplier before using summary billing (see Figure 22.7). Remember that savings should be based on an annual cost.

If the supplier were to provide summary billing, the number of times a year the task is performed would drop from 240 to 12. Because it takes longer to process a larger invoice, we estimated that the cost per invoice would increase to $100 from $35. Using these numbers, the savings to the customer would equal $7,200 for the year.

A critical point needs to be made about processes: They are generally considered "soft." Revenues, expenditures, and assets, on the other hand, are generally considered "hard." Hard saving means the customer will see a definite impact on operating profits. If you increase revenues or reduce possession costs, the customer *will* be more profitable. But unless overtime is eliminated, a person is laid off, or a worker is moved to eliminate a part–time position, the impact of process changes will not actually improve operating profit because the worker or workers are still provided a full paycheck. This type of change does, however, offer the customer the opportunity to better use the time of the employees impacted. Because it *might* impact profits, it is considered a soft saving.

Soft savings should still be measured and included in calculating total cost savings, but many customers do not like to accept them. Acceptance is important, because why should the supplier help improve productivity and reduce the time needed to perform operations if the supplier is not given credit for helping their customer? And in most cases the supplier is not asking to be paid for the savings, only to be given credit for having reduced the time requirements involved in performing an activity. For the supplier, pro-cesses are the second most commonly documented savings. If they are not given credit for the total cost savings from these process improvements, then a lower price often remains as the main value being added.

The assets: inventory category is the fourth savings area (see Figure 22.8). Inventory savings refer to any action the supplier takes that reduces the dollar value of supplies the customer is holding. Note that the amount of inventory reduction is not the amount saved. Inventory reduction is basically cash-flow improvement. However, there is a cost for carrying this inventory. So to measure the impact of inventory reductions, you need to find these two pieces of information.

Amount reduction ($). How much inventory, in dollars, was reduced?

Carrying cost (%). What is the annual cost for owning inventory? (Carrying costs generally include interest rate, insurance, taxes, shrinkage, spoilage, obsolescence, and some storage and handling costs.) Carrying costs are most often measured as a percentage of inventory.

If a supplier were to consign parts/supplies into the customer's inventory in the amount of $20,000, and the customer had an 18% carrying cost, the savings to the customer would be $3,600 (see Figure 22.9). Because it is consigned, the savings would be both hard and ongoing.

Inventory was used in this example because it is the most commonly reduced asset, but reductions in equipment and facility requirements can be measured in much the same way. As stated earlier, possession costs are most commonly designated as a percentage of the value of the asset. So an 18% possession or inventory carrying cost means that it costs the customer 18 cents for each dollar of inventory it carries. Equipment generally has a higher possession cost than inventory because of the maintenance and energy costs for usage involved with owning the equipment.

When documenting actual solutions, remember that most value-added solutions impact multiple categories. So it is not as simple as measuring one cost driver. A better fit-to-function substitution can impact all four categories. Thus, you need to combine these into a worksheet.

It is also advantageous to make the information electronic and store it in a database. Many companies create spreadsheets for some of the solutions they offer. But for

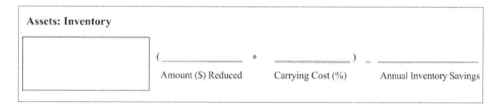

Figure 22.8 Worksheet for measuring assets: Inventory savings

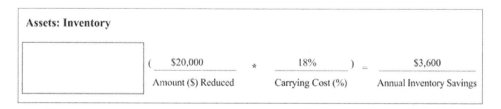

Figure 22.9 Completed assets: Inventory worksheet for inventory reduction example

companies that have a wide value-added offering, spreadsheets can become cumbersome. Companies that want to demonstrate value to strategic accounts need a database of the savings events by customer in order to run quarterly, annual, and multiyear savings reports to share with their customers. Without a database, they would have to spend a great deal of time compiling the savings by customer, industry, or other variables. For this reason, more and more companies are building their own software programs or turning to commercially available packages.

A supplier providing this kind of proof of savings creates a true competitive advantage because it helps the customer meet their cost-savings goals and proves that the supplier is truly the lowest total cost provider.

Having a database of the savings they have provided each customer over the years allows suppliers to report individual savings that are both proposed and already provided to their customers, to run reports across industries to show new customers the value they bring to that industry and potentially to that new account, and to run reports based on various time frames to work with their existing strategic accounts.

Much of the potential value suppliers add is through their products. These are often harder to report than services because of the breadth of products that a supplier might represent, and the different impact that each individual substitution can have on the customer's profitability. As such, when manufacturers sell through distributors, savings other than price are rarely documented unless the manufacturer helps to measure the value added from better fit-to-function products. Perhaps the best-known example of manufacturers providing solid support and tools is around lighting. Manufacturers such as GE Lighting and Philips Lighting have built tools to help their distributors better prove the savings from their products.

When used effectively, the documenting of value-added savings helps the supplier prove they are the lowest total cost, even if they are not the supplier with the lowest initial cost. But the numbers have to be reasonable and defendable. Customers often dismiss value-added savings because they do not think the savings are real. Because of this widespread skepticism by customers, the savings need to be spelled out and entered into a cost-accounting format that allows them to be proved. Otherwise, these very real savings will be seen as a "fabrication" of savings or as an exaggerated sales pitch that helps a supplier justify a higher price.

When documented effectively, these savings can help the supplier create and sustain a competitive advantage by proving how their product/services improve the customer's overall operating profits, beyond the price paid. Suppliers who learn to measure both cost savings and revenue enhancement based on cost-accounting principles, and who explain these to their current and potential customers, will be able to generate more sales, maintain key accounts more effectively, and even combat margin erosion. At the same time, they will be helping their customers achieve a competitive advantage through improved operating profits. Bottom line: documenting value-added savings can help demonstrate why they are the supplier of choice.

Part VII
Epilogue

23 A call to action

Value quantification in B2B buying and selling

Snelgrove, Todd C.

The salesforce is the principal messenger of value to the customer and must understand and effectively communicate value to the customer base. If the salesforce isn't fluent in these skills, customers will eventually perceive parity between their choices in the market. When this happens, organizational efforts to leverage the value of technology, product, process, or services will not achieve their true potential.

In 1996, a hit movie told the story of a sports agent, Jerry Maguire, and an aging football star, Rod Tidwell, hoping for a big contract. In one of the film's most memorable scenes, the two are talking on the phone, and Rod keeps saying to Jerry, "Say it . . . Yell it . . . Show me the money!" At the same time that *Jerry Maguire* became a hit, professional procurement was gaining traction in large companies. The procurement position and responsibility truly started the transformation from a tactical purchasing function, usually reporting into Finance, to a full-fledged group that has a seat with the CEO; the development of strategic procurement was rising. A gap we continued to see – and it continues to widen – was in the contractual negotiations with suppliers. Procurement seemed to want low costs (which translates into lowest price if you can't monetize your value) only (as we saw in the previous chapters), and salespeople would often wax on about this so-called value that they brought and others didn't and for which they therefore deserved a price premium. In the mid-1990s the users of the product or services, or business units, seemed to be the ones telling procurement what to buy and to just make sure all the terms and conditions were fair. Fast forward to the present, and now we see procurement, and rightfully so, challenging the internal customer, and asking whether a company can truly deliver on its promise and really help it become more efficient and thereby profitable.

This book is the first to my knowledge to feature best-in-class sales organizations that show how, in a tough B2B environment, they have been able to demonstrate real value, quantify that value in terms the customer understands, Total Profit Added™ and cares about (cold hard cash), and then negotiate on what will be measured and delivered for the customer, and how, all while supporting procurement's evolution into a more strategic role. A role in which there are three bids – and in which "buy the lowest" is not the primary strategy or choice – asks, "Who can bring us real measurable value by helping us become more innovative, differentiating our products and services, add revenue and/or take costs out of our operation?"

In the previous chapters you saw that the sales and buying relationship is not a zero-sum game and that when done properly, looking at real value, both the customer and the supplier can become more profitable. Pricing for that value can only occur once the customer believes that value is real and tangible.

DOI: 10.4324/9781003177937-30

Sales managers, new business development, marketing, and project managers should work with their pricing counterparts to understand how they can and will create more meaningful value for their customers. Procurement professionals should keep asking suppliers to demonstrate why they deserve to be bought not on the lowest price but on the best value. Finally, procurement should spearhead that value capturing for the organization, in order to continually be seen as a strong support function to the business, and show how it can get the best suppliers to bring their best resources and therefore value. Suppliers and customers should be sitting on the same side of the table and showing how we both sustainably win by measuring the best value created and received. The new era of collaborative procurement is coming to a customer or country near you.

24 Quotes and statistics to help you on your value-selling journey

Snelgrove, Todd C.

Selling on value

Companies that price for value are 24% more profitable than their industry average, 36% more profitable than those that price to cost.

Monitor Deloitte 2012
Closing rate increases of 25% by developing customized business case
Confidential B2B industrial company
Shorten sales cycle by 33%, reduce discounting by 18%, increased deal close 15%
B2B global software company

Buying on value

Bought and rewarded suppliers on TPA™ were 35% more profitable than industrial companies that did not.

Manufacturers alliance for productivity and innovation 2013 chief procurement officer survey

A 2007 study sponsored by the International Association for Contract and Commercial Management and the Strategic Account Management Association found buying companies realized 40% more value from their most collaborative suppliers than their least collaborative suppliers. The same report also found suppliers reported an average delivering 49% more value to their most collaborative key customers.

Memorable quotes

It is not how little you pay its how much you get
– Todd Snelgrove, Experts in Value

Suppliers often don't come to us with a business case. But it's what we want. Sell your value in our numbers to get our attention. But if you can't quantify your value – don't be surprised at the failure of procurement to do so.
– Paula Gildert President; Chartered Institute of Procurement and Supply

Even at Half the Price it can be Twice the Cost
– Todd Snelgrove, Experts in Value

DOI: 10.4324/9781003177937-31

Customers don't just want to know that you can help them make money or save money. They want to know how much and by when.
– Mike Wilkenson, Axia Value

Price Does Not Equal Cost.
– Todd Snelgrove, Experts in Value

Being different is not differentiation. Differentiation is being different in ways the customer values.
– Mike Wilkenson, Axia Value

Too many value propositions are high on proposition but low on value.
– Mike Wilkenson, Axia Value

Procurement and sales sometime confuse what ISO really means. . . . It's a conformance not performance standard.
– Rob Maguire, Maguire Izatt

My offering can be the highest price, but the lowest cost, and bring you the most profit.
– Todd Snelgrove, Experts in Value

Companies are not in the business of buying and products and services for no reason, the exists to do something of value for their clients. Can you help then m add value and sell that value?
– Todd Snelgrove, Experts in Value

Price is only an issue in the absence of quantified value.
– Todd Snelgrove, Experts in Value

25 Interview

The present and future of value quantification

Hinterhuber, Andreas and Snelgrove, Todd C.

Andreas Hinterhuber: What is value in B2B markets?

TODD C. SNELGROVE: Value is different for different persons and functions within a business: production, marketing, maintenance, and sales as all care about and value different things. For publicly traded companies all managers have an obligation to increase shareholders wealth – over the long term, while doing business in an ethical way for all stakeholders. Value is therefore the answer to the question: How do I make my customer more sustainably profitable than the next best alternative? Sustainably means over a period of time: Businesses that find a way to be "profitable" one quarter at the cost of next year's earning do not create but destroy shareholder value.

Some companies use total cost of ownership (TCO) approach to evaluate alternative products and services. However, my experience is that, although TCO approaches are widely used (Snelgrove, 2012), there is a lot of confusion around the elements that make up TCO. For example, procurement managers would say "TCO," but really mean "[l]anded cost or total cost of acquisition." As is well known, total costs of acquisition are only a small part of all the costs and benefits of an offer.

Over the years I realized that the concept of total costs of ownership should be updated to something more encompassing. The objective should be to identify the option that increases profits by the largest absolute amount. Therefore, I created the term "Total profit added" (Snelgrove, 2017a). Profit includes cost reductions, but also revenue improvements. If you help customers increase sales by increasing the production, helping the sales force to be more efficient, getting to market earlier than planned, enables them to upsell or cross-sell, discount less, etc., then all these factors drive revenue and profit, but they are not cost reductions.

Traditional TCO analysis is too much focus on costs and typically does not include revenue improvements (Hinterhuber, 2017; Hinterhuber and Snelgrove, 2017). Traditional TCO analysis therefore might push people to buy options that are not truly the best value.

To truly see all the benefits and costs you would look at the following three phases of use if you are the end user of the product or service (see Figure 25.1):

1. Acquisition phase: capital costs (CAPEX), initial purchase price, shipping, receiving, minimum order quantity, tariffs, taxation, currency conversion costs, risks, hedging fees, etc.
2. Installation, maintenance and operation: costs and benefit such as plus or minus the difference in operating costs (OPEX); also include benefits such as differences in

DOI: 10.4324/9781003177937-32

Total Profit Added™

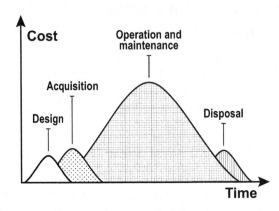

Figure 25.1 Total profit added (Snelgrove and Anderson, 2017)

    expected life of the machine, output differences, unscheduled downtime, production quality, etc.

3.   Disposal: can be a cost or benefit. Costs such as teardown, recycling, environmental, clean up, etc. Benefits result from the resale or the ability to refurbish the product.

ANDREAS HINTERHUBER: What about value quantification for intangibles?

TODD C. SNELGROVE: Great question, Andreas. I find this is the answer that is used most often so the supplier does not need to do the homework. First of all, and I paraphrase numerous VPs of Procurement I know: "If the supplier cannot or will not demonstrate and document why they can deliver more value, how am I, as the buyer, supposed to justify buying a higher priced alternative? They are supposed to be the expert."

    I hear companies in numerous industries around the world say, "*all of our customers are different, so no value formulae exist.*" I disagree. The calculation for energy savings, sales force productivity, reduced scrap, faster time to market or whatever is the same everywhere in the world. Whether that value driver has an impact, or the magnitude of that impact will vary by customer, segment, country. Also the numbers used in the calculation are different (downtime by industry, cost of capital, scrap value), but the formula is the same. With some research, customer knowledge, and good questioning skills you can get numbers that are close enough to build the first value model to start a conversation.

    Finally, numerous things customers value such as location of supplier, country of supply, supplier relationship, risk, etc., can be modeled. Again, these are not guarantees but allow someone to put some basic numbers to a value driver. I use an exercise called "So What." Pretend you're talking to your 5-year-old child that keeps asking "Why?," "Why?," "Why?" Coming from outside industries, I would ask this question numerous times and found that if I kept asking "So what?," a light would go off and I could quantify the related value.

MORE RELIABLE: *So what?* This means that it works when you need it to. *So what?* Then you don't need to keep lots of spare parts or back up machines or extra production or work in progress to minimize the risk of that production machine not working and missing deliveries. . . . I can quantify those things.

LOCAL SUPPLY: *So what?* We are closer to the customer? *So what?* If they have to buy from Asia (for a North American customer) they have to keep extra inventory as lead times are longer, they have to hedge currency, tariff, and freight costs as prices always exclude freight. I was able to quantify, demonstrate, and secure an order for a client where their price was 30% higher, but total profit added was 10% better after quantifying all these value drivers.

ONE OF MY FAVORITES: It runs cooler (industrial parts inside a machine). *So what?* I am told the operating temperature with this new bearing will be lower for the bearing – I am told "*everyone knows*" that a 10 Celsius reduction in operating temperature doubles the life of the lubricant. Well, I can surely quantify the reduced lubricant consumption, storage, disposal, labor to lubricate, etc. However, I didn't know that running cooler meant anything like this . . . Do not assume your customer can or will take the time to quantify your value.

ANDREAS HINTERHUBER: Why is value quantification important?

TODD C. SNELGROVE: You know the answer well (Hinterhuber, 2017; Hinterhuber and Snelgrove, 2017). In my experience without value quantification the customer focuses on what they can see and understand – the price. Without you quantifying the value of your offer, you are leaving it up to your customer to determine all the value below the waterline (see Figure 25.2). The things below the waterline with a profit impact might be tough to see or understand for the customer. Just imagine going to your boss right now and saying "I want to buy a machine for $100K" or "I want to buy a better version of a given product than we normally use." What do you think the response would be? "*Why? What is the benefit? Will we get a return? Are other similar options available to do the same thing but cheaper?*" If the user, the person that wants to buy your option, is not equipped with a reasonable business case, no wonder 80% of sales go to the "No decision" bucket. You're not losing to your competitor;

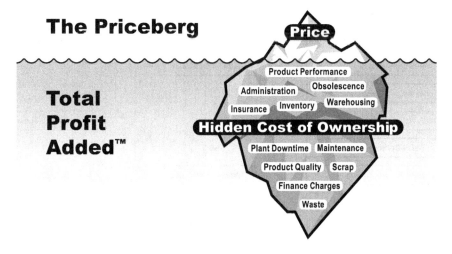

Figure 25.2 The Priceberg (Snelgrove, 2017b)

you are losing to your customer doing nothing. This is why it is so important to elevate the cost of doing nothing, as you say in your recent article (Hinterhuber, Pollono et al., 2018).

ANDREAS HINTERHUBER: What are current best practices around value?

TODD C. SNELGROVE: Great question. I think Figure 25.3 covers all the levers that should be addressed. Too often people come to me and focus on building or buying a tool that allows the sales or marketing team to generate customized business cases. Implementing value-based selling and value quantification requires more than a tool: it requires a set of capabilities, processes, structures, experiences, and structural adjustments that are geared to improving both the ability and the motivation to sell based on value (see Figure 25.3).

1. Value conceptualization: Understanding the value your solution offers (drivers, calculations, and expected ranges) for different customer segment. Without that it is a bunch of "If we could do this, then it would be worth this." The tool needs to have some "meat on the bone." Funny enough some good inexpensive research can usually pull the major numbers (cost downtime, average sales price, etc.). Also, whenever you're building a new product or service, ask yourself: *"What is this worth in monetary terms to customers versus the next best alternative?"* If you cannot put a number on it for a specific customer maybe you shouldn't invest the money in building something with the hope customers will figure out what it should be worth and buy it.
2. Value-selling process: Have you targeted your sales and marketing material to frame the discussion on your offering around anything but lowest price? The message needs to reach customers: where they learn about your products so when they get to the buying phase of comparing offers, they already are open to a discussion around quantified value, total profit added, etc. You should educate your customers so that at the request for proposal (RFP) stage your customers are prepared to rethink traditional

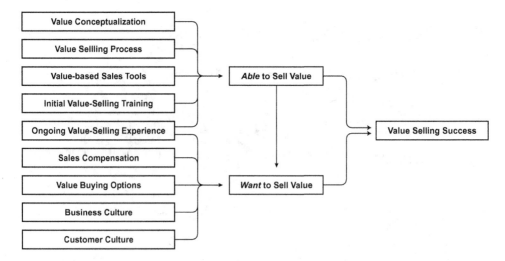

Figure 25.3 Key factors in implementing value-based selling (Snelgrove and Anderson, 2017)

weighting systems favoring lowest price and so that they are willing to purchase offers that optimize value, as opposed to price.

3. Value-based sales tools: Senior managers should equip customer-facing people with not only a tool to quantify value, but presentations, videos, examples, references to explain value and other material. Sales and account managers need to be able to explain customers the total lifetime value of the offering, they need to be able to model different value drivers based on specific use situations, and they need to high-light which elements beyond price (downtime, quality, speed to market) your offer improves and how these elements will influence key business metrics of the customer.

4. Initial value sales training: Companies need to train sales, marketing, customer ser-vice managers, etc., on selling value, on translating product features into quantified customer benefits, and on how to engage the economic buyer or senior executive in discussions around value (Liozu, 2015a).

5. Ongoing value-selling experience: Sales and account managers should constantly review sales strategies, review the value conversation, role-play sales and pricing strat-egies for large deals, etc. Companies expecting that a one-time training will change a company's 100-year-DNA will find efforts wasted unless a consistent focus is applied and updated to stay fresh.

6. Sales compensation: CEOs sometimes expect their sales teams to fight for value and reward volume or market share. This is crazy. CEOs need to reward the teams that fight for that extra 5%. If sales teams are given an "easy way" to cut a price they will do it and move on and say *"Boss, we will make it up in volume"* – which in 25 years in industry I have never seen happen sustainably.

7. Value buying options: Companies need to invest in pricing new products and ser-vices based on the value delivered so product launches are successful, as opposed to offering price cuts after introduction. The best companies offer customers choices where price is a direct variable and thus uncertain function of value. Any sales person can say how great they are, how much value they could create, but more and more procurement teams are asking *"Are you willing to get paid on delivering that value? Are you prepared to having some fee at risk?"* Without having these options, the story falls flat with customers. Performance guarantees add value, that is, the certainty of business outcomes for a B2B customer or piece of mind for B2C customers. Also, Andreas, these are not as risky as it might initially sound; they can be a small amount versus the discount you were going to give anyways. Choice is powerful

8. Business culture: This should not be understated. Is it in your company's DNA to be the best, to be the company that creates the most value? Does your CEO talk about it? Value was on our CEO's agenda, in our annual report, part of every corporate presentation. Companies that are suppliers of choice for their customers excel in creating, delivering, and quantifying value to customers. To this point, best-in-class companies actually have full-time resources to drive these corporate-wide initiatives. I was called Global VP of Value; my job was to focus on value quantification every day. I was focused on finding ways to demonstrate value to customers, on how to support our teams in selling value, on developing new products and services deliv-ering additional value, and on improving the resonance of our value messages to customers. Without focus, programs grow old and die. With a person responsible, it being live, updated, and a resource it has the chance to grow and get the rest of the organization better at it. Today I am hearing the term "Commercial excellence," which in my mind, is very similar to this also.

9. Customer culture: It all starts with customer obsession, with a genuine interest in enabling customers succeed in their business. We need to be actively trying to solve customer problems whether it is with our products or not. This attitude builds long-lasting customer relationships and trust. That is where we get the raves and endorsements and recommendations that mean we need to invest less in getting new customers. The development of true customer centricity requires a shift in mindset: from passively solving customer problems upon request to proactively solving customer problems, regardless of whether problems may be the customer's fault or may lay outside of our company's sphere of influence (Davidow, 2020). Customer centricity means that we solve problems, whatever it takes.

ANDREAS HINTERHUBER: Very well said. I appreciate the importance of true customer centricity. Let us get down to the individual sales manager/strategic account manager (SAM). What are in your view characteristics – that is, personality traits – of sales managers that excel in value-based selling/value quantification?

TODD C. SNELGROVE: I think you need people that have curiosity, think differently, and challenge themselves and customers. Of course, knowing your industry, competitors, customers business is of utmost importance but can be learned (Liozu, 2015b). Better be a team player and be able to marshal numerous different resources around your customer, all while being creative and adaptive is important. Maybe we get too much group think and "we have always done it this way" when we keep hiring the same types of people, with the same experiences, with the same type of education. My success is partly attributable from coming outside the industries I work in, my colleagues being patient enough to allow me to ask questions, and management creative enough to say, "Yes, we could learn from other industries."

ANDREAS HINTERHUBER: What are the next best practices of value quantification?

TODD C. SNELGROVE: I think that value quantitation should be used throughout the sales cycle. So, when you engage a customer, you start with a template (with some research) and move off a starting point: "We think based on the research, experience, etc., that this offer should deliver a given amount of quantified benefits." Then the case gets modified with the customer input and data, so now you have a refined case with customer buy in. Then when the customer buys the product or service this has now become a value order, an expected value in use is what they are buying. Finally, checking in and seeing how is the solution really delivering value. Is it better than expected? Worse? Maybe an update is needed, maybe a different implementation, maybe a different product specification, maybe a different way of working together with customers – all these factors should be examined so that the offer actually delivers the value that was originally quantified. This should not be a one and done; here is the case. I see the last stage is where a lot of companies stop. The value system has a bunch of business cases that are expectations. Whereas, over time we at SKF had over 80,000 cases in our system of actuals results. We could actually become predictive for clients – I have done this 55 times for this industry, and this is the average improvement, minimum, best, probability, etc. I remember the look of customers, saying that is what I am buying your knowledge and experience of how to do it; that creates real value not an excel spreadsheet with "What if" predictions. Now with fee-at-risk agreements this will help drive the move from "throwing up" a speculative business case to the business case being a living, iterative document that guides the relationship.

ANDREAS HINTERHUBER: How should companies start this journey?

TODD C. SNELGROVE: This depends on where they are. I have seen companies that have plenty of research on the value they deliver versus each competitive offer. In this case companies need to get this information into a financial model. However, some start with stating that their value proposition is "Local, been around 100 years, spend a lot of money on R&D, amazing amount of inventory." In that case some work needs to be done to move from features to benefits to quantified value. Start with one specific offering, for one specific segment or customer type where you think you have an advantage; over time you add more solutions and can start adding the value of your company (engineering support, turnaround time, small batch sizes, etc.). Once you have a solution with a few value drivers, formulas, and some ranges you can start vetting that with customers and see response. From that you make the decision to make a tool or buy. In my opinion buying a tool makes the most sense. I have also seen companies spending time and money trying to make an excel sheet look good and accurate; I have copies of numerous that were vetted and, in the marketplace, and are wrong (conflating ROI – Return *On* Investment, versus ROI – Return *Of* Investment – break even as an example). Put someone in charge of value quantification (it might be the product manager for that solution as example), then create a program to drive value quantification across multiple business units, and elevate that person or team to a senior position with high internal and external visibility.

ANDREAS HINTERHUBER: Todd, thank you for this thoughtful exchange of thoughts on the present and future of value quantification. I will summarize key points. Total costs of ownership (TCO) models are out; the next best practice are models that quantify the full range of benefits – including revenue increases, decreases in risk, reductions in costs, and capital expense savings (Hinterhuber, 2017). We could call them quite simply total benefit of ownership models. In the future, in this area we will likely see an increased focus on quantifying intangibles, including the quantification of non-economic benefits – likely even factors such as the value of a lower environmental impact. Value quantification capabilities are, and will be, a key differentiator between high- and low-performing companies. In the future, value quantification will be employed throughout the sales cycle, with an increased focus on value quantification in the new product development phase and an increased focus on innovative pricing models and performance-based, value-based pricing models. Finally, if value quantification is a recursive, iterative process, the availability of big data and experience will enable managers to make predictive assessments of customer quantified benefits based on both human and artificial intelligence.

Acknowledgment

Reprinted, with permission, from Hinterhuber, A. and Snelgrove, T. C. (2020) "The Present and Future of Value Quantification," *Journal of Creating Value* 6(2), 295–303. https://doi.org/10.1177/2394964320967521;

References

Davidow, M. (2020) "Counteracting value destruction," *Journal of Creating Value* 6(1), 86–96.

Hinterhuber, A. (2017) "Value quantification capabilities in industrial markets," *Journal of Business Research* 76, 163–178.

Hinterhuber, A., Pollono, E., et al. (2018) "Elevating the cost of doing nothing: An interview with Mark Shafer," *Journal of Revenue & Pricing Management* 17(1), 3–10.

Hinterhuber, A. and Snelgrove, T. (eds.). (2017) *Value First, then Price: Quantifying Value in Business Markets from the Perspective of Both Buyers and Sellers*, Milton Park, UK: Routledge.

Liozu, S. (2015a) "Pricing superheroes: How a confident sales team can influence firm performance," *Industrial Marketing Management* 47, 26–38.

Liozu, S. (2015b) *The Pricing Journey: The Organizational Transformation toward Pricing Excellence*, Stanford, CA: Stanford University Press.

Snelgrove, T. (2012) "Value pricing when you understand your customers: Total cost of ownership- Past, present and future," *Journal of Revenue & Pricing Management* 11(1), 76–80.

Snelgrove, T. (2017a) "Creating, calculating and communicating customer value: How companies can set premium prices that customers are willing and able to pay," in A. Hinterhuber and S. Liozu (eds.), *Innovation in Pricing: Contemporary Theories and Best Practices* (pp. 244–256), New York, NY: Routledge.

Snelgrove, T. (2017b) "Future view: Evolving the measurement of best customer value from using a total cost of ownership to total profit added methodology," *Journal of Creating Value* 3(2), 210–216.

Snelgrove, T. and J. Anderson (2017) "Muddling through on customer value in business markets?" in A. Hinterhuber and T. Snelgrove (eds.), *Value First, then Price: Quantifying Value in Business Markets from the Perspective of Both Buyers and Sellers*, Abingdon, UK: Routledge.

Index

Printed in the United States
by Baker & Taylor Publisher Services